THE PROBLEM OF FREEDOM

CONTEMPORARY PROBLEMS IN PHILOSOPHY
George F. McLean, O.M.I., *Editor*

Situationism and the New Morality, *Robert L. Cunningham*
Human and Artificial Intelligence, *Frederick J. Crosson*
The Problem of Scientific Realism, *Edward A. MacKinnon*
The Problem of Freedom, *Mary T. Clark*
The Problem of Religious Language, *M. J. Charlesworth*

THE PROBLEM OF FREEDOM

Mary T. Clark

MANHATTANVILLE COLLEGE

New York
Appleton-Century-Crofts
Educational Division
Meredith Corporation

Contents

Notes on contributors

SIR ARTHUR STANLEY EDDINGTON (1882-1944): born in Kendal, Westmoreland; English astrophysicist, graduate of Trinity College, Cambridge; Professor of Astronomy, Cambridge; Fellow of Royal Society; WRITINGS: *The Nature of the Physical World* (Cambridge: University Press, 1928); *The Philosophy of Physical Science* (Cambridge: University Press, 1939).

WERNER HEISENBERG (1901-   ): born at Wurzburg, Germany; physicist, graduate of the University of Munich; Fellow of Royal Society; worked under Niels Bohr at Copenhagen; Professor at Leipzig, Berlin, Munich.
Organized the Max Planck Institute for Physics at Gottingen, now at Munich. His name is associated with his theory of quantum physics published in 1925, when he was 23; won Nobel Prize for Physics, 1932.

EDMUND W. SINNOTT (1888-1968): born in Cambridge, Mass.; botanist, graduate of Harvard University and Northeastern University; Sterling Professor of Botany at Yale University 1940-1956; WRITINGS: *Cell and Psyche* (Chapel Hill: University of North Carolina Press, 1950); *The Biology of the Spirit* (New York: Viking Press, 1955).

JOSEPH NUTTIN (1909-   ):   born in Belgium; psychologist and
    philosopher, graduate of Louvain University, Belgium; Pro-
    fessor at the University of Louvain and Fordham University,
    New York;   WRITINGS: *La Structure de la personalité*
    (Paris: Presses Universitaires de France, 1965).

ERNEST NAGEL (1901-   ):   born in Novemesto, Czechoslovakia;
    philosopher, graduate of Columbia University; Guggenheim
    Fellow; Professor of Philosophy at Columbia University, New
    York;   WRITINGS: *Sovereign Reason* (Glencoe, Ill: Free
    Press, 1954); *Logic without Metaphysics* (Glencoe, Ill: Free
    Press, 1957).

ALFRED JULES AYER (1910-   ):   born in London; philosopher;
    graduate of Christ Church College, Oxford; Professor at Uni-
    versity of London; since 1959 Wykeman Professor of Logic,
    Oxford University;   WRITINGS: *Language, Truth and Logic*
    (London: V. Gollancz, 1936); *The Problem of Knowledge*
    (London: Macmillan, 1956).

C. ARTHUR CAMPBELL (1897-   ):   born in Scotland; philosopher,
    Professor Emeritus at the University of Glasgow;   WRITINGS:
    Scepticism and Construction (London: Allen & Unwin, 1931):
    Selfhood and Godhood (London: Allen & Unwin,) (New York:
    Macmillan, 1957).

RICHARD M. HARE (1919-   ):   born in England; White's Professor
    of Moral Philosophy at Oxford University; Fellow of Balliol
    College 1947-1966;   WRITINGS: *The Language of Morals*
    (New York: Oxford University Press, 1961).

JOHN DEWEY (1859-1952):   born in Burlington, Vermont; Social
    philosopher, educated at Johns Hopkins University; Professor
    at Universities of Michigan, Minnesota, Chicago, Columbia.
    Beginning as an idealist, he defended a naturalism in many
    writings;   WRITINGS: *Reconstruction in Philosophy* (New
    York: H. Holt & Co., 1920); *Experience and Nature* (Chicago:
    Open Court Publishing Co., 1925); *The Quest for Certainty*
    (New York: Minton, Balch & Co., 1929).

JEAN-PAUL SARTRE (1905-   ):   born in Paris; philosopher and
novelist; graduate of Ecole Normale Superieure; founder of
Les Temps Modernes; taught at lycees in le Havre and Paris,
then leader in French Resistance Movement, 1941-1944;
WRITINGS: *Being and Nothingness*, tr. Hazel E. Barnes (New
York: Philosophical Library, 1943); *Critique de la raison
dialectique* (Paris: Gallimard, 1960).

ALBERT CAMUS (1913-1960):   born in Mondovi, Algeria; literary
commentator on society; awarded Nobel Prize for literary
work in 1957; joined French Resistance during World War II,
edited *Combat*, an underground paper;   WRITINGS: *The
Plague*, tr. Stuart Gilbert (New York: Knopf, 1948); *The
Rebel*, tr. Anthony Bower (New York: Knopf, 1954).

AYN RAND (1905-   ):   born in Petrograd, Russia; American novelist
who claims her own philosophical framework for understanding man, called "objectivism";   WRITINGS: *We, the Living*
(New York: Macmillan, 1936); *The Fountainhead* (Indianapolis: Bobb-Merrill, 1943); *Atlas Shrugged* (New York:
Random House, 1957).

PIERRE THEVENAZ (1913-1955):   born at Neuchatel, Switzerland;
phenomenologist, close friend of E. Mounier; worked toward
developing "Protestant Philosophy"; Professor at University
of Lausanne;   WRITINGS: *L'homme et sa raison*, ed. Paul
Ricoeur (Neuchatel: Editions de la Baconniere, 1956).

WILLIAM A. LUIJPEN (1922-   ):   born in Holland; phenomenolo-
gist and historian of contemporary philosophy; studied at the
Sorbonne, the Angelicum in Rome, the Higher Institute of
Philosophy at Louvain, and University of Freiburg; Professor
at   Augustinian   Philosophicum,   Eindhoven,   Netherlands;
WRITINGS: *Phenomenology and Atheism*, tr. Stattivan de
Puttle, Pittsburgh; *Phenomenology and Metaphysics*, tr. Henry
J. Koren (Pittsburgh: Duquesne University Press, 1965).

PIERRE TEILHARD DE CHARDIN (1882-1955):   born in Auvergne,
France; paleontologist, educated in Jesuit schools; Jesuit

Priest; Professor of Geology at Catholic Institute in Paris, Director of the National Geologic Survey of China and of the National Research Center of France; WRITINGS: *Divine Milieu* (New York: Harper & Row, 1960); *Man's Place in Nature* (New York: Harper & Row, 1966).

KARL JASPERS (1883-1969): born in Oldenburg, Germany; philosopher and scientist, received his M.D. in 1909; Professor of Philosophy at Heidelberg, Basel; WRITINGS: *Man in the Modern Age*, tr. Eden & Cedar Paul (London: G. Routledge, 1933); *The Way to Wisdom*, tr. Ralph Manheim, (London: V. Gollancz, 1951).

JOHN MACMURRAY (1891-   ): born in Scotland; philosopher; educated at Glasgow University and Balliol College, Oxford; Professor at Oxford University, University of London, now Professor Emeritus of Moral Philosophy at University of Edinburgh; WRITINGS: *Persons in Relation* vol. 2: *The Form of the Personal* (London: Faber & Faber, 1961); *Conditions of Freedom* (Toronto: Ryersin Press, 1949).

AUGUSTE BRUNNER (1894-   ): born in Orschwir, Germany; philosopher-writer, educated at Ignatius-Kollege, Volkenburg; Professor at Pullach bei München until 1958; presently writing; WRITINGS: *A New Creation,* tr. Ruth Mary Bethell (London: Burns & Oates, 1955).

PAUL RICOEUR (1913-   ): born in Valence; Professor of Philosophy at the Sorbonne, Yale Terry lecturer 1967, collaborator on *Esprit*, foremost interpreter and translator of Husserl, leading historian of the phenomenological movement; WRITINGS: *Gabriel Marcel et Karl Jaspers* (Paris: Editions de Temps presents, 1948);*De l'Interpretation*, study of Freud's "Analytic hermneutic" (Paris: Editions du Seuil, 1965).

JOSEPH DE FINANCE (1904-   ):   born in France; metaphysician,
    educated at Seminaire des Missions, Valspres le Ruy, Haute
    Loire; Professor at Gregorian University, Rome;   WRITINGS:
    Essai sur l'agir, 1962; *Connaissance de l'Etre,* traité d'ontologie,
    Coll. Essais pour notre temps (Paris: Desclée de Brouwer, 1966).

Foreword

This volume on the problem of freedom by Mary T. Clark is located appropriately in the series, "Contemporary Problems in Philosophy," since it concentrates upon a basic problem in man's continuing search for meaning. But because freedom has seldom been reflected upon until after it has come under attack, man's concern for it often has not extended beyond the elaboration of tactics for warding off external threats. Philosophical reflection is intended to accomplish much more. Rather than merely responding to external dangers, it must investigate the issue at a depth sufficient to transform threats into creative tensions and to uncover the resources in the human spirit for drawing from tension authentic growth.

The volumes in this series share a common structure calculated to aid the reader to live out this process within himself. To do this, they include an extensive introductory essay that begins by tracing the history of the issue. This is intended to isolate the key factors and elucidate the precise nature of the contemporary problem. The introduction then surveys the types of work now being done and makes special note of the new insights that show the greatest promise. The major part of each volume consists of an extensive selection of substantial passages from writings that best illustrate the kind of work now in progress. These passages are ordered in a manner that assists the reader gradually to enter into the problem and coordinate his own reflection upon it.

This volume by Mary Clark fully illustrates the creative possibilities of philosophic reflection upon a key problem. Certainly, no issue has been more central in the dramatic shifts from ancient to medieval, medieval to modern, and modern to contemporary thought than that of freedom. As analyzed in the introduction, each step of this transformation is seen to imply a more radical question. Finally, the contemporary problematic stemming both from scientific determinism and existential self negation opens the road to an examination of the very existence and nature of freedom.

The reader will find of special value the works of the many philosophers, especially as coordinated in this volume. Together they do more than respond to the problem of freedom by a defense of its minimal meaning. By searching into the components of freedom and the conditions for its realization by man and society they generate a new level of awareness concerning the phenomenon of human freedom. Reflection upon this by the reader should generate a deeper appreciation of its meaning and a better understanding of the way in which it can be lived.

Perhaps it is inevitable then that this volume should have a special and extended conclusion. It is not that the last word now can be written, but that philosophical reflection upon the problem of living freely opens the road to rich insights into the meaning of human life and the bases upon which it can be lived. Having presented the materials for this reflection Mary Clark does well to point again towards that which each person must ultimately discover for himself, because that discovery is life itself.

G. F. McL.

Introduction

Revolution is a theme and also an ongoing reality of contemporary life. Revolutions are begun — and usually justified — in the name of freedom. The desire for freedom has been publicized in our day by the protest movements erupting on all sides: on the campus, in the ghetto, on the street, in the conference hall. Wars continue to be waged, grainfields are turned into battlefields, and the declared purpose of it all is freedom.

What is this that is called freedom? Martin Luther King who led the most recent freedom movement in America has said :

> There is nothing in all the world greater than freedom. It is worth paying for; it is worth losing a job for; it is worth going to jail for. I would rather be a free pauper than a rich slave. I would rather die in abject poverty with my convictions than live in inordinate riches with the lack of self-respect.[1]

In this passage there is the message that freedom may not be equated with security. Nor does it simply come with human nature. The possibility may be present in all men to account for the universal yearning for freedom, but the reality of freedom is related, it seems, to what man does. Again, it was Dr. King who said :"Freedom is the act of deliberating, deciding and responding within our destined nature."[2] The apparent need that there is

[1] Martin Luther King, Jr., *I Have A Dream*, ed. Lotte Hoskins (New York: Grosset & Dunlap, 1968), p. 45.
[2] Martin Luther King, Jr., *Strength to Love* (New York: Harper & Row, 1959), p. 81.

for every generation to take part in some special way in the advancement of human freedom seems to point out that certain conditions are required for freedom to be real. Some conditions that have been proposed involve the individual agent, the environment, the society — that is, man as he is: human, individual and social.

HISTORICAL SURVEY

Freedom has had a varied reference in different cultures and at different times. What man wants, what people feel threatened by, what the possibilities are for progress in any age, all these factors help to formulate a certain conception of freedom. An inquiry into the history of the development of the idea of freedom shows that our understanding of it has been a very gradual process. How men of different decades regarded freedom largely depended upon the particular aspect of freedom that the temporal conditions challenged them to emphasize. At times the challenge came from social conditions, at other times from political circumstances, and then again from the conditions of human ignorance or human knowledge. As long as there are many levels of human experience, there will be many ways in which freedom is experienced as a problem. Whenever any one aspect of freedom or any one level of the experience of freedom as problematic is taken to be the whole reality, there is a danger of missing the meaning of freedom. We should expect that the social evolution of mankind insofar as it affects and changes man's self-consciousness would bring with it a more total approach to the understanding of freedom so that all the aspects uncovered through the historical process would find their rightful place.

EASTERN AND WESTERN THOUGHT

Freedom has been diversely interpreted in the East and in the West. Easterners have tended to see freedom as liberation from the internal constraint of egoistic desires and anxieties in the interest of unity and self-control.[3] Self-knowledge is sought as the prelude to this inner

[3]Franz Rosenthal, *The Muslim Concept of Freedom* (Leiden: E. J. Brill, 1960). Karl H. Potter, "Freedom and Determinism from an Indian Perspective", *Philosophy East and West*, 17, 113-124. Ja. O. 1967.

freedom. Eastern sages have long felt that Westerners tended to overemphasize the role of the scientific and practical intellect and have thereby drained energy from the human spirit, the contemplative spirit of man.

In the West, on the other hand, there has been a notable absence of agreement as to what freedom means. The Eastern insight into freedom as liberation, as integrity, as unifying the self to make possible a union-with-the-All has been retained by some Western philosophers and by some religious thinkers. Other Westerners consider freedom chiefly as the absence of external constraint upon an individual's ability to act freely. And of late years a greater emphasis has been put upon freedom as control. Scientific and political know-how is applauded because it does extend this freedom-power. It is not too difficult to see that a freedom identified with any one of these aspects to the exclusion of the others would prove to be unreal or futile or fatal. Today's ideal is that freedom should be something enjoyed by all men, and it should serve to humanize man. But it is evident that if freedom-power is unduly cultivated, extreme competition between man and man, between nation and nation becomes inevitable. Moreover, unless the possessor of such freedom-power is liberated from his passions of fear and greed, his so-called freedom will achieve the dehumanization of many men as well as his own self-defeat.

A whole volume of readings could be devoted to the problem of freedom in the East, but the vastness of the topic in western thought forces us to confine our remarks to this.

WESTERN THOUGHT ON FREEDOM

A constant element in Western culture is the consensus that man is personally responsible for his actions and therefore accountable to society for what he does. All moral and legal or political judgments presuppose that men are capable of acting freely, and it is believed that they do so unless proof to the contrary is produced. The philosophers, however, have not held a unanimous opinion on this point.

From the time of the earliest philosophers we can detect the emergence of what eventually became three positions on the existence or nonexistence of freedom.

1. Man considered as *a part of nature* was thought to be subservient to natural events or destiny.

2.   Man considered as someone *apart from nature* was thought to
      be free from the material cosmos, a master of himself.

3.   Man considered to be *within nature but related to that which
      was beyond nature*, namely truth or goodness or beauty, was
      thought to have power over the cosmos and over himself within
      certain material and spiritual conditions.

As human knowledge evolved, "nature" became a variable; with
man's changed view of nature there also developed a changed view of
freedom or non-freedom. At first nature was looked upon as made up of
the famous four elements; later it was thought to be one vast organism
with all things internally related; today nature is viewed as an open,
evolving process called cosmogenesis. These changing conceptions of
nature would affect the notion of freedom according to the way a thinker
would relate freedom to nature.

THE CLASSICAL-CHRISTIAN PERIOD

The history of the problem of freedom has been constituted
by the interweaving through time of the abovementioned three positions
on freedom's relation to nature; it is also the content of the contemporary
problem of freedom.

For Democritus (460-360 B.C.) and for the Epicureans (342
B.C.-   ) the real world consisted of a plurality of material atoms
constantly moving and just as constantly swerving according to some
physical law. For Chrysippus (282-209 B.C.) and for the Stoics (350
B.C.-   ) there was one principle or *logos* guiding the single, interrelated
cosmos. Man, whether merely a part of the loose mechanism of the
Epicurean cosmos or a part of the world organism of the Stoics, was just as
necessitated as the rest of the world, without choice or control.

The Sophists (481 B.C.-   ), whom some call the pragmatists of the
classical world, apparently took it for granted that in a world of
Heraclitean flux all things are indetermined. In the shifting situation this
was most true of what men might want to do.

Socrates (469-399 B.C.), Plato (427-347 B.C.) and Aristotle
(384-322 B.C.) considered that the humanness of man placed him above
ordinary natural transactions; this going beyond the nature in which one

participates is often called transcendence. Nevertheless, although man transcended physical nature, classical philosophers taught that those actions were most human which were in harmony with what was known to be true. It is above all in Plato, and to some extent in Aristotle, that the eastern notion of freedom as self-control by surrender to a higher reality is somewhat developed. Just as Socrates is said to have taken to heart the admonition of the Delphic Oracle, *Know Thyself*, and thereby discovered the soul as moral personality, Plato can be seen as having pointed the way to personal freedom. In this he joins the Eastern sages. The Platonic plan of education aimed to bring into perfect harmony all man's powers. Plato was certain that there is such complexity in man's relation to his world that his desires or emotions will affect the way things appear to him. Before being able to control things effectively, man must learn to control his affections. The "guardians" were to be educated toward this self-mastery. But only a few who leave the "cave" and live in the sunlight of the "Forms" (permanent principles of truth) would be able to educate the guardians.[4] These educators were to be the philosopher-kings; such men would know not only what to do but why. In the power to think truly, Plato located human autonomy or freedom. Most men would remain in the cave unless they are forced to give up their life of illusory sensation by being provoked to think. Only in the light of intellectual knowledge will they be able to recognize their cave-life as an enslavement.

Aristotle was the first to speak of choice as distinct both from sense appetite and rational wish and from knowledge. He spoke of it as a decision following upon deliberation of whether to take or to avoid a good or an evil. Aristotle's description of decision as something "chosen before" other things places it within man's psychic life as an interior aspect of human action, and thus he arrived at defining choice as "a deliberate desire for things that are within our power."[5] That choice is free follows from the fact that men share the responsibility for their own characteristics and

---

[4] Plato, *The Republic*, 443 c d: "Righteousness pertains to the inner action not the outer, to oneself and to the elements of the self, restricting the specific elements in one's self to their respective roles, forbidding the types in the *psyche* to get mixed up in one another's business; requiring a man to make a proper disposition of his several properties and to assume command of himself . . . becoming in all respects a single person instead of many . . ."

[5] Aristotle, *Jicomachaean Ethics*, III, 3-4-5.

"because the ends we set up for ourselves are determined by the kind of persons we are."[6] Thus, although Aristotle attributes a certain material and teleological necessity to the play of cosmic forces, he speaks of human events as contingent or indetermined. Whereas he teaches that moral activity as a matter of choice is free, he restricts choice to the means of obtaining the ends fixed by nature. The end that Aristotle envisions is an activity in accordance with reason, the contemplation of the Unmoved Mover, and the choice of moral action is for the sake of freeing man from the disturbing desires of his sensible nature. Like Plato, Aristotle is not in complete opposition to the Eastern notion of freedom as self-control. In this context the Greek City-State was to enable ordinary men to live the good life of dutiful citizens. The State rather than the philosopher-king provided the conditions for human perfection. We may conclude that Aristotle concerned himself with the problem of human responsibility and was not anxious about the problem of free will. He firmly faced two factors that would eliminate human responsibility: 1) ignorance of the true state of affairs; 2) violence — that is, the effecting of action by a source outside the personal agent. Aristotle presupposed that man was free from natural necessity; reason placed man beyond nature and was the source of human responsibility.

The first philosopher of the post-pagan period was Philo (20 B.C.-40 A.D.) of the Jewish community at Alexandria at the time of the reign of the Emperor Augustus. Philo taught that man participated in God's own freedom from natural laws. He spoke eloquently of spiritual liberty as a free obedience to God. This kind of freedom was not too remote from that cherished by Eastern sages and which St. Paul (-c.67 A.D.) and St. Augustine (354-430 A.D.) experienced in their conversions and advocated for Christians. It involved the following of the will's natural orientation or dynamism towards God as total Goodness through the choice in each situation of what is morally good.

The first speculative challenge to the existence of freedom arose within the religious context and came specifically from reflection upon the doctrine of creation. It was clearly seen that the Creator would have attributes such as omniscience and omnipotence and omnipresence and

---

[6]Ibid., III, 6. "It is absurd, then, to blame things outside us instead of our own readiness to yield to their allurements, and, while we claim our noble acts as our own, to set down our disgraceful actions to pleasant things outside us." *Nic. Eth.* III, 1.

that He was the source of all that is real. But if God knows not only all that man has done and is doing but all that he is going to do, is man not necessitated to act in accord with God's knowledge? And if there is one Creator rather than two principles of good and evil, must not evil also be attributed to God? This was the problematic articulated by Augustine.[7] With the aid of Plotinian philosophy he showed that evil as non-being (the negation of what should be) required no efficient cause, but that the positive content of any human action — the intention and the deed — could be freely chosen. Thereupon God's knowledge of the action — never really foreknowledge for an eternal Being — would include the knowledge that it was done freely, if indeed the conditions for freedom were present. Later, against Pelagius, Augustine argued that grace does not determine man's will as something coming from outside the agent. The gift that it is, the power to love God, is a delight (*delectatio*), which becomes the "weight" or inclination of the will itself towards God. Grace inclines but does not determine the will; the will, under the weight of love, determines itself.[8]

THE MEDIEVAL PERIOD

In the Middle Ages, thinkers did not so much argue whether or not man could choose freely as produce arguments to explain how man can freely choose. Like Augustine, they rooted man's free choice in the relation to Infinite Goodness by an analysis of the formal objects of the faculties of knowing and willing. They found that the dynamism towards Infinite Being is implicit in the experience of willing anything, and discussion focused upon whether freedom was rooted more in reason than in will.

St. Thomas Aquinas (1224-1274 A.D.) emphasized the contingency of choice or free judgment as the reconciliation of the respective dynamisms of intellect and will. This he did by accepting the Aristotelian suggestion that causes are causes of each other in different orders. The total good apprehended by intellect acts as final cause, and the partial good apprehended by intellect acts as formal cause specifying the will,

---

[7] Augustine, *De libero arbitrio (On Free Choice)* (Westminster, Md.: Newman Press, 1960).
[8] Mary T. Clark, *Augustine, Philosopher of Freedom* (New York: Desclee Co., 1959).

..uch, as efficient cause, moves the practical intellect to a decision that the will then elects. There is a priority of speculative knowledge giving rise to the love of what is apprehended, but when truth is for the sake of action, the practical judgment is formed under the influence of the will. This is because the will is the power for attaining the end of man, an end attained in the order of action or finality. Insofar as man's other powers are concerned with action, the will moves these powers. That is why the practical intellect proposes the formal cause of action under the influx of the will as efficient cause in pursuit of its end.[9]

The metaphysical basis for the radical indetermination of the practical judgment and the active domination of the will before all partial goods is the incommensurability of any finite thing to the totality of being. Left to itself, the practical intellect remains undetermined to a final judgment. Acting as a formal cause, revealing the *ratio* of this good thing both in itself and in relation to the end and thereby channeling the influx of the final cause, the intellect can be determined to judge conclusively that this act should here and now be done only when the will, acting as efficient cause with the dynamism that belongs to it by its ordination to total being, freely identifies "this good" with man's good. No finite reality can fulfill the infinite capacity of the will for good. No motive is absolutely and infallibly sufficient to actuate the will. If it becomes sufficient, the will has made it so. Choice is a free response arising from an infinite well of desire that no particular good can fill. The immateriality of the speculative intellect is the root of liberty; the consequent indetermination of the practical judgment is the proximate cause of free human acts; and the immediate explanation of free choice is the active domination of the free will whose formal object is never proposed to it for choice in the here and now.[10] Aquinas' view of freedom is rooted in the subtle intricacy of a metaphysical explanation of why man must be free.

---

[9]Thomas Aquinas, *De Veritate (On Truth)*, q. 24, a. 1. For St. Thomas free choice means a "free judgment about acting or not acting." Cf. *Summa contra Gentiles*, II, 48.

[10]Ibid., q. 22, a. 4, c: "And so a rational nature's inclination is not determined for it by anything else but by itself."
Ibid., q. 22, a. 7, c: "But man has implanted in him an appetite for his last end in general, so that he naturally desires to be complete in goodness. But just what that completeness consists of, whether virtues or knowledge or pleasure or anything else of the sort, has not been determined for him by nature."

THE MODERN PERIOD

The problem of free will was accentuated when Newton announced the physical laws that determine the state of nature.[11] Scientists began to assert their certainty as to the over-all description of the functioning of nature and by the experimental method they proceeded to the prediction of future events. At that point the early deterministic view of nature suggested by Democritus and the Epicureans reached a sophisticated form and made use of the machine-model for interpreting the universe as a closed system wherein all is necessitated. It would be difficult to withdraw the human body from the effects of this view, and to many the close identification of man with his body placed human freedom in jeopardy. It would be possible for philosophers to argue that the human mind is free only if they made a sharp dichotomy between soul and body.

If natural laws alone accounted for material changes and events, man's decisions made within the realm of mind might be free but futile or fruitless. Yet if man's decisions did affect and direct his human acts that involved changes in the physical world, then all physical actions would not be subject to physical laws and the mechanistic view of the universe with its corollary of universal determinism is false. The crack in the claim for universal determinism came first with the realization that the laws so confidently formulated were corrigible, and that the knowledge of nature might never be complete, and at last by the discovery that the great law of matter was that it was a law of contingency, of indeterminism.

Modern determinism was never a philosophical position but a scientific hypothesis. This early hypothesis has been replaced by another. Nevertheless the scientific intelligence so dominated man that whereas in Greek culture freedom was taken for granted, in modern times determinism became an assumption.

It was in such a climate of opinion that Rene Descartes (1596-1650) began to philosophize; he taught that man chooses freely. This he was able to do by a drastic separation of man as mind from nature as extended matter. Thus the operation of the material universe according to its own "mechanical" laws could take place without bringing man's freedom into question.

[11] Edwin A. Burtt, *The Metaphysical Foundations of Modern Physical Science* (New York: Harcourt, Brace and Co., 1932).

On the other hand, there is evidence that Spinoza (1632-1677), Leibnitz (1646-1727), and Hume (1711-1776) were determinists. By uniting mind and extension as two aspects of one world-substance, Spinoza made human decisions to be as determined as had been Descartes' material events. In speaking of pre-established harmony between body and soul, Leibnitz was saying that everything within the windowless monad that is man is so regulated that reason has the power to overcome desire; man is free because he is determined by the best reason. Although not a rationalist like Spinoza and Leibnitz, the empiricist Hume concurred with Spinoza's opinion that certain human acts are thought to be free only because we are ignorant of their determining causes.

Immanual Kant (1724-1804) was another philosopher who bypassed the question of nature's conditioning or eliminating human freedom when he divided the universe into two worlds: the world of freedom and the world of nature. The world of freedom is to be found within human subjects where man himself determines what is morally right for him to do and thereby becomes his own lawgiver. What a man intends within his own subjectivity is the source for judging the action good or bad. This power over his own goodness or badness was called "autonomy" by Kant. In Kant's view the weight and the interference of the material domain did not affect the act of man which was entirely free because it was his own.

Two more recent modern philosophers, Hegel (1770-1831) and Marx (1818-1883) have openly avowed the cause of freedom, which they appear to have greatly esteemed. Their positions well illustrate the importance of the way freedom is interpreted. Hegel agreed with Kant that the will is thoroughly rational; in fact, will is just another name for the practical aspect of reason. Whereas for Kant the moral law was the highest expression of human freedom and ruled the inner world, Hegel espoused a freedom that expressed itself objectively in the whole social order. Hegel echoed the Greeks when he taught that the perfect life was life in the perfect State. Certainly Hegel has accented two very important aspects of human freedom: its need for externalization and its political character. His deep appreciation of the value of freedom is manifested in the fact that he made freedom to be the end of the State. But in the dialectical opposition and reconciliation that marks the process of the development of Spirit to which Hegel refers as the stages of freedom, where precisely is there room for man to choose freely? Although materialism is usually associated with determinism, in Hegel's doctrine we find a spiritualism joined with what at least appears to be the determinism of men in history. It would seem that the lack of any room for transcendence where Spirit or rationality is the whole of reality has effectively removed any place for freedom. In the self-development of a Spirit that is both mind and reality, subject and object, there is nothing to transcend. The dialectic of Hegel was his principle of progress, but freedom was evacuated; among the classical thinkers the principle of transcendence acted as the principle of progress as well as the foundation of freedom.

Karl Marx, on the other hand, saw man, as a part of nature, liberating himself in a dialectical process and becoming himself in relation to the world. He is helped to do this by a human society — although when Marx wrote in the nineteenth century, the socioeconomic determinisms operative in society had not yet produced that human society. Marx predicted that the dialectic in society will bring about a classless society where man will produce beyond his individual needs for the human race. It remains difficult to see how this prediction was made at the same time that Marx recognized that man's freedom is a factor in bringing about revolution. Nevertheless, it is worth remarking that although he does not escape classification as a determinist, Marx spoke of freedom in social rather than in individual terms. The social aspect of human freedom was an important aspect to uncover. The perfect society will come, he thought, when each man identifies his own interests with the interests of all.

For many nineteenth-century theorists, freedom was to exist only in the future. Leaning heavily, if unconsciously, upon a concept of freedom that identified it with the lack of coercion or of control by others, they prophesied rather than explained. Auguste Comte (1797-1857)[12] awaited a future when scientific knowledge would allow man to control all things so that the unpredictable would be forever eliminated. Saint-Simon (1760-1825) asserted that technology would achieve the absence of poverty. For Marx and Engels (1820-1895), freedom would arrive upon

[12]Comte was the founder of Positivism, a materialism. Logical Positivism was a name given in 1931 by A. E. Blumberg and Herbert Feigl to a set of philosophical ideas announced by the Vienna Circle, a group of Viennese philosophers much influenced by the scientific tradition. The logical positivists considered themselves to be prolonging a 19th century Viennese empirical tradition close to British empiricism, and culminating in the antimetaphysical, scientifically oriented teachings of Ernest Mach. These thinkers rejected transcendental metaphysics on the ground that its assertions were meaningless, since there was no possible way of verifying them through sensible experience. By meaningless they meant a lack of "cognitive meaning."

the elimination of social classes. In one sense the only prophet among these futurists was Karl Marx who did see that community was a prerequisite for justice, and that without justice all forms of freedom are illusory. But this is not to say that Marx provided a suitable rationale for the coming of community.

We have seen that the history of philosophy reveals sharp differences of opinion as to whether there is such a thing as human freedom. On the subject of the essential character of human freedom, the diversity is still greater. This becomes more urgent today as there is more profoundly realized the severe consequences of not reaching consensus upon freedom's meaning for nations that claim the right to freedom, fight for freedom, and fix freedom as their national purpose.

REFLECTION UPON THE ASPECTS OF FREEDOM

In modern times it has become customary to set up a so-called model to assist in the understanding of nature; but the dictation of our understanding of nature and hence of freedom by an inadequate model-theory has disastrous effects. During the modern period when nature was viewed as mechanized, the model for thinking about nature was the "machine". We should not be surprised to find that this machine-model played its part in draining vitality from man and likewise from his choices. This vitality was restored when the organism-model was used to understand nature; it gave to freedom the function of self-realization as its direct endeavor. But just as any view of society as organic is defective when it tends to regard men as parts existing for the sake of the whole body-politic, so the contemporary thinkers who substitute the organism model for the mechanism model cannot authentically interpret human freedom. By proposing intrinsic self-movement they improve upon the scientific determinists' merely extrinsic movement of man. Nevertheless, the modern biological model signifying the dynamic attainment of independent existence is little better than the Greek substance that signified the rather static possession of independent existence.

Independence alone seems scarcely sufficient for the self. Personal development and fulfilment cannot be achieved in a context of self-sufficiency. Psychologists have shown that one may in some measure realize potentialities through a kind of material or cultural metabolism interacting with the cosmic environment, but personal creation occurs only through ex-centric, not ego-centric action. Psychological studies on the use of freedom point the way toward the need to reinterpret human reality not as atavistic substance but as interpersonal process. This reinterpretation would lead to a readjustment of human ambitions regarding freedom. *Community* would gradually replace *autonomy* when referring to freedom. Decision, necessary as it is for the free act, may not dispense with the consensus that seems increasingly necessary for true freedom to exist.

This is why *community* is being suggested as a more appropriate model for understanding freedom than the mechanism and organism models have been. Within the over-all pattern of community, choice and control are best developed since there is cooperation rather than competition, coexistence rather than conflict. If freedom is illuminated by the model of community, education for freedom would become education in giving. Civic education would concern itself with the inculcation of intergroup relationships, since justice that is merely legislated and unsupported by right relationships remains unreal. *Rights* are empty words without the good will of all citizens. This suggests why socialism can never be the complete answer to the misery of the masses. And political democracy is only the framework for equality. Friendship is a prerequisite for justice, and arises only out of that freedom which glories in the interdependence of authentic community. The coming of such freedom to mankind will no doubt await a more universal conviction that to be human is to be interdependent. Personal freedom cannot develop nor stand alone. It has a communal origin and its consequences are cosmic. Independence, disguised as freedom, needs to be unmasked and recognized as spurious; it is not freedom's concretion but its contradiction.

Nevertheless, independence has always had its appeal for man and this needs to be accounted for as a value. Perhaps this stems from the fact that a decision must be mine if it is to affect me and thereby be self-creative. One can affect things by carrying out decisions made by others, but only one's own decision is self-determining, self-changing, self-creative. In this sense there is a point to the yearning for independence, since without it there can be no personal growth.

For a long time it has been almost a cliché to say that the great problem in the individual, family, society, State, or Church is the problem of freedom versus order. What is suggested here is that the truly basic problem is the fully personal one of putting order within freedom. This touches upon the two factors in the history of freedom controversy: the either/or of freedom's existence and the meanings of freedom. Men reached maturity in philosophy when they became self-conscious to the point of being fully aware that to be human is to be free. The escape from freedom into determinism was in its own way an escape from responsibility for the way things are. How unconsciously modern man argued for a mechanized view of life with his escape in view we shall not attempt to say. But he has emerged from the cave into the full light of freedom-consciousness. Contemporary literature abounds with man's effort to understand himself as free. There are philosophic pleadings that freedom be understood as choice or control. But voices are also raised to say that neither one can be really in order apart from the third aspect of freedom, creative responsibility or the power-to-be exercised through love. In the exercise of this freedom, community is born and man is more profoundly personalized. Here is validated the conclusion reached by Pierre Teilhard de Chardin: love unites, and union differentiates.

With freedom understood as creative responsibility in the light of the community-model, all three aspects of freedom are harmoniously interwoven within the "order of love." The dialectic between order and freedom reaches a higher synthesis of order-within-freedom. True personal freedom does not have to be ordered from the outside. With this freedom it is not a case of finding itself checked or constrained by laws nor is it a case of flouting laws, which indeed have no other purpose than that of promoting or safeguarding the fundamental law of brotherly love. The reality of love is a synthesis, a higher reality within which both order and freedom thrive. Choice as personal commitment is here insured by the presence of love; control or freedom-power is here rooted in the desire to fulfil the wishes and the needs of those who are loved. Freedom as creative responsibility generates an atmosphere where choice and control can be fully themselves as legitimate factors of freedom.

No model for understanding freedom should be adopted unless it makes room for all these aspects of human freedom — choice, control, and creative responsibility. Differ as they do, the mechanism and the organism models fail for the same reason, namely, their origin in infrahuman reality. Man is, after all, the one who was proclaimed to be created as the image of

God. St. Bernard may be quite correct in seeing freedom as that which marks man as God's image — an open human nature with infinite possibilities germinating in human freedom. The model of community illuminates the creativity of personal freedom because it is within community that personality develops and provides for responsible choice and control by offering objective standards and public accountability.

The order within human freedom has its paradigm in God's creative love as trusting and total. The freedom to choose and the freedom to control arise and are motivated not out of the fear of being dominated by others but out of love for the others with a view to promoting their well-being. Within this reality of friendship or interpersonal process choice, control and creativity mingle harmoniously as indeed they do in God's creative work. In friendship, which is a matter of gift and not of conquest inasmuch as no one can demand friendship, man identifies with the friend in whose interest his creative intelligence is used. Because friendship is a gift, it flourishes only in an atmosphere of freedom. But if love cannot be demanded, it never ceases to be desired. There will never come a time when man can live as self-sufficient and this is a sign that freedom itself can never claim exemption from human interdependence.

DEVELOPMENT OF THE CONTEMPORARY PROBLEMATIC

IS THERE ANY FREEDOM?

The Scientific View

Our brief history of the argument on freedom has shown that the view that man is determined is in accord with the philosophical position of monism, the theory that reality is nothing but matter or nothing but spirit. Determinism is especially characteristic of materialistic monism, which explains reality in terms of matter in motion. Among the earlier monists were Democritus and the Stoics; and among the later, Spinoza, Hegel, and Marx. Except for Spinoza and Hegel, these were

. From the seventeenth century onward, the scientist who regarded the world as a physical mechanism became so ...ᴜnzed by the predictive features of the scientific method that science became a kind of matrix for the consideration of all things. Without declaring themselves to be philosophical monists, many modern men were unconsciously influenced by a scientific outlook. When finally the method of science was deliberately taken up by philosophers as universally valid, it turned into the principle of verification used by the logical positivists. On the basis of this principle they declared that only those statements are true which are verifiable through referring the terms to what can be sensed. [13] The general principle subscribed to by the scientific mentality was that what could not be scientifically demonstrated could not be said to exist. If only the protons and electrons in man fall within the scope of science, it is easy to conclude that man is subject to the principle of necessity as this operates in the whole of nature. Such views were not confined to Newtonian physicists. Although Darwin (1809-1882) substituted an organic view of the world for a mechanical one, his process of natural selection suggested to man that there was little scope for liberty. Herbert Spencer (1820-1903) molded the Darwinian theory of evolution into sociological laws of progress so necessitating that they could be regarded as irresistible as the physical laws of gravitation. Freud (1856-1939) also led many to question whether their conscious choices were entirely free from the compulsion of psychic forces.

This materialistic view so contradicted human experience that philosophers like Descartes and Kant and Sartre completely separated what is human in man from any influence of the material. Thus set apart from nature, man's freedom was portrayed almost as angelic, limited only by lack of knowledge, or as arbitrary, a law unto itself.

In the course of time both these exaggerated views gave way to the conviction that the experience of freedom reveals men simultaneously to be immersed in nature and to transcend nature. Thus man has come to accept and even to glory in his responsibility for nature and its development. Scientists of this century affirm that no investigation of natural processes can turn up conclusive evidence for or against the existence of human freedom. Some aspects of the human act are open to scientific investigation; others like motivation, decision, intention are not. If the whole history of a human act does not fall within the purview of

[13] Vienna Circle, the group of logical positivists with whom Ludwig Wittgenstein was at first associated.

science, then in being faithful to their proper methodology scientists have nothing to say about the existence or nonexistence of free choice. Such statements as "everything is determined" lie beyond the scientific instruments for measuring the particular and the concrete, and we no longer hear these statements from scientists. In fact, since the announcement of the "principle of indeterminacy" with regard to the smallest particles of material things by Werner Heisenberg (1901-), [14] the scientists have even been careful to say that "everything we deal with is indetermined." All the scientific evidence is now on the side of a nonmechanized universe.

Thus in Parts I and II we shall hear a discussion of physical, biological, psychological, and historical indeterminism where contemporary man gradually frees himself from the fixation of the early scientific deterministic outlook.

But the philosophic argument about the either/or of freedom's existence continues. The prestige of scientific methodology is still strong among those who moved it from one method among many to the only method whereby truth can be delivered. Nonsensible realities will, of course, escape sensible verification. A certain doubt as to their status as facts is simply raised by the repetition of Hume's statement that they cannot be known to exist (by sense impressions). In this tradition it can still be said today that human freedom cannot be known to exist. Such philosophers are the rapidly diminishing group called logical positivists who accept the philosophic doctrine of Auguste Comte and his Vienna disciples that knowledge is based upon and restricted to sensible facts.

On the other hand, as the passages in Part I show, scientists who are led to wonder about whether or not there exists that freedom claimed by men and implied by moral law and the legal courts are finding – in physics, biology, psychology, and sociology – factors that favor an open or nondetermined universe. The physicist Sir James Jeans (1877-1946) once said that "the universe seems to be nearer to a great thought than to a great machine." [15] The philosopher Arthur Balfour (1848-1930) has

---

[14] Werner Heisenberg along with Max Planck and Niels Bohr revolutionized science. They elaborated the quantum theory; before the quantum theory appeared, the principle of the uniformity of nature – that like causes produce like effects – had been accepted as a universal and indisputable fact of science. As soon as the atomicity of radiation became established, this principle had to be discarded.

[15] Sir James Jeans, *Physics and Philosophy* (Michigan: University of Michigan Press, 1958).

asserted that "we now know too much about matter to be materialists." [16]
Today's scientists know too much about matter to be determinists and too
little about man to be dogmatic.

The Philosophic View

Yet it would give a decidedly false impression to say that there
is no longer any philosophical disagreement about the existence or reality
of human freedom. For this reason we present in Part II a confrontation
by two contemporary philosophers on the question of the reality of free
choice. Alfred J. Ayer (1910-   ) argues that necessity rather than
freedom characterizes human action; C. Arthur Campbell (1897-   )
argues in defence of the freedom of human actions. Here the opposition is
apparently between nature and experience. The personal experience of
freedom that most men think they enjoy is interpreted by Professor Ayer
in the light of nature and its mode of functioning. Professor Campbell, on
the other hand, interprets human nature in the light of personal
experience. From this he draws the conclusion that freedom is a
permanent quality of man.

Not only is the scientific tradition now heavily on the side of
indeterminism in nature, but the philosophers who grew out of logical
positivism and gave their attention to the mere analysis of language have
said that the way freedom has appeared as a problem in philosophical
literature is the result of linguistic confusion. In this vein, R.M. Hare
(1919-   ) clarifies the notion of predictability and shows that it has
erroneously been opposed to the presence of freedom in action. The work
of these linguistic philosophers is akin to that of contemporary scientists.
Both indicate that certain presuppositions that formerly put freedom into
question either are unjustified as premises or are not, in fact, incompatible
with the reality of free decision and free action.

THE CONTEMPORARY PROBLEM OF FREEDOM

In Part III we are faced with the new forms in which freedom

[16] Arthur James Balfour, *Theism and Humanism* (London: Hodder & Stoughton,
1915).

has become problematic today. It appears on all horizons as the vital problematic of acting freely, of being free, of becoming truly free. In the attempt to cast some light upon such an urgent problematic we must not disregard any aspect of freedom that the history of philosophy has brought forward. If the theoretical question of freedom's existence could not be answered as long as man was mistakenly regarded either as a part of nature or as apart from it, the practical question of becoming free as a person will go unanswered to the extent that any partial account of freedom is taken for the whole.

We have seen that a burning human question has been that of order versus freedom. Scientists once felt that natural order excluded freedom; political scientists wondered how much freedom man could be allowed if order was to be retained. Today, in the name of freedom and starting from the base, it is being asked how much order should be tolerated by man. The contemporary problem that is central to life and therefore to our considerations in Part III has become the problem of order within freedom. The human aspects or factors involved in freedom such as control, choice, action, and creativity must be so ordered that they do not destroy or devour but enhance human freedom as a concrete reality. Freedom without its content of these factors is only a word, an abstraction. Concrete freedom demands that they be ordered aright.

In a world where science no longer denies the existence of freedom but has become man's partner in enhancing freedom, in a world where philosophers regard freedom as fundamental and, in some quarters, even equivalent to human existence, the main question has become: What does it mean to be free?

In the section on history we saw that for some thinkers freedom has meant the subordination of willing to whatever knowledge man possessed (the rationalists), while for others freedom meant the subordination of reason to willing (the voluntarists). The former position has spawned various forms of socialism, the latter various forms of individualism. Now that the old problem of the relation of man to nature has reached a plateau status in the rather general admission that man is sovereign over rather than subservient to nature, the problem of freedom has expressed itself in the new terms of the relation of man to society.

Thus the current problematic of order within freedom is bound up with the question of how man is related to society. In this age human freedom is first in the hearts of men, but how fully, how deeply and accurately is it understood by their minds? Moreover, the problematic of

freedom as a practical question has assumed an urgency that was not
present in the era of theoretical formulation.

Part III identifies and discusses the various ways of understanding
freedom that are manifest in the writings of some leading spokesmen for
freedom. Freedom understood as control was supported and publicized by
John Dewey (1859-1952). He wished to eliminate all discussion of free
will and insisted that we should attribute decision to the practical
intelligence.

> We are free in the degree in which we act knowing what we are
> about. The identification of freedom with "freedom of will" locates
> contingency in the wrong place. Contingency of will would mean
> that uncertainty was uncertainly dealt with; it would be a resort to
> chance for a decision.[17]

Instead of free will, Dewey spoke of free action. In this context freedom
means being capable of action that produces situations having qualities of
added significance and order. Choice as an internal aspect of freedom is
here rejected, and the source of knowing whether the "added significance"
is ultimately good is at least ignored. Does it not seem that freedom is
being limited here to those whose state in life allows them to exercise
social control? What of the others? Moreover, when action is for the sake
of arriving at better situations, there still remains the question of who is to
decide what "better" means. Dewey has said that this is the social good.
But may social good be attained in any way whatsoever? And if free action
is that which betters social institutions, does it not raise the question of
whether society's goals are in harmony with human goals?

The question of how control or power is best exercised in the
modern world for the common good of all mankind has aroused deep and
agonized reflection among twentieth-century thinkers. It is vividly seen
that independent power can be self-defeating. Just as in modern times the
old affirmation that the Sabbath is made for man, not man for the
Sabbath, was secularized to nature is made for man, not man for nature, so
it is now being readjusted once again to the newest man-society polarity.
In this context there is no easy answer, for the either/or does not hold,
inasmuch as man is present in both sides of the polarity. There can be no

[17]John Dewey, *The Quest of Certainty* (New York: Minton, Balch & Co.,
1929).

question of simply resolving the problem by making society serve the individual, and still less may we view man as the mere servant of society.

Jean-Paul Sartre (1905-   ) equates freedom with a knowing subject's choice of its mode of being, which he calls the individual's project. Every project is expressed by action directed toward a particular end. It is important to note that in a Sartrian world the word *transcendence* has a special meaning. It means the process by which the conscious self or the for-itself goes beyond or surpasses the given in the pursuit of its project. In this transcending of the given, the subject objectifies or brings low all others, even other subjects. The projects are called absurd because the ends being pursued by them are unattainable. Yet he gives the fine name of *total responsibility* to human freedom when it acts as choice in the absence of any need to conform to truth or to be loyal to fixed values. Man is responsible for everything except his responsibility, of which he cannot rid himself.

> Freedom is existence, and in it existence precedes essence and is not to be distinguished from its choice, that is, from the person himself.[18]

In the spirit of Nietzsche, the Sartrians go beyond good and evil in their ·affirmation of freedom from the constricting force of all schemes of values. Sartre, following Kierkegaard, is rejecting the Hegelian definition of man as spirit or mind with its corresponding admission of the universal. Sartre's knowing subject is an individual existing for-itself. Because man is his freedom, human freedom is absolute and at the same time destined to frustration since all man's projects are in pursuit of an ideal self, in pursuit of being God, the In-Itself-For-Itself. Sartre calls God a self-contradiction inasmuch as the In-Itself, the plenitude of being, cannot coexist, he says, with the For-Itself, which requires the admission of nothingness. But this view makes no allowance for the very different ontological structure that characterizes a divine mind which is pure spirit and capable of self-intuition. Thus the freedom analyzed by Sartre is grounded in nothingness. For such freedom to exist, God must not exist. Sartre was thus one of the first of our contemporaries to declare the death of God on behalf of a so-called humanism.

[18]Jean Paul Sartre, *Existentialism and Human Emotions* (New York: Philosophical Library, 1957), p. 66.

Albert Camus (1913-1960) is so far from agreeing with Dewey's notion of freedom as signified by social achievement that he asserts rebellion to be a legitimate use of freedom. In making this assertion, he speaks for the alienated whose freedom is exercised apart from society's aims. But Camus' position on freedom should not be frozen since he died too early to untangle some of the ambiguities in his work. Thus in his novel *The Plague* men are restored to their authentic selves by exercising neighborly concern and selfless friendship for the sick and thereby overcoming their self-alienation.

Ayn Rand (1905-   ) concentrates on choice as an individual's freedom to act for his own sake. Every individual is a world unto himself with the right not to be interfered with in the pursuit of a free and happy life. In the universe of individuals, the State's function is to prevent anyone from interfering with another's freedom of action. This view raises the question whether such individualism is the truth of the human condition and whether action should be unrelated to the quality of human life when that quality is not necessarily in direct ratio to the exercise of a man's right to acquire all he needs and to use it as he wants.

If some of the most clamorous voices of our century have not offered entirely satisfactory views on freedom, they have certainly challenged others to respond to their views. In the philosophic world it has been considered a prime necessity to adopt, in this search for the essence of freedom, a method that is presuppositionless.

THE PHENOMENOLOGY OF FREEDOM

Part IV is given over to the phenomenological method used by Pierre Thevenaz (1913-1955) and William A. Luijpen (1922-   ) to describe freedom. It is a reflective and subjective method for discovering what we are experiencing. Its intent is to leave aside all assumptions, presuppositions, positions, and dogmas in order to become as objective as possible in describing whatever is being subjectively experienced in the act of knowing. Edmund Husserl (1859-1938) called this suspension of beliefs the *epoche*.[19]

[19] Quentin Lauer, *Phenomenology: Its Genesis and Prospect* (New York: Harper & Row, 196).

A phenomenology of freedom attempts to separate the subjective or reflective experience of freedom from its natural and cultural setting in order to look at freedom as it is. The writers in this section show that when viewed in this way, human freedom presents elements of transcendence and of incarnation, that is, intentionality and embodiment. The logical positivists taught that there is nothing beyond the sensible world with its sense qualities and its imaginative constructs. But the experience of freedom as analyzed by the phenomenological method points beyond the material world to the existence of a personal center called the self, and even beyond the self to the community. Community in turn points to a superior source of its union — an Absolute Being to whom men are open through an experience of truth, goodness, and love, and which guarantees their fidelity in friendship and promotes their creativity in freedom.

This phenomenological investigation provides a knowledge of freedom as it is disclosed in the direct experience transpiring within the world of persons and things. It can deliver a concrete knowledge. A philosophy that is not derived from the life-world will never aid man to live freely. But this is what is expected of philosophy today.

The work of Pierre Teilhard de Chardin (1881-1955) is included in Part IV because it is a related phenomenology of the sciences wherein the whole of man is described as it appears throughout the long past and in its present process.[20] Teilhard is concerned to describe all the manifestations of man, including human history and human values. Because man appears as a process, Teilhard is not content to evaluate him in terms of his origin but seeks to define the world-process in terms of its direction. He observes the process of human convergence to be tending to a final state called *point omega* as opposed to the alpha of elementary particles. The attainment of freedom coincides with cosmic evolution and the process of personal maturation.

A developed human being, as he [Teilhard] rightly pointed out, is not merely a more highly individualized individual. He has crossed the threshold of self-consciousness to a new mode of thought, and as a result has achieved some degree of conscious integration — integration of the self with the outer world of men and nature,

[20]Pierre Teilhard de Chardin, *The Phenomenon of Man* (New York: Harper & Row, 1959).

integration of the separate elements of the self with each other. He is a person, an organism which has transcended individuality in personality. This attainment of personality was an essential element in man's past and present evolutionary success: accordingly its fuller achievement must be an essential aim for the evolutionary future.. . .

He realized that the appearance of human personality was the culmination of two major evolutionary trends — the trend towards more extreme individuation, and that towards more extensive interrelation and cooperation.[21]

Pierre Teilhard de Chardin has given a synthesis of scientific findings about man in an attempt to reveal the whole phenomenon. He has pointed out the curve of freedom in function of space and time. Teilhard and the phenomenologists are not using the same methodology, but they are all trying to let freedom show itself through the phenomenon of human experience. As observations and descriptions they do not replace philosophical interpretations but they prepare well for them.

THE PHILOSOPHY OF FREEDOM

THE PHILOSOPHICAL INTERPRETATIONS OF FREEDOM

Karl Jaspers (1883-1969) and John MacMurray (1891-) suggest that what is of prime importance to the freedom issue is the quality of the relation between man and other men. When friendship qualifies this relation, it initiates community. Because community fosters rather than threatens man's freedom, in this instance we may say both that man is made for community and that community is made for man. The passages in this Part represent some of the most thoughtful analyses of freedom in recent literature. They warrant careful reading because of their delicate handling of the subtle ordering of all the aspects of freedom, especially those of control and choice.

Both philosophers reject the machine-model of the determinist-materialist and the organism-model according to which each part develops

[21] Ibid., Preface, pp. 19-20.

its own lifestyle distinctively as inappropriate for the understanding of freedom. The model they offer is that of community. When society is made up of persons who are related to one another, not as parts within a wider whole where they function for the sake of the whole but as interrelated wholes where each acts for the sake of the other, the result is human community. Within community, freedom is neither excessive dependence nor exaggerated independence, but it is very real interdependence. When we say that freedom is interdependence, we are saying that true freedom exists only when it arises not merely from what one person desires but also from the desires of others. If Reinhold Niebuhr[22] (1892-1971) is right in saying that freedom is born as a response to the other, then, while requiring both choice and control or power to achieve, freedom is more directly described as responsibility. The response that is born of what others want, what others believe possible, gives to a man's freedom a creative quality of spiritual power. The needs and the rights of others to which man responds help him to escape his own egoism. In this community-model for understanding freedom there is provision for that liberation from fear and greed so emphasized by Eastern sages. If free choice without power is empty, power that is accumulated and used out of fear is perilous. Whereas men should not forsake their freedom for the sake of material security, ultimate moral security is the fruit of freedom exercised as responsibility.

THE METAPHYSICAL FOUNDATION OF FREEDOM

The work of Auguste Brunner (1814-), Paul Ricoeur (1913-), and Joseph de Finance (1904-) brings this investigation to some metaphysical understanding of freedom as a totally human experience of transcendence. There is scarcely the need to note here that the conclusions reached are not final, since contemporary man's historical consciousness has made him aware that nothing finite is ever final. If philosophy is an interpretation of human experience, philosophy will

---

[22] Reinhold Niebuhr, *Man's Nature and His Communities*; essays on the dynamics and enigmas of man's personal and social existence (New York: Scribner, 1965).
Richard R. Niebuhr, *Responsible Self* (New York: Harper & Row, 1963).

develop along with that experience, and therefore philosophical insight into the meaning of freedom will be aided by an expanding human consciousness. Because freedom is a tension of many factors such as man's relation to the cosmos, man's creation of culture, man's interpersonal attitudes, and man's responsibilities for others, there is every indication that freedom will be enlarged as those relations and creations, attitudes and responses are improved. Enlargement here connotes something qualitative, not quantitative. Progress in freedom is, after all, human progress.

Freedom today is asserted as a fact; the increase of freedom is desired as a value. A correct philosophical interpretation of freedom is crucial for both the enhancement of freedom and its extension to an ever greater number of persons.

When philosophers analyzed the free act as one that transcends motivations and goals, they noted some of the ontological conditions for this transcendence, conditions that pertain to its very being or existence: an openness to the totality of being along with participating of the person in community. That which mediates the influence of their relation to Total Being is the challenge that their community makes upon them to respond to a growing consciousness of values not yet incarnate in social institutions.

There can be no metaphysical understanding of freedom without questioning why man can surpass, as he so often does, his material structures as well as the psychic and social forces he undergoes, and why every so often he is able to recreate his political institutions. In other words, the material parts of man cannot account for the thinking and the longing, the planning, the projecting, and the achieving that characterize human living. Human conceptions and goals are not reducible to the material components of man. The fact that men can transcend their inner environment of mood and motivation and also transcend their social environment with its demand that they conform to customs and the expectations of society indicates that they are not bound by any metabolism that insists that they take in and become whatever the environment offers and thereby adjust themselves to the times. But it is above all in the revolution that men have brought about in the political structures governing them that we can recognize that into man's freedom has been given the power not only of liberating himself from the brute forces of nature but even from the rational forces of his culture to which, as to a second nature, he has been subservient in former times. The criterion for human action is found not in what natural environment or the inherited culture impose upon man and require in the way of reaction, but in what other men propose through their human needs and personal hopes. Limitless possibilities for the evolution and enlargement of human freedom are opened up by the challenges facing every generation. Much has been said of individual initiative as the source of great changes in the world. But if our analysis is correct, the future is forged by persons who respond to the needs and the desires and even the dreams of others. A philosophical analysis of the conditions for human creative change of social and political institutions reveals that relationship to others is the ontic (pertaining to being or existence) foundation of creative freedom and its evolution.

Thus at its most profound level freedom appears as love. It is clear then both why community is the work of freedom and why freedom is its fruit. Since community is never achieved once and for all, the primary task of freedom is never finished. As an ongoing process, community is constantly awakening man to responsibility for his choices, for his exercise of power, but chiefly to his responsibility for community.

If freedom is achieved and develops most favorably within community, any age that makes interpersonal relations difficult or impossible will be a dehumanized age, and even if freedom is explicitly lauded in that age, it will nevertheless be implicitly compromised. As we have seen, the scientists and the linguistic analysts of our day leave ample room for the possibility of human freedom. Why then do so many contemporary writers complain about the dehumanization and the enslavement of man in a scientific age? Science has made technology possible, but many of the aspects of a technological society decrease the possibilities for freedom. The psychological disturbances undergone by many people today are rooted in a personal frustration related to the lack of community.

The ontological foundation of community is the existence of interpersonal relationships, which are rooted somehow in the primitive condition of each one's relation to God. It is true that all nature of which for so long man was deemed to be merely a part is related to God by the act of creation. But man knows or can know that he is related to God and that he remains open to His power. This is a basis for the belief in the unlimited possibility for human development. Man's rootedness in and continued relationship to this transcendent source frees him from the compelling conditions of nature and society. This relationship is not only the foundation of free choice, as was pointed out by the medieval metaphysicians, but it is also the basis of that free personal commitment to friendship that is the matrix for the growth of human freedom. A natural need of man is not only to transcend the immediacy of sensible life through a life of thought, which humanizes existence into a civilization, but to transcend the isolation of individuality by relating to other persons in a communal situation. If the I-Thou relationship is the foundation of every human existence, any disregard of this in the living out of life will take its toll.

CONCLUSION

When all the facts and the conditions of freedom are probed, it becomes clear that freedom is not merely something transpiring within the self, nor is it merely exemption from all kinds of constraint; it is neither wholly inner nor wholly outer freedom. Personal unity, self-unification, and the control of physical and social forces are all factors within freedom as a totality. In its authentic form as qualifying the human person, freedom is affected by the interdependent status of human being. Therefore freedom embraces the other no less than the self; it requires the openness of both to that which is greater than both, namely, Infinite Being, which marks the horizon of the experience of willing. The unlimited character of this pole of human action is nature's guarantee of human freedom. Of course, this intrinsic dynamism of the mind-will to Absolute Being does not depend upon being explicitly known in order to be operative. It is required simply by the experience of willing freely as philosophers have interpreted that experience.

A philosophy of freedom also has the critical function of assisting us in detecting the false forms of freedom that in each age plead for allegiance. This criticism is not merely an academic pursuit but has the practical purpose of making man free. The common good of the world community toward which we all must work is freedom in common. This freedom is the taking of responsibility, not only for ourselves, but in love for every man. The phenomenologist who illumines freedom's meaning and the philosopher who provides an ultimate explanation of freedom as experienced make important contributions to mankind. A senseless life, far more than the unexamined life, is not worth living; but only if we can make sense of freedom can we indeed make sense of human existence. The understanding of freedom, however, is no substitute for the task of becoming free, a task that is not the privilege of a few philosophers but both the destiny and the duty of every human person.

Part **I**

CONTEMPORARY SCIENTIFIC VIEWS CONCERNING THE QUESTION: DOES FREEDOM EXIST?

1

The decline of determinism

Sir Arthur Stanley Eddington

The "uncertainty" that recent scientific method has revealed as characteristic of the sub-atomic particles is more credible to man — who is very aware of his own uncertainty — than was the old mechanized-world reality.

Two things have happened here. First, the generalization of determinism in which scientists had included man's choosing has been found untrue even for inorganic things. Second, Spinoza's old argument that our consciousness of freedom is a consequence of our ignorance of what is determining us has now been drastically reversed to read: our ignorance of the true nature of nuclei resulted in the belief that all movement was determined — which was untrue.

Ignorance has never been a valid basis for a conclusion; but man's awareness of his own experience of freedom may prove to be a better point of departure for understanding the universe.

Thus from the outset we can be quite clear about one very important fact, namely, that the validity of the law of causation for the world of reality is a question that cannot be decided on grounds of abstract reasoning.   Max Planck, *Where is Science Going?* p. 113.

The new theory appears to be well founded on observation, but one may ask whether *in the future*, by development or refinement, it may not be made deterministic again. As to this it must be said: It can be shown by rigorous mathematics that the accepted formal theory of quantum mechanics does not admit of any such extension. If anyone clings to the hope that determinism will ever return, he must hold the existing theory to be false in substance; it must be possible to disprove experimentally definite assertions of this theory. The determinist should therefore not protest but experiment.

Max Born, *Naturwissenschaften*, 1929, p. 117.

Whilst the feeling of free-will dominates the life of the spirit, the regularity of sensory phenomena lays down the demand for causality. But in both domains simultaneously the point in question is an idealisation, whose natural limitations can be more closely investigated, and which determine one another in the sense that the feeling of volition and the demand for causality are equally indispensable to the relation between Subject and Object which is the kernel of the problem of perception.

Niels Bohr, *Naturwissenschaften*, 1930, p. 77.

We must await the further development of science, perhaps for centuries, before we can design a true and detailed picture of the interwoven texture of Matter, Life and Soul. But the old classical determinism of Hobbes and Laplace need not oppress us any longer.

Herman Weyl, *The Open World*, p. 55.

Ten years ago practically every physicist of repute was, or believed himself to be, a determinist, at any rate so far as inorganic phenomena are concerned. He believed he had come across a scheme of strict causality

From A. S. Eddington, *New Pathways in Science* (New York: Cambridge University Press, 1935), pp. 83-91. Reprinted by permission.

regulating the sequence of phenomena. It was considered to be the primary aim of science to fit as much of the universe as possible into such a scheme; so that, as a working belief if not as a philosophical conviction, the causal scheme was always held to be applicable in default of overwhelming evidence to the contrary. In fact, the methods, definitions and conceptions of physical science were so much bound up with the hypothesis of strict causality that the limits (if any) of the scheme of causal law were looked upon as the ultimate limits of physical science. No serious doubt was entertained that this determinism covered all inorganic phenomena. How far it applied to living or conscious matter or to consciousness itself was a matter of individual opinion; but there was naturally a reluctance to accept any restriction of an outlook which had proved so successful over a wide domain.

Then rather suddenly determinism faded out of theoretical physics. Its exit has been received in various ways. Some writers are incredulous and cannot be persuaded that determinism has really been eliminated from the present foundations of physical theory. Some think that it is no more than a domestic change in physics, having no reactions on general philosophic thought. Some decide cynically to wait and see if determinism fades in again.

The rejection of determinism is in no sense an abdication of scientific method. It is rather the fruition of a scientific method which had grown up under the shelter of the old causal method and has now been found to have a wider range. It has greatly increased the power and precision of the mathematical theory of observed phenomena. On the other hand I cannot agree with those who belittle the philosophical significance of the change. The withdrawal of physical science from an attitude it had adopted consistently for more than 200 years is not to be treated lightly; and it provokes a reconsideration of our views as to one of the most perplexing problems of our existence.

*   *   *

The future is never entirely determined by the past, nor is it ever entirely detached. We have referred to several phenomena in which the future is *practically determined*; the break-down of a radium nucleus is an example of a phenomenon in which the future is *practically detached* from the past.

But, you will say, the fact that physics assigns no characteristic to the radium nucleus predetermining the date at which it will break up, only means that that characteristic has not yet been discovered. You readily agree that we cannot predict the future in all cases; but why blame Nature rather than our own ignorance? If the radium atom were an exception, it would be natural to suppose that there is a determining characteristic which, when it is found, will bring it into line with other phenomena. But the radio-active atom was not brought forward as an exception; I have mentioned it as an extreme example of that which applies in greater or lesser degree to all kinds of phenomena. There is a difference between explaining away an exception and explaining away a rule.

The persistent critic continues, "You are evading the point. I contend that there are characteristics unknown to you which completely predetermine not only the time of break-up of the radio-active atom but all physical phenomena. How do you know that there are not? You are not omniscient?" I can understand the casual reader raising this question; but when a man of scientific training asks it, he wants shaking up and waking. Let us try the effect of a story.

About the year 2000, the famous archaeologist Prof. Lambda discovered an ancient Greek inscription which recorded that a foreign prince, whose name was given as Κανδεκλης, came with his followers into Greece and established his tribe there. The Professor anxious to identify the prince, after exhausting other sources of information, began to look through the letters C and K in the *Encyclopaedia Athenica*. His attention was attracted by an article on Canticles who it appeared was the son of Solomon. Clearly that was the required identification; no one could doubt that Κανδεκλης was the Jewish Prince Canticles. His theory attained great notoriety. At that time the Great Powers of Greece and Palestine were concluding an Entente and the Greek Prime Minister in an eloquent peroration made touching reference to the newly discovered historical ties of kinship between the two nations. Some time later Prof. Lambda happened to refer to the article again and discovered that he had made an unfortunate mistake; he had misread "Son of Solomon" for "Song of Solomon". The correction was published widely, and it might have been supposed that the Canticles theory would die a natural death. But no: Greeks and Palestinians continued to believe in their kinship, and the Greek Minister continued to make perorations. Prof. Lambda one day ventured to remonstrate with him. The Minister turned on him severely, "How do you know that Solomon had not a son called Canticles? You are not omniscient". The Professor, having reflected on the rather extensive character of Solomon's matrimonial establishment, found it difficult to reply.

The curious thing is that the determinist who takes this line is under the illusion that he is adopting a more modest attitude in regard to our scientific knowledge than the indeterminist. The indeterminist is accused of claiming omniscience. I do not bring quite the same countercharge against the determinist; but surely it is only the man who thinks himself *nearly* omniscient who would have the audacity to enumerate the possibilities which (it occurs to him) might exist unknown to him. I suspect that some of the other chapters in this book will be criticized for including hypotheses and deductions for which the evidence is considered to be insufficiently conclusive; that is inevitable if one is to give a picture of physical science in the process of development and discuss the current problems which occupy our thoughts. I tremble to think what the critics would say if I included a conjecture solely on the ground that, not being omniscient, I do not know that it is false.

I have already said that determinism is not disproved by physics. But it is the determinist who puts forward a positive proposal and the onus of proof is on him. He wishes to base on our ordinary experience of the sequence of cause and effect a wide generalisation called the Principle of Causality. Since physics to-day represents this experience as the result of statistical laws without any reference to the principle of causality, it is obvious that the generalisation has nothing to commend it so far as observational evidence is concerned. The indeterminists therefore regard it as they do any other entirely unsupported hypothesis. It is part of the tactics of the advocate of determinism to turn our unbelief in his conjecture into a positive conjecture of our own — a sort of Principle of Uncausality. The indeterminist is sometimes said to postulate "something like free-will" in the individual atoms. *Something like* is conveniently vague; the various mechanisms used in daily life have their obstinate moods and may be said to display something like free-will. But if it is suggested that we postulate psychological characters in the individual atoms of the kind which appear in our minds as human free-will, I deny this altogether. We do not discard one rash generalisation only to fall into another equally rash.

When determinism was believed to prevail in the physical world, the question naturally arose, how far did it govern human activities? The question has often been confused by assuming that human activity belongs to a totally separate sphere — a mental sphere. But man has a body as well as a mind. The movements of his limbs, the sound waves which issue from his lips, the twinkle in his eye, are all phenomena of the physical world, and unless expressly excluded would be predetermined along with other physical phenomena. We can, if we like, distinguish two forms of determinism: (1) The scheme of causal law predetermines all human thoughts, emotions and volitions; (2) it predetermines human actions but not human motives and volitions. The second seems less drastic and probably commends itself to the liberal-minded, but the concession really amounts to very little. Under it a man can think what he likes, but he can only say that which the laws of physics preordain.

The essential point is that, if determinism is to have any definable meaning, the domain of deterministic law must be a closed system; that is to say, all the data used in predicting must themselves be capable of being predicted. Whatever predetermines the future must itself be predetermined by the past. The movements of human bodies are part of the complete data of prediction of future states of the material universe; and if we include them for this purpose we must include them also as data which (it is asserted) can be predicted.

We must also note a semi-deterministic view, which asserts determinism for inorganic phenomena but supposes that it can be overridden by the interference of consciousness. Determinism in the material universe then applies only to phenomena in which it is assured that consciousness is not intervening directly or indirectly. It would be difficult to accept such a view nowadays. I suppose that most of those who expect determinism ultimately to reappear in physics do so from the feeling that there is some kind of logical necessity for it; but it can scarcely be a logical necessity if it is capable of being overridden. The hypothesis puts the scientific investigator in the position of being afraid to prove too much; he must show that effect is firmly linked to cause, but not so firmly that consciousness is unable to break the link. Finally we have to remember that physical law is arrived at from the analysis of conscious experience; it is the solution of the cryptogram contained in the story of consciousness. How then can we represent consciousness as being not only outside it but inimical to it?

The revolution of theory which has expelled determinism from present-day physics has therefore the important consequence that it is no longer necessary to suppose that human actions are completely predetermined. Although the door of human freedom is opened, it is not flung wide open; only a chink of daylight appears. But I think this is sufficient to justify a reorientation of our attitude to the problem. If our new-found freedom is like that of the mass of ·001 mgm., which is only allowed to stray $\frac{1}{5000}$ mm. in a thousand years, it is not much to boast of. The physical results do not spontaneously suggest any higher degree of freedom than this. But it seems to me that philosophical, psychological, and in fact commonsense arguments for greater freedom are so cogent that we are justified in trying to prise the door further open now that it is not actually barred. How can this be done without violence to physics?

If we could attribute the large-scale movements of our bodies to the "trigger action" of the unpredetermined behaviour of a few key atoms in our brain cells the problem would be simple; for individual atoms have wide indeterminacy of behaviour. It is obvious that there is a great deal of trigger action in our bodily mechanism, as when the pent up energy of a muscle is released by a minute physical change in a nerve; but it would be rash to suppose that the physical controlling cause is contained in the configuration of a few dozen atoms. I should conjecture that the smallest unit of structure in which the physical effects of volition have their origin contains many billions of atoms. If such a unit behaved like an inorganic system of similar mass the indeterminacy would be insufficient to allow appreciable freedom. My own tentative view is that this "conscious unit" does in fact differ from an inorganic system in having a much higher indeterminacy of behaviour – simply because of the unitary nature of that which in reality it represents, namely the Ego.

We have to remember that the physical world of atoms, electrons, quanta, etc., is the abstract symbolic representation of something. Generally we do not know anything of the background of the symbols – we do not know the inner nature of what is being symbolized. But at a point of contact of the physical world with consciousness, we have acquaintance with the conscious unity – the self or mind – whose physical aspect and symbol is the brain cell. Our method of physical analysis leads us to dissect this cell into atoms similar to the atoms in any non-conscious region of the world. But whereas in other regions each atom (so far as its behaviour is indeterminate) is governed independently by chance, in the conscious cell the behaviour symbolises a single volition of the spirit and not a conflict of billions of independent impulses. It seems equations and the conservation of energy. In this case I am by no means anxious to stress the fact (if it is a fact) that the operations of my mind are unpredictable. Indeed I often prefer to use a multiplying machine whose results are less unpredictable than those of my own mental arithmetic. But the truth of the result $7 \times 11 = 77$ lies in its character as a possible mental operation and not in the fact that it is turned out automatically by a special combination of cog-wheels. I attach importance to the physical unpredictability of the motion of my pen, because it leaves it free to respond to the thought evolved in my brain which may or may not have been predetermined by the mental characteristics of my nature. If the mathematical argument in my mind is compelled to reach the conclusion which a deterministic system of physical law has preordained that my hands shall write down, then reasoning must be explained away as a process quite other than that which I feel it to be. But my whole respect for reasoning is based on the hypothesis that it *is* what I feel it to be.

I do not think we can take liberties with that immediate self-knowledge of consciousness by which we are aware of ourselves as responsible, truth-seeking, reasoning, striving. The external world is not what it seems; we can transform our conception of it as we will provided that the system of signals passing from it to the mind is conserved. But as we draw nearer to the source of all knowledge the stream should run clearer. At least that is the hypothesis that the scientist is compelled to make, else where shall he start to look for truth? The Problem of Experience becomes unintelligible unless it is considered as the quest of a responsible, truth-seeking, reasoning spirit. These characteristics of the spirit therefore become the first datum of the problem.

The conceptions of physics are becoming difficult to understand. First relativity theory, then quantum theory and wave mechanics, have transformed the universe, making it seem fantastic to our minds. And perhaps the end is not yet. But there is another side to the transformation. Naive realism, materialism, and mechanistic conceptions of phenomena were simple to understand; but I think that it was only by closing our eyes to the essential nature of conscious experience that they could be made to seem credible. These revolutions of scientific thought are clearing up the deeper contradictions between life and theoretical knowledge. The latest phase with its release from determinism is one of the greatest steps in the reconciliation. I would even say that in the present indeterministic theory of the physical universe we have reached something which a reasonable man might *almost* believe.

to me that we must attribute some kind of unitary behaviour to the physical terminal of consciousness, otherwise the physical symbolism is not an appropriate representation of the mental unit which is being symbolized.

We conclude then that the activities of consciousness do not violate the laws of physics, since in the present indeterministic scheme there is freedom to operate within them. But at first sight they seem to involve something which we previously described (p. 64) as worse than a violation of the laws of physics, namely an exceedingly improbable coincidence. That had reference to coincidences ascribed to chance. Here we do not suppose that the conspiracy of the atoms in a brain cell to bring about a certain physical result instead of all fighting against one another is due to a chance coincidence. The unanimity is rather the condition that the atoms form a legitimate representation of that which is itself a unit in the mental reality behind the world of symbols.

The two aspects of human freedom on which I would lay most stress are *responsibility* and *self-understanding.* The nature of responsibility brings us to a well-known dilemma which I am no more able to solve than hundreds who have tried before me. How can we be responsible for our own good or evil nature? We feel that we can to some extent change our nature; we can reform or deteriorate. But is not the reforming or deteriorating impulse also in our nature? Or, if it is not in us, how can we be responsible for it? I will not add to the many discussions of this difficulty, for I have no solution to suggest. I will only say that I cannot accept as satisfactory the solution sometimes offered, that responsibility is a self-contradictory illusion. The solution does not seem to me to fit the data. Just as a theory of matter has to correspond to our perceptions of matter so a theory of the human spirit has to correspond to our inner perception of our spiritual nature. And to me it seems that responsibility is one of the fundamental facts of our nature. If I can be deluded over such a matter of immediate knowledge – the very nature of the being that I myself am – it is hard to see where any trustworthy beginning of knowledge is to be found.

I pass on to another aspect of the freedom allowed under physical indeterminacy, which seems to be quite distinct from the question of Free Will. Suppose that I have hit on a piece of mathematical research which promises interesting results. The assurance that I most desire is that the result which I write down at the end shall be the work of a mind which respects truth and logic, not the work of a hand which respects Maxwell's

2

Dialogue concerning science and philosophilcal positions

Werner Heisenberg

This discussion by scientists is very relevant to the topic of the scientific retreat from determinism, especially because it includes statements by Werner Heisenberg with whose name the principle of indeterminacy has been associated. We hear one member of the discussion conclude that the philosopher's use of dialectic and categories is diametrically opposed to the scientist's experiment and quantitative measurement. While Professor Heisenberg agrees that scientists only imagine philosophy to be an extension of science, he thinks it necessary to ask whether Plato's theory, according to which the ultimate particles of "earth" are cubes and those of "fire" tetrahedrons, is philosophy or science?

The dialogue also indicates that the human factor in our knowledge of science has gained ascendancy over the scientific factor in our knowledge of man. The impossibility of bracketing one's beliefs and attitudes when engaged in the "phenomenological epoché" seems foreshadowed in Heisenberg's realization that the nineteenth-century scientific attempt to "photograph" nature was in a sense an abortive effort, inasmuch as when atomic physicists try to photograph nature, they alter its character.

Albert Picot

Werner Heisenberg has expounded to us how nineteenth-century science was founded on ideas of Newton and Descartes. Absolute time, absolute space, absolute causality shut us in and have enclosed the scientists in a relatively narrow area. On the other hand, with the new discoveries of which we spoke last night and above all with the quantum theory and relativity, we have arrived at the concept of which Heisenberg is the chief proponent, the uncertainty principle, a concept that casts doubts on the general theory of causality and on determinism. In a parallel manner in the eighteenth, nineteenth and twentieth centuries, a series of great philosophers affirmed the liberty of man, even independently of science. Three of these appear to us as the proponents of liberty: Kant, Charles Secretan, Karl Jaspers.

And here is my question — a rather critical question, almost indiscreet, since it compels us to ask Professor Heisenberg what his convictions are. Do these philosophers find support in the theory of uncertainty, in the new orientation of science, which recognizes the role of liberty in nature? Is it not strange that a man like Karl Jaspers does not support these discoveries? Is it a new element to prove the liberty of man or is it only a momentary stage in science, which one day will again show causality in quanta? Can we join together, or must we separate, the philosophers who affirm liberty on the basis of philosophy and the scientists who have expounded the uncertainty concept on principles that seem very solid?

Heisenberg

The problem of the relation between uncertainty and liberty has been dealt with too imprecisely and superficially, particularly in the press. It cannot be said that the uncertainty principle opens the door wider to liberty.

We must try to approach the problem of uncertainty and liberty by means of the theory of knowledge, such as Kant also used. The question of what I can do or cannot do is, however, very different from the question what another must do or not do. And there are always many complex questions related to these problems.

Even when we have to do with apparently identical questions, very different replies are obtained; this depends on the way such questions are approached. When we have to do with apparently completely different questions, which often are only different facets of the same problem, very similar answers are sometimes obtained. Summarizing, I do not think that the uncertainty principle has a direct relationship to the concept of liberty. The relation is rather indirect; the introduction of uncertainty into physics has put us on guard against taking too definite a position.

Giacomo Devoto

Before addressing two questions to Professor Heisenberg, I will take the liberty of making a very brief comment on the discussion which has taken place up to now.

1. The relationships to philosophy: It is a very different thing to say that the progress of physics has repercussions on philosophy and that the progress of physics has given a new aspect to the relationship between science and philosophy. In the first case, we must never forget that philosophy is something that precedes science. For centuries it oscillated between a realistic and idealistic vision of the world. The discoveries of science can influence it in one direction or another, but they are never decisive.

2. I associate myself with Professor Heisenberg's point of view about the concept of liberty. Defining moral liberty by basing it on the

uncertainty principle is as absurd as saying: since we cannot put all men into one prison or compel them to live in the same manner from morning till night, we may as well acknowledge their liberty.

Since the uncertainty principle means only one thing — man and science are not in a position to photograph nature down to its last details — it is ridiculous to try find in it a basis for liberty. A definition of liberty cannot be based on a phenomenon of inability.

I now come to the two questions to Professor Heisenberg that I have already announced.

Since the passage of science from the nineteenth to the twentieth century does not imply a change in philosophical position, is he willing to limit it to a change in definitions?

Up to the nineteenth century, science hoped or pretended to photograph nature. The science of the twentieth century limits itself to describing it. The science of the twentieth century is a language. Being a language, it must arouse the same problems that present themselves in the study of a language. And the fundamental question is the following: In physics there is the relationship between physical facts and mathematical interpretation; in the study of languages, what is there? On the one hand there is historical observation, the history of languages; on the other, the pedagogic application by the grammarian, who tries to establish and describe the conventions that everyone observes in a linguistic context.

Now the second question I ask Professor Heisenberg is the following: Does he accept my suggestion to set up a parallel between physics and the history of languages, of that language which is the new science of which the mathematician is only the grammarian? I know that this definition does not please the mathematician; but nevertheless this is one way of putting the question and above all of ending the discussion between those who believe we can describe facts mathematically and those who do not. Mathematics is a way of describing physical phenomena, just as the rules of grammar are a way of describing a language but are not the language.

Heisenberg

In broad outline I perfectly agree with what you state. It is really possible to say, when recapitulating, that the nineteenth century attempted to photograph nature, while the twentieth century describes nature in a mathematical language. The physicist, however, has realized that, when he believed he was photographing, he was not always doing so.

The physicist in the nineteenth century did not have to discuss philosophy or religion. It was even believed that these doctrines could be kept completely aside and that it would thus be possible to achieve what Professor Devoto calls "a photograph of nature." But it was found that this point of view could not be confirmed experimentally, and very often, when atomic physicists try to photograph nature, they alter its character.

Furthermore, it is observed that the physics of quanta, where uncertainty intervenes, must always be based on deterministic physics. It is hardly possible to do otherwise, and it seems that indeterminateness brings a correction to classical, deterministic physics.

I think it would undoubtedly be useful to study more closely and develop this problem of parallelism between science and language, but I will not do so here. I believe that Professor Devoto is more qualified to attempt it, and perhaps he has already done so. However, we must not forget that the sciences are "between" nature and man.

*   *   *

Heisenberg

I resume with some further details of the example of the hydrogen atom. When a simple hydrogen atom is considered and its collision with an electron is studied, a disturbance in the hydrogen atom is observed. The classical physicists believed this collision occurred in a completely analogous manner to that which would have been produced between a planet and comet. In more modern physics the result of this collision is nevertheless not completely predictable, even though it depends on the initial conditions. There exists one probability of finding an electron in the excited hydrogen atom, another of finding the nucleus deprived of its electron. And these probabilities are fixed and cannot be modified. The hydrogen atom that is found after the collision is, however, no longer exactly what it was before. It is in fact known that, when an interaction contains enough energy, there exists the probability that the hydrogen is not found again, but instead something completely different is found. Several different cases are possible, and these cases are connected among themselves by relations of probability. In fact, what is thus found as a result of an interaction, of any action, is not always objects, but forms — forms of that energy which is the fundamental basic material of modern physics, capable of taking different forms in which we recognize objects.

Umberto Campagnolo

I am wondering whether a physicist can really speak as philosopher and if his considerations will have the precision that a philosopher must observe in his subject.

I believe that there lies the chief danger of the discussion of which is to be ascribed, at least from appearances, to the bringing together of scientists and philosophers. The problem a philosopher puts to himself is always of a radically different nature from that which the scientist puts to himself. The scientists assume that there is always the possibility of arriving at quantity and measurement, at calculations and equations. The philosophers, on the contrary, seek categories and try to link them by means of a process that, if you allow me to use the word, has nothing in common with that of science, that is, by dialectics.

Concluding, I think that we would have much to gain in our discussions by eliminating here the references to philosophy, because philosophical thought is very different from scientific thought. Scientists often tend to imagine philosophy as an extension of science, as a general way of considering their problem from a particular point of view. But I believe that they deceive themselves; it is the philosophers who are and remain responsible for philosophy.

Heisenberg

I completely agree with this way of posing the problem, but I ask Professor Campagnolo if Plato's theory, according to which the ultimate particles of "earth" are cubes and those of "fire" tetrahedrons, is philosophy or science?

3

Biology and freedom

Edmund W. Sinnott

Professor Sinnott sees freedom as characterized by goal-seeking, a search that the biologists detect already in the living embryo; thus as part of human life man's purposes can triumph over the familiar frustrations of any life. As a prefiguration of this in nature, Professor Sinnott discusses the equifinality shown by some embryos where, if one course of development is blocked, the organism reaches the same end by quite a different route.

The spontaneity of imagination is a primary hint that human action transcends the functioning of a simple mechanism. We may not know how great poems and symphonies are created, but at least we know that they are not manufactured.

A creativity in man's way of living is more related to the order of human goals than to any capacity for caprice.

The problem of creativeness is closely involved, of course, with that of freedom and determinism. If man is physically a mechanism only, there can be in him no real creativeness and thus no freedom, for in a universe the fate of which is fixed there are no novelties at all.

The underlying questions in philosophy which man must face keep coming back in different formulations as one historical era succeeds another. The "freedom of the will" is one such problem. Whether man has a soul is an important question, but a shackled soul is hardly any soul at all. Is man really *free*, we ask, to do what he wishes and therefore endowed with moral responsibility, or is he caught in the great snare of fate which drags him on whether he will or no? To common sense and our deep inner conviction the answer can be made with no uncertainty — we *are* free, obviously and inescapably. The successful conduct of our lives, the very pursuit of science itself, depends on a belief that we can choose our course. No hypothesis has ever been confirmed more fully than has this one by its practical results, and no belief more amply justified.

And yet this belief has been most seriously challenged. As theologians in the Christian tradition pondered the attributes of God three centuries ago they were bound to ascribe to him not only omnipotence but omniscience and complete foreknowledge of the future, which thus must already be determined. On this assumption man's course is obviously predetermined and his fate is fixed. But if he is not free to act, how can God hold him morally accountable for what he does? Over this problem men long suffered agonies of doubt and apprehension. If sinners in the hands of an angry God were predestined to sin, why should they suffer the pains of hell for something they could never help? The injustice of this was obvious but the alternative seemed to be denial that God was all-foreseeing. The horns of the dilemma were a limited God or a helpless man. The stern Puritan creed endeavored to break a pathway through this wilderness, and its best answer is to be found in Jonathan Edwards' "The

Reprinted by permission of Harper and Row and George Allen & Unwin Ltd. From pp. 124-132, 137-138 in MATTER, MIND AND MAN (hardbound edition) by Edmund W. Sinnott, copyright 1957 by Edmund Ware Sinnott.

Freedom of the Will." This carries little comfort to ordinary men — especially those not predestined to divine grace! — nor is it acceptable to many nowadays.

In the nineteenth century another reason was invoked for denying man his freedom, not the omniscience of God this time but the uniformity and predictability of nature which science had revealed. This great conception implies that every event in the universe is rigidly determined by physical causes and cannot in the least degree be diverted from its destined course. A complete knowledge of the universe at any instant and of the laws which govern it would make possible, at least in theory, a prediction of its entire future history.

> The first morning of creation wrote
> What the last dawn of reckoning shall read.

Freedom or any degree of uncertainty, in living or lifeless nature, is incompatible with this assumption of complete determinism, which justified itself by the triumphant advance of science through the century. The problem of freedom troubled many still but the horns of the dilemma now were expressed in scientific rather than in theological terms. The deadlock remains today, but it is the custom now to look at the freedom of the will as an outdated and rather meaningless problem, one chiefly of semantics and no longer requiring serious attention from philosophers.

Such a conclusion, I believe, is far from sound. It has been proposed not because freedom no longer is important but because to reconcile it with scientific orthodoxy seems impossible. Where there is such a sharp conflict, however, between the deterministic requirements of scientific theory and an assumption of freedom based on almost universal human conviction, an assumption which underlies most of our philosophy and morals, every effort should be made to reconcile the two. The problem of freedom is by no means academic only. Many of our ills today are the result of a growing acceptance of the idea that we are puppets, pushed around by fate and circumstance and no longer masters of our own destiny. The moral and philosophical implications of such a belief are momentous.

Aside from the general question of physical determinism and the uniformity of nature, there are two more immediate sources — psychology and genetics — from which the conclusion has commonly been drawn that man is not free. They often oppose each other but each has many supporters.

Psychology, like science in general, is so committed to determinism that although it often speaks of choice and purpose it uses these terms largely for convenience and sidesteps the basic problem. Sherrington comments that "from the human standpoint, the important thing is less that man's will should be free than that man should think that it is free." But until the science of the mind can develop a foundation of theory that can satisfy its own data and at the same time bring them into harmony with the universal conviction of mankind and thus reinforce his sense of moral responsibility, it will fail in its chief service. Somewhere, somehow, the barriers between theory and experience must be breached. Professor Allport speaks wisely about psychology's attitude toward freedom, though perhaps for a minority of his colleagues.

> No other issue [he says] causes such consternation for the scientific psychologist. One may look through a hundred successive American books in psychology and find no mention of "will" or "freedom." It is customary for the psychologist, as for other scientists, to proceed within the framework of strict determinism, and to build barriers between himself and common sense lest common sense infect psychology with its belief in freedom. For the same reason barricades are erected against theology. But to our discomfort recent events have raised the issue all over again. Existentialism insists on freedom; much of the psychotherapy now in vogue presupposes it; psychology's new concern with values is at bottom a concern with choices, and therefore revives the problem of freedom. Up to now the tug of war between free will and determinism has been marked by naiveté. Just as we have learned with some success to transcend the monolithic oppositions between mind and body, nature and nurture, we should strive for better perspective in our view of freedom and determinism.[1]

At present a substantial body of psychological opinion looks on man as an "empty" organism, a *tabula rasa* on which his environment writes everything and he, nothing. On an earlier page this position was presented briefly. To quote Professor B.F. Skinner again:

[1] Gordon W. Allport, *Becoming* (New Haven: Yale University Press, 1955), pp. 82-83.

Man, we once believed, was free to express himself in art, music and literature, to inquire into nature, to seek salvation in his own way. He could initiate action and make spontaneous and capricious changes of course. Under the most extreme duress some sort of choice remained to him. He could resist any effort to control him, though it might cost him his life. But science insists that action is initiated by forces impinging upon the individual, and that caprice is only another name for behavior for which we have not yet found a cause.[2]

For Professor Skinner, freedom is mere caprice. Unless it turns out to be more than this, however, we may well agree that it is meaningless. No one will go to the barricades to defend mere randomness and aimless whimsey. We can agree that *something* determines what we do. The great question, standing at the very foundation of our inquiry into man's nature, is whether this factor comes entirely from outside man himself, determining everything he is and does, or whether there is something within him that shares in the directiveness. No one can doubt, of course, that much of our behavior is the result of influences in our environment — upbringing, education, culture pattern and conditioning. The son of an Episcopalian is likely to be an Episcopalian and of a Democrat, a Democrat. One brought up in a family of wealth will acquire different economic views from those of a laborer's son. The pattern of culture south of Mason and Dixon's line imparts a different attitude toward race relations than one common in the north.

A belief in the supreme importance of environment is adopted by much of sociology today. We are told that the way to improve mankind is by giving us better conditions under which to live — better food, housing, medical care and other things that minister to safety and well-being. Many students of ethics maintain that morals are imposed on us by our culture and are without any inner authority. Criminals are not really culpable but simply the unfortunate victims of a poor environment.

Certainly much hope for man lies in the proper manipulation of his environment, for he is very sensitive to it and is highly educable. So to condition him that he will cooperate with his fellows unselfishly and value qualities that will make him healthy, wise and productive offers to the

[2]B. F. Skinner, "Freedom and the Control of Men," *American Scholar*, 25:52-53, 1955-56.

practitioners of applied psychology a challenge to remake the world. This has a tremendous appeal, for it is essentailly the same challenge that has inspired teachers and reformers and missionaries and evangelists from the beginning. What is new in it, however, is the assumption that these external agencies are all-important and that the individual himself has no control over his own behavior. The freedom he seems to possess is only illusion.

But in their conviction that factors outside the organism are of paramount importance in determining its behavior, psychologists have too much neglected the organism itself. It certainly is by no means the empty, neutral thing that many assume it to be. For over half a century the science of genetics has accumulated a vast amount of evidence that what an organism is and does depends to a great extent on its inborn hereditary constitution. Two individuals may react very differently to the same environmental factor. Less is known about the genetics of man than of many lower organisms because of the difficulty of getting extensive data, but it is certain that the general principles of heredity apply to him as fully as to other living things and not only to his physical traits but to his mental ones. This does not mean that inheritance is everything, for environment obviously exerts a profound influence. It is well recognized that what a gene controls is not a specific trait but a *specific way of reacting to the environment*. Both heredity and environment are major influences on an organism, and neither should be emphasized to the exclusion of the other. Let us not forget, too, that protoplasm is not a nonspecific system. It has a physical and chemical constitution that is remarkably uniform throughout the organic world. We should expect it to have certain qualities and predispositions of its own which will resist the influence of either environmental or genetic factors and such, I believe, is actually the case.

Some geneticists are as dogmatic as some psychologists. As the latter would try to persuade us that man is a puppet and under the complete control of his environment, so the former, especially when they are considering the human species, stress the paramount importance of inheritance. Professor C.D. Darlington[3] in a recent book tries to convince his readers that a person's hereditary constitution determines most of what he is and does. There is indeed some very striking evidence of the often subtle role heredity must play, notably in cases of identical twins who

[3] C.D. Darlington, *The Facts of Life* (New York: The Macmillan Company, 1952).

have been reared apart but in whose lives events are remarkably parallel. Most geneticists, however, would not draw such sweeping conclusions as does Professor Darlington. This book will serve as an excellent counterpoise to one by Professor Skinner[4] for both are extreme statements of their particular points of view.

Either of these theories, however, or any division of man's fate between them would mean that freedom is drastically abridged or wholly lacking. One can be as much the slave of his genes as of his conditioning. Indeed, genetics has more often been cited in support of a deterministic philosophy than has psychology. Certainly neither of these sciences, at least in their more thoroughgoing applications, seems likely to provide a theory of behavior that will be scientifically acceptable and at the same time offer a satisfying interpretation for man's conviction that what determines his behavior, at least in part, is something within himself over which he, as a person, has control. One can hardly expect this ancient question to be settled now by any new insight, but it certainly should not be neglected or suffer from a conspiracy of silence. It is here, perhaps, that the suggestion offered in these pages may prove useful.

Causation is an abstruse subject upon which we need not enter here. It is clear, however, that our acts are not random happenings but follow some sort of orderliness, some kind of law, else chaos would be supreme. If the laws of chemistry and physics with which we are familiar and which are the basis of mechanistic philosophy do not explain what we do, then some new principle must be invoked. We should not be afraid to explore widely in the field of unconfirmed and unorthodox ideas for new principles of this sort, even if what is found upsets some cherished preconceptions. Biological organization may be considered as such a new principle. What, we may ask, can it do for an interpretation of the problem of freedom?

Its contribution is a simple one but not, I think, without value. This centers in the concept of the self, of what each of us actually is. The self-regulation of protoplasm, its basic quality, means that all its activities tend to realize goals — in man, goals of many kinds in the same individual. The important fact is that the self is *the sum of all the goals of the individual*, all its purposes, desires and aspirations, the total of its organizing relations. We *are* what we *want*. Wanting — goal-seeking — is at

[4]B. F. Skinner, *Science and Human Behavior* (New York: The Macmillan Company, 1953).

the center of biology. The self is the essence of man's aspirations, of the things he seeks. It is not a static, nebulous, ghostly thing but a search and a desiring; a pattern in living stuff which seeks to be fulfilled.

If this be once admitted, it seems to me that the problem of freedom has been moved a long step onward toward interpretation. Since the behavior of an organism results from the tendency of its living system to conform to goals or purposes that are set up within it, and since the self is the sum of these purposes, the self is obviously a part of the means by which purpose is translated into deed. The purpose and the purposer are one, and both are aspects of the regulatory power of living stuff which moves it to the consummation of the purpose. If this is so, a purpose in the mind is not something alien to the deed, a different category of things; part of a system about which we can argue as to whether it is "free" to do the deed or not. In a sense it *is* the deed for it is our experience of the protoplasmic goal which the deed will realize. There is no *compulsion* here to act, for the very act is an expression of the self. Obviously, we do what we will to do. Among the various choices open to us, we make the one which we want most to make. Freedom is the coincidence between ourselves and our acts.

Of course not every want can be satisfied or every goal realized. There are forms of outer compulsion which bind us and prevent our doing many things we want to do. Lack of physical strength, the determination of others who are more powerful than we, absence of opportunity and many more. These are life's familiar frustrations but are not limitations to our fundamental freedom to choose our course. Against these obstacles our purpose holds. Like the equifinality shown by some embryos where, if one course of development is blocked, the organism reaches the same end by quite a different route, so a man whose motives are strong enough will try one course after another to overcome these obstacles and reach his goal. His will is free but cannot always bring to pass the thing it wills.

*   *   *

What determines our choice involves the problem here discussed so often — how, in an organism or within the brain, are protoplasmic goals for action set up? Until the laws which govern these are understood the concept of freedom will still remain incomplete. Here is the nub of many problems. There must be *some* sort of physical correlate in the process of choosing a course of action, and that correlate, I believe, is the protoplasmic pattern to the realization of which its activity conforms. That something more than the classical laws of matter and energy may here be involved is suggested by the remarkable developments in the physical sciences during the past half century. This is an active field of debate by philosophers and theoretical physicists today but so full of technical complexities that a layman has difficulty in understanding all the points involved and should not draw from it conclusions which are not supported by those who are able to speak here with authority. Many of these men, however, have become convinced that the doctrine of simple mechanical determinism has passed into limbo. The radically new ideas which produced the great revolution in physics encouraged open-mindedness on the part of physicists. This open-mindedness caused them to entertain ideas about the universe and its history and inhabitants which would have been cast aside a century earlier as violating the basic conclusions that science had been so long in establishing. To such men, physical indeterminism is not as shocking to contemplate as it had been to their predecessors.

One of the early indications of this change in attitude had to do with natural law itself, the very citadel of science. Many kinds of law — some say all — are now regarded not as rigid and inviolable necessities in the universe but rather as the large-scale result of the random behavior of a vast multitude of tiny physical units.

*   *   *

The difficulty frequently experienced of providing a scientific justification for the concept of freedom is doubtless in part responsible for the feeling in many minds today that freedom is not the indispensable thing our fathers thought it was; less to be desired than security, a pleasant life and intelligent supervision of our doings. Why should we fight for freedom if actually we are puppets anyway? But despite the defeatist attitude of a minority and its inculcation by totalitarian theory, most men still eagerly want freedom. They believe that they *can* break their chains and choose their course and stand on their own feet, and that no clap-trap about determinism, psychological or genetic, can make them slaves to matter or energy despite all theories about the unbreakable sequence of events. Their inspiration comes from men like Milton and Jefferson and Lincoln, not from Marx. Man is never so like a god as when he gives up everything else for freedom. Life would be a ghastly travesty if the freedom for which through the ages men have lived and died proves, when at last they win it, to be mere illusion. What profit is there if they overcome external tyranny only to find this triumph meaningless since they are bound in the unyielding and impersonal web of matter and energy, and freedom turns out to be a mockery?

> For what avail the plough or sail,
> Or land or life, if freedom fail?

The deep question about freedom is, *what* is free? A freedom that was mere capriciousness would have no value. If something beyond genetic determinism and environmental conditioning controls our acts, what is this something? I believe it is the inborn, native tendencies of life; the creativity that is inherent in every organism and most especially in man; the inner protoplasmic directiveness, moving toward goals of many kinds and at many levels. To seek an answer to this question we must therefore consider in more detail the highest aspect of man's goal-seeking.

4

The unconscious and freedom

Joseph Nuttin

Depth psychology has replaced scientific determinism in the
minds of some, revealing unconscious forces motivating
actions that men believe to be free. Psychic determinism is also
linked with a certain self-deception. The strength of this threat
to human freedom lies in the fact that it would make
irrelevant any feeling of freedom experienced by the subject.
In this passage, Professor Nuttin argues that an unconscious
tendency is no different from a conscious tendency in the
making of a free act. Neither one nor the other receives from
man an automatic reaction. The experiencing of tendencies
does not release man from responding to values. Man's very
mistakes about his motives indicate the complexity of his acts
of choice. Psychic mechanisms do not destroy man's conscious
responses to value; in fact, the awareness of mechanisms can
increase one's freedom. Freud has done no disservice to man
by accenting these impersonal forces. Yet a certain distrust of
the feeling of freedom has been communicated to all those
who think that Freud succeeded not merely in discovering the
existence of impersonal forces but in destroying personal
choice by revealing such forces to be dominant.

Having presented the doctrine of the unconscious and shown the influence it has had on the psychological view of man, it remains for us to consider our central problem: to what extent is the influence of unconscious factors on conduct compatible with a spiritual belief in *the freedom of human acts?*

1.   Post-Hypnotic Suggestion

To begin with, let us consider the hypnotic phenomena, from the consideration of which Freud's ideas concerning the influence of the unconscious on conduct began.

Acts performed during hypnosis are not particularly relevant to our problem; for these acts do not form part of normal behaviour. But it is known that a hypnotized person, *after* coming out of a trance — and therefore back *into a normal state of consciousness* — may perform acts ordered during the trance, and do this without knowing that he is obeying an order.

These are cases of post-hypnotic suggestion, a phenomenon studied particularly at the school in Nancy. Here is how the director, Dr Bernheim, describes it:

The patient heard what I said to him while he was in the trance, but he remembers nothing about it, not even that I spoke to him. The suggested idea comes back into his mind when he wakes up; having forgotten where it came from, he believes it to be original. Facts of this kind have been proved by Bertrand, General Noiset, Dr Liebault and Charles Richet. I have tried them out successfully again and again and am convinced that the people concerned are telling the truth.

At eleven o'clock I suggested to C. that at one o'clock in the

From PSYCHOANALYSIS AND PERSONALITY by Joseph Nuttin, copyright 1953 Sheed & Ward Inc., New York. Pp. 123-129.

afternoon he would be seized by an irresistible desire to go all the way up Stanislas Street and back again, twice. At one o'clock I saw him come out into the street, walk from one end to the other, and then come back again, stopping in front of the shop-windows as though he was just taking a stroll.[1]

The phenomenon can be taken as established. It has been studied experimentally and checked both for its length and for its effectiveness.[2] An order given during hypnosis may not only be obeyed immediately after the person concerned has wakened up; it may remain efficacious for many days and even for weeks afterwards.

For what concerns us, it must be assumed that the given order stays in existence *unconsciously* in the individual. Imagination of the act and the need to perform it rise into consciousness at a set moment, *but the source of the image and the need remains unconscious*. The act is performed as though it were a spontaneous achievement of the person himself.

It seems doubtful whether such an act, arising from the unconscious, can be called free, and, if this is so, whether any form of unconscious influence on action is compatible with freedom of behaviour.

The first important fact to realize when faced with this question is that *suggestions made during hypnosis are not invariably carried out*. Some authors have asserted the contrary and said that post-hypnotic suggestion is accomplished necessarily and invariably.

Thus Liebault, and after him Beaunis, declares, "One characteristic of actions performed a long time after the suggestion has been made is that the urge to do them seems to the individual to come from his own initiative, whereas in reality he goes towards his object under the influence of a decision which he has been made to take with the fatality of a falling stone, not as a result of that controlled and intentional effort which is the source of all our reasonable actions." "In short," adds Beaunis, "he thinks himself free but he is not free. This is a 'direct hit' at the argument for free will which is drawn from our *feeling* of freedom."[3]

[1]Cf. Bernheim, *De la suggestion* (2nd ed. Paris, Doin, 1888), pp. 45 and 47.
[2]See particularly E.R. Kellogg, "Duration of the Effects of Post-hypnotic Suggestion," *Journal of Experimental Psychology*, 1929, XII, pp. 502-514; also the recent account by A.W. Weitzenhoffer, "A Note on the Persistence of Hypnotic Suggestion, *The Journal of Abnormal and Social Psychology*, 1950, XLV, pp. 160-162.

If this were so, post-hypnotic phenomena would provide an illustration of Spinoza's maxim. For Spinoza, our consciousness of freedom is simply ignorance of the causes that make us act.[4]

It seems quite certain that in *abnormal* cases such as hysteria and abulia, post-hypnotic suggestion produces its effect quite automatically, despite the occasional feeling of spontaneity and freedom. Beaunis himself stipulates one condition, to ensure the accomplishment of suggestion: the individual must have been frequently hypnotized by the same person. But this, as is well known, means a weakening in the force of resistance.

And it is quite certain that in some cases the individual fights hard against performing the act, when it goes against strong tendencies. Thus Bernheim admits, as Charcot has also admitted:

The effect of post-hypnotic suggestion is not absolutely a matter of fate; some people fight against it . . . Here are a few examples . . . To young G. I suggest that when he wakes up he must stand on the table. When he wakes up he looks at the table but he does not get up on to it. The desire to do so is no doubt there but respect for the people present gives him the strength to overcome the desire.[5]

Another case quoted by Bernheim brings out very clearly the inner conflict that can take place in the individual:

One day I told one of my hypnotized patients, a girl, to kiss one of the men on duty when she woke up. As soon as she woke up she went up to him and took hold of his hand; then she hesitated and looked round, seeming embarrassed by the attention that was being paid to her. She remained like this for a few moments, with an anxious look on her face, obviously experiencing the acutest distress. When she was questioned, she finally confessed that she wanted to kiss Mr X but that she could never bring herself to behave so improperly.[6]

[3]Cf. J. Morand, *Hypnotisme et Suggestion* (Paris, 1889), pp. 322-3.
[4]Cf. Spinoza, Letter XXXII: "This is the human liberty of which men are so proud; fundamentally, it means that they are conscious of their appetites but not of the external causes which determine them."
[5]Cf. Bernheim, *De la suggestion*, pp. 52-3.
[6]This case is quoted from Dr J.S. Morand, *Hypnotisme et Suggestion* (Paris, Garnier, 1889), p. 320.

2.   The Unconscious Source of Normal Needs

There are then three main points established by the study of post-hypnotic phenomena. First, the individual *experiences a conscious inclination* to perform an action. Second, this inclination emanates in actual fact from *psychic contents which are not conscious* (for example, from an order given previously), and the act which is performed rises from these unconscious contents. Third, the individual may, or may not, give way to his inclination.

The crucial point is this, that the inclination — and consequently the behaviour — *has an unconscious source*, i.e. derives from an *unconscious* order.

Now an analysis of human behaviour soon reveals that it is not at all unusual for an inclination to arise or start from the unconscious layers of the personality. Most of our tendencies and natural needs — hunger, thirst, sex — have their source in unconscious biological states of the organism. From these dynamisms a single thing emerges into consciousness: at a fixed moment, and in pursuance of the satisfaction of a need, we feel drawn or driven to perform an act whose image rises up in our mind. The source or basis of this desire is not immediately given to consciousness. Or, again, we may be mistaken about the source of our desires. What we take to be our real motives for being attracted towards a certain object may merely be pretexts for justifying our behaviour. The real source of a tendency can often only be discovered by scientific research into its antecedents and the factors which brought it into existence.

From this comparison with the process of normal need it should be clear that in both cases the problem of the unconscious is the same. Nevertheless there is an interesting difference between the two processes. In post-hypnotic suggestion it is a forgotten *psychic content* — the command or order received — which is the unconscious source of the image and need which rise up in the individual; whereas in natural needs the inclination emanates fundamentally from *physiological states* of the organism itself. Neither, however, is in itself *directly or fundamentally conscious*. Notice, finally, that the problem is the same both for Freud's dynamic unconscious and for post-hypnotic suggestion. In both cases unconscious psychic contents are the starting-point for images and inclination which rise up into consciousness. And, as we have shown, it was in post-hypnotic phenomena that Freud found the prototype of his active unconscious.

3.   Freedom and Tendencies Rising from the Unconscious

We have now to inquire whether facts such as these can be reconciled with activity that can properly be called free. But what exactly is the process known as a free act?

The fact that we are impelled by a certain need — which has its own *source* — towards such and such a form of behaviour, does not mean that the act is not free. It is not so much the *source* of the need, conscious or unconscious, that interests us, as the *felt need itself* and *the way it influences* behaviour.

When behaving freely, in fact, the individual takes up an attitude towards the different elements of "value" — the motives — which are *actually being lived* in the given situation, i.e. are being experienced. The "attractive power" or value of each motive depends on the power of the *aspirations and impulses which are being experienced at the moment*. The ultimate source of these aspirations and impulses does not come into it, either into any scrutiny of the motives or into the attitude which the individual may adopt towards them. In other words, *it is to the extent that they are actually "felt" that the "motives" are to be considered as forces influencing freedom of action.* Ignorance of their source does not alter the case at all.

Whether the act is free or determined will therefore depend on the way the dynamic factors which the individual experiences within himself release the activity. The act will *not* be free when the "motives" or motive forces cause a reaction which is like a link in a chain, materially determined by natural processes. On the other hand there *will be* a free act when the individual *faces motives as value-elements which he recognizes intellectually without being completely absorbed by them*; for in this case, in an act of full self-possession he transcends the impression or the attraction experienced *hic et nunc* and consents to motives to which *he himself gives a value, according to the concrete system of values which makes up his own personality.*

From this it should be clear, then, that because a certain act arises from an unconscious dynamic source, this does not raise any *special problem* as regards its freedom. As with all other acts, the freedom or necessity depends on whether the dynamism behind the act has developed and acted on the spiritual level. This depends on whether the individual *transcends* the actual impression he experiences or is simply "affected" by it. The question whether this spiritual level of activity exists in man, whether there is a certain element of freedom — i.e., spirituality — involved in human conduct, does not arise here. It is a question for philosophical psychology, and outside the scope of this treatise. Here it is sufficient to have shown that no *new* problem is raised by the fact that certain tendencies *derive from the unconscious.*

As we have said, there seem to be a great number of acts, arising out of unconscious tendencies or suggestions, which are *not* performed automatically. It can even happen that a person *fails to* perform the act he has been told to perform because of a tendency to respect propriety or the conventions. Occasionally, again, a compromise will be reached and the patient will simply shake hands with someone he has been told to kiss. In some cases, however, it really does seem as though certain acts — especially those performed as a result of post-hypnotic suggestion — can actually be performed just like so many *automatic reactions.* This is particularly true of certain hysterical and abulic cases which have been interestingly described by Janet.

Janet maintains that for some patients the performance of a voluntary act demands considerably more effort than the act of obeying a post-hypnotic suggestion. He maintains, for instance, that a woman patient suffering from abulia and lacking the will-power to perform a certain act which she had been asked to do, performed the same act without any effort as the result of an unconscious suggestion. After hypnotizing this patient Janet said to her: "When I knock on the table, take this hat and hang it on a peg." He goes on:

> I woke her up. A little later I called her, as though I wanted her to do something for me. "Would you mind taking this hat? It is getting in my way while I am writing. Hang it up on the peg, will you?" "Of course I will," she replied. She tried to get up, shook herself and stretched out her arms, but her movements were uncoordinated, so she sat down; then she stood up again. This went on for twenty minutes. Then I knocked on the table. Immediately she got up, took hold of the hat, hung it up, and went and sat down again. The action

had been done by suggestion in a moment; she had not been able to do it by an effort of will in twenty minutes.[7]

In cases of this kind the suggestion seems to act rather like a force of impulse and lead directly to the action without any interference from the individual concerned.

This kind of unconscious behaviour does not present any *special* problems either: such examples can be classed with ordinary automatic actions.

The conclusion seems to be that as regards this question everything depends on the psychic equilibrium of the person concerned. When he has no will at all — i.e., when the psychic powers do not appear at the spiritual level — the dynamism roused by an unconscious order is released automatically or impulsively in behaviour. But when the individual is normally balanced and has the normal psychic powers, *the tendency roused by suggestion does not have any different effect on behaviour from that of any of man's other tendencies which arise either from biochemical or physiological factors or ultimately, even, from cosmic forces.*

4. Freedom and Unconscious Sexuality

The Freudian psychology of the unconscious does not merely claim that motives and inclinations may have their source in the "dark depths of personality". The thing that has so profoundly changed the picture of man that it presents to us is its thesis that conscious motives, as we experience them, are a *deception.* Even so-called higher motives are held to be nothing but disguised forms of libido, the only constructive power in human behaviour.

Hence when anybody follows any conscious motive he is quite simply deceived; what has happened is that impulses which he refused to follow in their naked reality now govern his behaviour in disguise.

In the next chapter, when we discuss the dynamic structure of personality, we shall examine the thesis that the libido is the only driving-force in human personality. For the moment we need only concern ourselves with the problem of the connection between *unconscious*

[7]Cf. Pierre Janet, *Les Medications Psychologiques* (Paris, Alcan, 1925), I, p. 226.

transformations and *disguised* tendencies, on the one hand, and freedom, on the other.

It is quite clear both from clinical data and from ordinary, every-day psychology that so-called lower or instinctive tendencies can motivate conduct in disguised ways. When we strip this idea of the theoretical trimmings which psychoanalysis has added to it, all we find is something that helps us towards a fuller view of the *complex dynamism* behind human activity.

Besides psychoanalysis, Adler's Individual Psychology has made important contributions to this field of knowledge. Individual Psychology shows that not only the libido but also the inferiority complex and the need for self-assertion can lurk, in a highly disguised form, behind "motivations" of human conduct.[8]

The fact that an individual can be completely mistaken about the real nature of the motives governing his conduct has not, as we have said, escaped the notice of everyday psychology. The positive contribution made by depth-psychology in this field lies simply in its having helped us towards deeper knowledge of the processes involved in such mistakes, and also in its attempt to uncover the mechanism of these processes. Their bias and their hasty generalizations have, however, done considerable harm to the new ideas which Adler and Freud introduced into this field.

The particular point about human freedom is that psychoanalysis, not content with showing how instinctive dynamisms affect all "higher" motivation, used the facts it had discovered to construct a theory that reduced *all such motivation* to a disguised form of libido.

The fact that in certain circumstances a person misunderstands the real character of the tendency by which he is being moved does not prevent the act itself, performed consciously as a result of this mistaken tendency, from being free. Here, as in the case of tendencies whose source is unconscious, what counts is the fact that the individual "personally" accepts the tendency as it presents itself to him. The only thing that would make freedom of behaviour an impossibility would be if all motivation *were essentially a disguised form of escape* for the libido.

When a man makes occasional mistakes about the nature of his motives the fact that he "personally" *agrees* to act in accordance with the mistaken motive implies that this inclination exists as a "value" for him at

[8]The word "motivation" is used here in the sense defined below, which it has acquired in contemporary psychology.

the spiritual level of his personality; otherwise he would not be able to adopt towards it a positive attitude reached by deliberation. Thus, when a man *consciously agrees* to bear his suffering for the love of God, this assumes that "doing something for the love of God" is for him an inclination or a value existing on the intellectual level of his personality. If on the other hand, to keep to the same case, it becomes obvious that the man *likes* to be ill *so as to assert himself*, it can be said that he is mistaken about the motive that impels him to "accept" his suffering. Nevertheless, the fact that the conscious motive of resignation to the will of God is *accepted* at the level of consciousness, *adds* to the unconscious dynamism of wanting to be noticed a new element which must be included in the total motivation behind this person's behaviour. This new element is the *conscious intention* of the person performing the act, which appears to the performer to be an act of resignation to the divine will. The total dynamism behind the person's behaviour will in this case be a complex of several dynamic elements.

If, on the other hand, the tendency to resign oneself in suffering to the will of God is held to be intrinsically mistaken, then man's whole dynamism is reduced to a process which excludes all spiritual development as a real dynamic factor.

After such theoretical consideration let us, with the help of a few examples, try to see more clearly into the concrete reality of the motives behind certain forms of behaviour. In this way it will become clearer that the real motivation is a *complex of several components* and not simply an unconscious mechanism. The real problem will then be reduced to seeing *how, in this context of complex motivation, freedom of behaviour is to be understood.*

Let us take as our first example the motives behind a generous acceptance of trials and suffering. This is in fact a central point in the Christian attitude to life.

It is certainly not only in abnormal cases that the motive-forces "recognized" in this acceptance of suffering *are found to be mixed with tendencies arising from deeper layers of the personality.*

To take one example from many: A young woman of about twenty-five had been unwell for several years with asthma, headaches and so on. Weeks of illness would alternate with days of activity and relatively good health. This girl was a good influence on a number of other girls in the district, directing their work and being a great help to them in all sorts of difficulties.

A variety of circumstances led this invalid girl to develop a deeper insight into her psychic condition. Analysis of the events of her childhood brought to light the fact that her life at that time had been dominated by a conflict between an inner feeling of perversion (the result of childish sexual practices) and the general opinion of her both at school and at home, where she was held up as a model child from every point of view. This feeling of contradiction between her inner perversion and her social "perfection" she found agonizing. A number of fairly distressing events occurred to her during her childhood, and these she interpreted, in the light of this conflict, as punishments sent by God, and accepted them eagerly as an expiation of her sins.

Later, when she was about eighteen, she became ill, suffering a great deal from a feeling of neglect, of not being sufficiently surrounded with affection. Her feeling of inner perversion had in the meantime managed to create an attitude that encouraged her tendency to feel sure of "coming out on top", not so much by her *actual* virtues or moral perfection as through her penitence. During her two years' illness she had been told of the special value of sacrifice and suffering, by which man rises far above the easy perfection that is to be reached through the active life or the apostolate. About this she said later: "These words made such an impression on me that the years when I was ill in bed were the best years of my life."

Though she had been cured of her illness, she never recovered her health completely. This was the beginning of that invalid state we have already mentioned. During her course of psychotherapy, she came to see more clearly into some of the details of her condition and her behaviour; she began to understand certain things that had remained "vague" in her consciousness because she did not want to recognize them. Faced with the naked truth of the situation, she ended by making a kind of confession, very rarely obtained in such cases:

> I had nothing positive in my life when so many others were getting so much. Sometimes I felt a secret satisfaction at the thought of being interesting and important because I was ill. In my deepest being I began to feel sorry when a new crisis did not arise. I was so self-engrossed in it all! . . . When I made an offering of my sufferings, that cost me very little because it flattered my own ego so much. With all my whole being I want to be cured, and yet I'm terribly afraid of it because my ego would lose so much by it. I am unhappy

because I realize so clearly now that all this isn't as I would like it to be — and so I never dared confess it to myself. I wish I could change it all!

The important thing in this case is that we are concerned with someone who cannot simply be described as hysterical. Undoubtedly this person was of high moral worth, animated by a desire for sincerity that sometimes went very deep indeed. Her attitude towards her illness was not simply one of fraud; but her elevated feelings and noble motives were inextricably mixed up with all kinds of other forces. Such is the complex reality that we have to respect. This girl would not have felt so genuinely unhappy when she realized the duplicity of her feelings if she had not had aspiration of genuine nobility, utterly different from the mere desire of wanting to be "interesting". It is this *complex of elements* in the acceptance of suffering that needs to be emphasized; it would be wrong to reduce the whole thing to one component only.

*　　*　　*

Therefore the essential problem as regards the freedom of human behaviour is to know *whether, and to what degree, man is deceiving himself when he imagines that he is consenting to conscious, rational motives.* When he believes his actions to be guided, for instance, by the spirit of abnegation, to what extent is he being moved by a disguised form of self-assertiveness? It is not so much the unconscious *source* of these tendencies that we need to concern ourselves with, as the question whether the needs as felt and experienced, and as motives of action, do not completely hoodwink "rational man".

In answer to this question let us observe that a "transformed" motive, or a partly unconscious need, is not normally the *whole* dynamic force behind a man's actions: this has been shown plainly in our earlier analyses. His system of motivations is a complex whole of tendencies and values *to some extent or other* recognized in their real form and *to some extent or other* spiritually created. In the next chapter we shall be able to show in greater detail the *psychological foundations* of this complexity. Here the question is *whether this complexity of our system of motives makes impossible any idea of a free will intervening in our actions*, or whether, on the contrary, in any satisfactory theory of the freedom of behaviour, this complexity appears as the normal condition of human conduct.

Free will is not to be looked upon as a "spiritual force" separate from the complex dynamism of the human psyche. As we have already remarked, free will means that these complex motive-forces do not release any kind of behaviour directly, or blindly, but only after they have been taken up into the transcendent individual *ego*.

An act that derives *at least partially* from such a grasp of the "motive-powers" by the transcendent *ego* is to that extent a *free act*. The element of freedom in such an act means that in concrete fact it is not the resultant pure and simple of a process governed by influences of environment and physiological factors but that there is also another principle behind it — the self-determination of a person.

Our actions always only *partially* derive from the activity of spiritual motive-forces. *People and things act upon us from all directions — physiological and psychological, conscious and unconscious — because our organism opens out upon the world in all directions. Any concrete situation affects us in all these ways at once and either invites or compels us to reply to it by means of some kind of reaction — which is our behaviour.*

Our behaviour is, therefore, a "reply" to an action which reaches us *by various ways.* In it the spiritual element is always one component only, because in *our very being* the spiritual element is simply one component amongst many. There is no such thing as a *purely spiritual* reply to the situations with which life presents us; there is only a "human" reply. *The action of the situation on the person, and the reply, are at once spiritual and material, like the person himself*: i.e., our activities are absorbed into a process of physical, biochemical and physiological reactions, but at the same time transcend this process to the extent that they are faced up to and consciously grasped by our *ego*.

Thus we can say that our behaviour is free to the extent that the situation and the reply are built up as a function of the autonomous personality of the individual. Freedom *varies* according to the *level* reached by any man in this kind of personal development of his activities.

Looked at from this psychological point of view, our behaviour cannot satisfactorily be divided into two categories, the free and the unfree. Freedom is not a static property of a few limited kinds of behaviour. On the contrary, all human activity is characterized by a certain degree of freedom, i.e., *a varying degree of spiritual activity*. There are very few kinds of behaviour, whether morally good or morally bad, which do not to a certain extent, at least, feel the influence of the transcendent activity of the human personality. This influence reveals itself somehow, even if only in the kind of check that sometimes prevents people from succumbing without scruple to irresistible impulse, or which moderates the enthusiasm with which they follow their instincts. It would, on the other hand, be just as much an illusion to imagine that any of our acts derive from *purely spiritual* activity, and that they do not have their dynamic origin in the vital centres and unconscious bases of our personality. These are levels of activity which contribute towards the attitude freely adopted in any given situation; physiological or unconscious layers of the personality which may be behind the irresolution that makes one hesitate to appreciate a value or the tendency of an argument, for example; but from these depths of the psyche may arise too the certainty that renders a conviction unshakable and the inspiration that takes the place of the will.

Seen in this way, freedom, like the spiritual element in our personality, is not so much a permanent possession as a *task* which each man fulfils in his behaviour to a greater or less degree throughout his life.

It is worth noting in this connection the complementary nature of the positions adopted by the Freudian theory and traditional psychology. Psychoanalysis reduces all dynamic activity to *impersonal* forces, so that man is dominated by the vital, unconscious force of the "id"; he does not govern or dispose of himself at all. Traditional psychology, on the other hand, concentrated on the other aspect of this dynamic activity and represents self-determination, or the conscious will, as a force which can govern human conduct in sovereign fashion absolutely. The real dynamism of human behaviour is, in fact, a varying combination of all these components, biological and spiritual, conscious and unconscious, known or disguised.

It is a task for the personality itself to increase its capacity for self-government and its knowledge of its own motives. It will best realize this aim by seeing ever more deeply into the complexity of the dynamic factors in its behaviour. The depth-psychology of Adler and Freud supplies us with *data* that can enrich our psychological insight. With its help we can rid ourselves of certain illusions about our freedom, and so become *more truly free* from the compulsions of the secret mechanisms in human nature through which men so often lose their real personality.

5

Determinism in history

Ernest Nagel

In a helpful and comprehensive study, Ernest Nagel here reviews the findings of scientists, psychologists, and historians. He reminds us that for believers in historical inevitability even "indeterminacy" and "evolution," whether cosmic or personal, still witness to law. Static reality may have been replaced by reality-in-process, cosmology by history, but there are many who regard this as the discovery of more deep-lying forces subservient to unknown patterns of development.

Although Professor Nagel does not think that historical inevitability has been or can be demonstrated, he seems to hold that historical actions are necessitated by certain conditions. Hence the retention of the principle of determinism as a general regulative principle would help, Nagel thinks, to reveal the various conditions determining the existence of human traits and actions. He holds that retaining the objective inquiry would be in the interests of the human subject's freedom insofar as it would constitute a liberation from illusion.

In the 1920's a historian of note examined the apparently decisive influence exercised by a number of famous persons upon such important historical events as the Protestant Reformation in England, the American Revolution, and the development of parliamentary government. He then assessed the supposedly critical role which the decisions and actions of these men played in bringing about those events, generalized his findings, and concluded as follows:

> These great changes seem to have come about with a certain inevitableness; there seems to have been an independent trend of events, some inexorable necessity controlling the progress of human affairs ... Examined closely, weighed and measured carefully, set in true perspective, the personal, the casual, the individual influences in history sink in significance and great cyclical forces loom up. Events come of themselves, so to speak; that is, they come so consistently and unavoidably as to rule out as causes not only physical phenomena but voluntary human action.
>
> So arises the conception of *law in history*. History, the great course of human affairs, has not been the result of voluntary efforts on the part of individuals or group of individuals, much less chance; but has been subject to law.[1]

The view expressed in this quotation is a variant of a conception of human affairs that is familiar and continues to be widely held. It is a conception that has sometimes been advanced as ancillary to a theodicy; sometimes to a romantic philosophy of cosmic organicism; sometimes to an ostensibly "scientific" theory of civilization which finds the causes of human progress or decline in the operations of impersonal factors such as geography, race, or economic organization. Despite important differences

From THE STRUCTURE OF SCIENCE by Ernest Nagel, © 1961 by Harcourt Brace Jovanovich, Inc. and reprinted with their permission. Pp. 593-602.
[1] If $E\lambda$ is the energy associated with a ray whose wave length is λ, T the absolute temperature of the radiating black body, h Planck's constant, the velocity of light, and k Boltzman's gas constant, then Planck's radiation law is given by

$$E\lambda = \frac{hc^2}{\lambda^5} \frac{1}{e^{hc/kT}\lambda-1}$$

between them, these various doctrines of historical inevitability share a common premise: the impotence of deliberate human action, whether individual or collective, to alter the course of human history, since historical changes are allegedly the products of deep-lying forces which conform to fixed, though perhaps not always known, patterns of development.

The doctrine of historical inevitability has been repeatedly shown to be untenable by historians as well as philosophers; and it is not the aim of the present discussion to exhibit once more its many deficiencies. It will suffice to note that in some of its variant forms the doctrine has no empirical content, since no conceivable empirical evidence can ever be relevant for testing those versions of the doctrine for their truth or falsity. Moreover, when the doctrine is formulated so that it can be empirically tested, the available evidence supports neither the thesis that all human events illustrate a unitary, transculturally invariant law of development, nor the thesis that individual or collective human effort never operates as a decisive factor in the transformations of society. However, the rejection of these claims is not to be construed as denying that in many historical situations individual choice and effort may count for little or nothing, nor that there frequently are ascertainable limits to human power for directing the course of social changes — limits that may be set by facts of physics and geography, by biological endowment, by modes of economic production and available technological skills, by tradition and political organization, by human stupidity and ignorance, as well as by various antecedent actions of men.

On the other hand, many recent critics of historical inevitability have gone much beyond denying the manifestly exaggerated claims of the doctrine. They have proceeded to challenge what they believe is the basic premise upon which it rests — the view, namely, that human events generally occur only under determinate and determining conditions. Accordingly, these critics have tried to show that a thoroughgoing determinism is incompatible with the established facts of human history as well as with the assumption, underlying all discussions of moral problems, that human beings are genuinely responsible for their deliberate choices and actions. Moreover, many thinkers who reject the doctrine of historical inevitability are also severe critics of current trends in psychological and social research; they maintain that, since the behavioristic (or "naturalistic") methodology adopted in these inquiries allegedly rests ultimately on the deterministic premise, contemporary social science is destroying the belief in human freedom and is therefore undermining the foundations of moral effort.

It is with some of these criticisms of determinism that the remainder of this chapter is concerned. However, these criticisms seldom make explicit how 'determinism' is to be construed as a general thesis; and, although critics of the thesis sometimes identify it with the doctrine of historical inevitability,[2] a much more comprehensive notion is usually intended. We must therefore briefly recall the account given in Chapter 10 of the sense in which 'determinism' is commonly understood in the natural sciences, since this appears also to be the sense in which determinism is frequently said to be the premise underlying the doctrine of historical inevitability.

It will be convenient to summarize our earlier discussion of determinism with the help of an example of a physicochemical system generally acknowledged to be deterministic.[3] The system consists of a mixture of soda water, whiskey, and ice, contained in a sealed vacuum bottle. It is assumed that no air is present in the bottle, and that the mixture is completely isolated from everything else, such as sources of heat in the environment. Moreover, the only characteristics of the system that enter into the discussion are the "thermodynamical variables," such as the following: the number of components of the system (the components in the example are water, alcohol, and carbon dioxide), the phases or types of aggregation in which the components occur (in the example, water occurs in a solid, liquid, and gaseous phase), the concentrations of the components in each phase, the temperature of the mixture, and the pressure on the walls of the container. It is well known that for a given temperature and pressure, each component in the system will occur in the various phases with definite concentrations, and conversely. Thus, if the pressure of the mixture is increased (e.g., by pressing down the stopper of the bottle), the concentration of water in the gaseous phase is reduced, but its concentration in the liquid phase is increased; and analogously for a change in temperature. The variables of the system thus stand to each

---

[2] According to one historian, for example, determinism is the doctrine "according to which we are helplessly caught in the grip of a movement proceeding from all that has gone before." – Pieter Geyl, *Debates with Historians*, New York, 1956, p. 236. But this is not a representative view.

[3] The example is borrowed from Lawrence J. Henderson, *Pareto's General Sociology*, Cambridge, Mass., 1935, Chap. 3, where it is used to illustrate the sense in which, according to Pareto, a social system is deterministic.

other in definite relations of interdependence, so that the value of a variable at any given time may be said to be "determined" by the values of the other variables at that time.

Now suppose that at some initial time the system is in a definite "state" (i.e., the variables have certain specific values), and that because of some change induced in one or more of the variables at that time the system is in some other definite state after an interval of time t; but suppose also that the system is brought back in some way to its initial state, that exactly the same changes are induced in the variables as before, and that after the same interval t the system is again in the second state. If the system behaves in this manner no matter what state is taken to be the initial state, and no matter how large the interval t, the system is said to be "deterministic" with respect to the specified set of thermodynamical variables.

If the reference to the physicochemical example is dropped, 'determinism' may therefore be defined quite generally as the thesis that for *every* set of attributes (or "variables") there is *some* system which is deterministic with respect to that set. Accordingly, 'determinism in history' is the thesis that, for every set of human actions, individual or collective characteristics, or social changes that may be of concern to the historian, there is some system which is deterministic with respect to those items — where the state variables of the system are, however, not specified. We can now turn to the task we proposed for the remainder of this chapter, to discuss various criticisms of determinism in history. The objections to the deterministic thesis to be examined fall under the following heads: (1) the argument from the falsity of the doctrine of historical inevitability and from the nonexistence of "laws of necessary development" in human affairs; (2) the argument from the unpredictability of human events; and (3) the argument from the incompatibility of determinism with the reality of human freedom; but we will conclude the examination with (4) some reflections on the validity of the thesis itself.

1.   The first argument can be briefly stated and also quickly dismissed. It is directed primarily against those grandiose philosophies of history, whether religious or secular in orientation, which claim to find a fixed pattern of development in the manifold succession of events that have taken place since the beginnings of the human race, or at the very least to detect an invariable order of sequential change repeatedly manifested in different societies or civilizations. From the perspective of

some of these philosophies, every human act appears to have a definite place in an unalterable structure of changes, and each society must necessarily pass through a fixed series of antecedent stages before it can achieve a subsequent stage. Moreover, though human individuals are the ostensible agents that bring about the movements of history, human actions are seen in many of these philosophies as at best only the "instruments" through which certain "forces," operating and evolving in conformity with timeless laws, become manifest.

Philosophies of history of this type often possess the fascination of great dramatic literature; and few of their readers would be willing to deny the remarkable imaginative powers and amazing erudition that frequently go into their construction. But as has already been mentioned, when the evidence of what has actually happened is at all relevant for judging such philosophies, it is overwhelmingly negative. Critics of these philosophies are on safe ground in rejecting them as false.

Does it nevertheless follow from the falsity of the doctrine of historical inevitability that there are no causal connections in human affairs, and that determinism in respect to the events discussed by historians is a myth? Those recent critics of the doctrine who believe that this does follow offer no explicit grounds for their claim, and appear to base their contention on an extraordinarily narrow conception of what a deterministic system must be like. They seem to think that, since the human past does not exhibit anything like the regular periodicities of a well-constructed chronometer, the events in that past cannot possibly be elements in a deterministic system. However, although a given system may fail to illustrate some relatively simple schema of changes, it may nevertheless manifest a more complex and unfamiliar pattern of relations of dependence. Moreover, even if it should be the case that a particular system is not deterministic in respect to a specified set of characteristics, the system may not be sufficiently well isolated from external influences (as in the case of a clock whose motions show "irregularities" because of the influence of a fluctuating magnetic field); and there may therefore be some other system (perhaps the system which includes these external influences together with the initial system) that is deterministic in respect to the given set of characteristics. In any event, granting that the doctrine of historical inevitability is false and that there are no laws of necessary development in human history, there is competent evidence to show that, for example, the decline of Spanish power in the seventeenth century was in part the consequence of Spanish economic and colonial policy, or that a necessary condition for the success of the Bolshevik Revolution was the leadership supplied by Lenin. In short, the first argument against determinism does not achieve its objective.

2.   Critics of determinism tend to place great weight on the objection that human events are in considerable measure unpredictable. Two senses of the latter word are usually distinguished in this connection. An event is "technologically" unpredictable if, because of limitations in the knowledge or technology men possess at a given time, they lack the effective ability either to foretell the event at all, or to foretell it with more than a certain degree of precision. However, it is obviously not a serious objection to determinism that events may be unpredictable in this sense; and no critic of the deterministic thesis is likely to argue that earthquakes, for example, do not have necessary and sufficient conditions for their occurrence, on the ground that we are unable at present to anticipate when the next earthquake will take place.

On the other hand, an event is "theoretically" unpredictable if the assumption that its occurrence can be calculated in advance with unlimited precision is incompatible with the "laws of nature," that is, with the corpus of scientific knowledge, and in particular with established scientific theory. The stock example used to illustrate this sense of the word is the limited precision with which, according to current quantum theory, subatomic processes can be predicted. It will be evident, however, that, even if human events are assumed to be theoretically unpredictable, this supposition has force as an objection to the deterministic thesis only if the thesis is identified with the claim that in principle events can be predicted with absolute precision.[4] To be sure, a connotation can undoubtedly be *assigned* to 'determinism' so that in consequence its meaning will coincide with that of 'predictable.' But the equivalence that would thus be established between the connotations of the words would be the result of an arbitrary *fiat*, since the words are not in fact generally employed as synonyms. If they were, it would be absurd to suppose that something which is admitted to be theoretically unpredictable might nevertheless be

[4]Such an identification was made by Moritz Schlick: " '*A* determines *B*' can mean nothing else than: *B* can be calculated from *A*. And this means: there is a universal formula, which attests to the occurrence of *B*, when certain values are substituted for the initial conditions *A* and in addition definite values are assigned to such variables as the time *t*. ... The word 'determined' thus means exactly what is meant by 'predictable' or 'calculable in advance.' " — Moritz Schlick, "Die Kausalitat in der gegenwartigen Physik," *Gesammelte Aufsatze*, Vienna, 1938, pp. 73-74.

determined. However, despite the circumstance that quantum mechanics belongs to the current corpus of scientific theory, it is not self-contradictory (though it may be mistaken) to hold, as Planck, Einstein, and others have held, that subatomic processes have determining conditions for their occurrence, and that an alternative to quantum theory is desirable which would set no upper bounds, as does the latter, upon the precision with which certain of those processes are predictable.

But in any event, nothing comparable to quantum mechanics is available in the social sciences upon which to rest the assumption that human events are theoretically unpredictable. Nor does the actual evidence establish the claim that human actions are utterly unpredictable in fact. It would be ridiculous to maintain that every detail in man's future can be predicted, or even to pretend that every event in the human past can be inferred from the available data. On the other hand, it is no less ridiculous to hold that we are completely incompetent to predict anything about the human future with any assurance of being correct. It is almost truistic to note that our personal relations with other men, our political arrangements and social institutions, our transportation schedules and our administration of justice, could not be what they are unless fairly safe inferences were possible about the human past and future.

*   *   *

3. The remaining argument we will consider is that a thoroughgoing determinism is incompatible with the fundamental axiom of moral theory that human beings can properly be said to be responsible for their decisions and deliberate actions. This objection to determinism has been a theme of philosophical and theological debate since antiquity, but has been revived in current discussions of human history and social science. We shall examine some of the issues raised by it in the form they are presented in a book by Isaiah Berlin.[5] The book is primarily a devastating critique of philosophies of history which view the human scene as the unfolding of an inevitable destiny that cannot be altered by human effort; and it also maintains that these philosophies are simply corollaries to the assumption that human affairs are strictly determined. We shall ignore this reason Berlin advances for rejecting determinism, since we have already shown that the deterministic thesis does not entail the doctrine of historical inevitability; but we must discuss two further arguments he directs against the thesis.

[5] Isaiah Berlin, *Historical Inevitability*, London and New York, 1954.

a.   Berlin's point of departure in the first of these arguments is the generally acknowledged commonplace that an individual cannot appropriately be held morally responsible for some action if he was coerced into performing it and if he did not elect to do it of his own free volition. Accordingly, if a person is genuinely responsible for an action, he *could* have acted differently had his choice been different. But Berlin also believes that on the deterministic thesis (understood by him to deny that there is any area of human life not exhaustively determined by law), the person could *not* have chosen differently from the way in which he did in *fact* choose, apparently because the individual's decision at the time it was made was determined by circumstances over which he had no control, such as his biological heritage or his character as formed by prior actions. In consequence, to anyone who accepts the deterministic thesis, the supposition that a man could have decided otherwise than he did decide must ultimately be an illusion which rests on our ignorance of the determining facts of his choice. Berlin therefore concludes that determinism entails the elimination of individual responsibility, since it is not a man's *free* choice, but rather the conditions determining his choice, that according to determinism explain the man's action. He declares, for example,

> Nobody denies that it would be stupid as well as cruel to blame me for not being taller than I am, or to regard the color of my hair or the qualities of my intellect or my heart as being due principally to my own free choice; these attributes are as they are through no decision of mine. If I extend this category without limit, then whatever is, is necessary and inevitable. ... To blame and praise, consider possible alternative courses of action, damn or congratulate historical figures for acting as they do or did, becomes an absurd activity.

And he adds:

> If I were convinced that although choices did affect what occurred, yet they were themselves wholly determined by factors not within the individual's control (including his own motives and springs of action), I should certainly not regard him as morally praiseworthy or blameworthy.[6]

[6]Isaiah Berlin, *op. cit.*, pp. 26-27.

Two comments are in order.

i.   In the first place, it is far from clear what is the conception of the "human self" with which Berlin operates. For on his view, the human self must apparently be distinguished not only from the human body but also from any of the choices, no longer within a man's control, which determine at least in part the choice he is about to make, as well as from his springs of action, his disposition, and his motives insofar as these latter are also beyond his control. It is therefore difficult to know what does remain of the self, when all the things are eliminated that in the slightest way influence a man's conduct during the knife-edge instant of the immediate present.

The difficulty is not diminished when we try to understand Berlin's conception of the self whose decisions are "free" in his sense of the term, in the context of imagining some person deliberating over a course of action he ought to adopt, and finally deciding between several alternatives he has been contemplating. The individual is usually unaware that the decision he finally makes may be the expression of a set of more or less stable habits, transient impulses, the careful attention he gave to some of the alternatives but not to the others, and so on — any more than he is normally aware of his own heartbeat or of the organ that produces it. It seems certainly unlikely that, when the individual recovers from his perplexed surprise on being asked whether the choice he finally made was really his own, he would hesitate to say that of course it was. But should the individual become aware of these things about himself, as he sometimes may become aware, would he regard his choice as any less his *own* choice? This too seems unlikely, just as it is unlikely that he would disclaim the pulse beat in his temples as his own, when he discovers that it is being produced by the rhythmic contractions of his heart.

According to Berlin, however, the answer to the question as to whether the decision was the individual's own must in either case apparently be negative. Berlin is therefore faced with a puzzle that is nothing short of being irresolvable — the puzzle of finding some activity or trait that is an intrinsic attribute of the human self, but with the proviso that anything which is causally dependent on something else is thereby automatically disqualified from being a genuine part of the self. His problem is like the one with which he would be confronted were he to set himself the task of describing a moving baseball, for example, without mentioning any attributes which owe their presence in the ball to any agency (such as the manufacturer who made it, the batter who struck it, or the sun which shines upon it) — for the reason that, since familiar attributes of the ball like size, shape, color, and state of motion have been determined by external factors, they are not genuinely intrinsic to the ball itself.

Just how and where the boundaries of the individual human self are to be drawn are undoubtedly not easy questions to decide; and the answers to them may vary with different contexts of self-identification, and may even depend on cultural differences in the ways the human self is conceived. But however they are drawn, the lines should not be so drawn that in the end nothing can be identified as the self. Certainly an artificial and insoluble puzzle should not be made of the fact that we are frequently conscious of acting of our own free volition and without external constraints, even if we recognize that some of our choices are the products of our dispositions, past actions, and present impulses.

    ii.   A second comment must be made on Berlin's argument. On the face of it, his discussion of the conditions under which human beings can be properly regarded as responsible agents closely resembles the reasoning often used to show that in the light of the findings of modern physics the common-sense view of the world is an illusion. For example, it has been argued that since, according to physics, common-sense objects like tables are complex systems of rapidly moving minute particles separated by relatively great distances, it is illusory to suppose that tables are "really" hard solids possessing continuous surfaces. But, as has been frequently noted, such an argument is a nest of fallacies. It commits the fundamental error of supposing that, since common-sense terms such as 'solid,' 'hard,' and 'continuous' are admittedly not applicable, when used in their ordinary meanings, to things like congeries of molecules, the terms are therefore not correctly applicable to macroscopic objects like tables.[7]

Berlin's discussion suffers from a similar flaw, for it argues in an analogous way that, if there are determining biological and psychological conditions under which responsible behavior occurs, men cannot be genuinely responsible for any of their acts, for the reason that responsibility (in the same sense of the term) cannot be properly ascribed

[7] J.C. Maxwell, *Matter in Motion*, New York, 1920, p. 13. But recent developments in physical cosmology suggest that Maxwell's formulation of the principle of causality may require modification.

to those *conditions*. It is nevertheless an empirical fact, as well attested as any, that men often do deliberate and decide between alternatives; and nothing we have discovered or will discover about the physiological and psychological *conditions* that make deliberation and choice possible can be used as evidence (except on pain of a fatal incoherence) for denying that such deliberative choices *do* occur.

Part **II**

CONTEMPORARY PHILOSOPHIC VIEWS CONCERNING THE EXISTENCE OF FREEDOM

6

Freedom and necessity

Alfred Jules Ayer

Professor Ayer handles freedom in the form of <u>free action</u>. Like Ernest Nagel, he welcomes a deterministic theory that signifies that acts are not done by chance. The possibility of predicting events means for him simply that human action can be explained. In other words, there is a conjunction of law and facts, but the facts are certainly man's doing. Yet what man does is no accident, reasons Ayer, or we surely would not hold man responsible. He therefore does not agree with John Dewey that responsibility is the assurance of a better future rather than an accountability for the past.

Ayer distinguishes <u>causality from constraint.</u> He wants the problem set in the terms of freedom or constraint. He would insist on freedom, but he does not hold that being caused or determined is opposed to being free. Freedom in this context refers to action rather than choice, and ordinary usage warrants this understanding of freedom as action.

When I am said to have done something of my own free will it is implied that I could have acted otherwise; and it is only when it is believed that I could have acted otherwise that I am held to be morally responsible for what I have done. For a man is not thought to be morally responsible for an action that it was not in his power to avoid. But if human behaviour is entirely governed by causal laws, it is not clear how any action that is done could ever have been avoided. It may be said of the agent that he would have acted otherwise if the causes of his action had been different, but they being what they were, it seems to follow that he was bound to act as he did. Now it is commonly assumed both that men are capable of acting freely, in the sense that is required to make them morally responsible, and that human behaviour is entirely governed by causal laws: and it is the apparent conflict between these two assumptions that gives rise to the philosophical problem of the freedom of will.

Confronted with this problem, many people will be inclined to agree with Dr. Johnson: 'Sir, we *know* our will is free, and *there's* an end on't'. But, while this does very well for those who accept Dr. Johnson's premise, it would hardly convince anyone who denied the freedom of the will. Certainly, if we do know that our wills are free, it follows that they are so. But the logical reply to this might be that since our wills are not free, it follows that no one can know that they are: so that if anyone claims, like Dr. Johnson, to know that they are, he must be mistaken. What is evident, indeed, is that people often believe themselves to be acting freely; and it is to this 'feeling' of freedom that some philosophers appeal when they wish, in the supposed interests of morality, to prove that not all human action is causally determined. But if these philosophers are right in their assumption that a man cannot be acting freely if his action is causally determined, then the fact that someone feels free to do, or not to do, a certain action does not prove that he really is so. It may prove that the agent does not himself know what it is that makes him act in one way rather than

From Alfred J. Ayer, *Philosophical Essays* (New York, St. Martin's Press, Inc., 1954), pp. 272-279, 282-284. By permission of St. Martin's Press, Inc., and Macmillan & Co., Ltd.

another: but from the fact that a man is unaware of the causes of his action, it does not follow that no such causes exist.

So much may be allowed to the determinist; but his belief that all human actions are subservient to causal laws still remains to be justified. If, indeed, it is necessary that every event should have a cause, then the rule must apply to human behaviour as much as to anything else. But why should it be supposed that every event must have a cause? The contrary is not unthinkable. Nor is the law of universal causation a necessary presupposition of scientific thought. The scientist may try to discover causal laws, and in many cases he succeeds; but sometimes he has to be content with statistical laws, and sometimes he comes upon events which, in the present state of his knowledge, he is not able to subsume under any law at all. In the case of these events he assumes that if he knew more he would be able to discover some law, whether causal or statistical, which would enable him to account for them. And this assumption cannot be disproved. For however far he may have carried his investigation, it is always open to him to carry it further; and it is always conceivable that if he carried it further he would discover the connection which had hitherto escaped him. Nevertheless, it is also conceivable that the events with which he is concerned are not systematically connected with any others: so that the reason why he does not discover the sort of laws that he requires is simply that they do not obtain.

Now in the case of human conduct the search for explanations has not in fact been altogether fruitless. Certain scientific laws have been established; and with the help of these laws we do make a number of successful predictions about the ways in which different people will behave. But these predictions do not always cover every detail. We may be able to predict that in certain circumstances a particular man will be angry, without being able to prescribe the precise form that the expression of his anger will take. We may be reasonably sure that he will shout, but not sure how loud his shout will be, or exactly what words he will use. And it is only a small proportion of human actions that we are able to forecast even so precisely as this. But that, it may be said, is because we have not carried our investigations very far. The science of psychology is still in its infancy and, as it is developed, not only will more human actions be explained, but the explanations will go into greater detail. The ideal of complete explanation may never in fact be attained: but it is theoretically attainable. Well, this may be so: and certainly it is impossible to show *a priori* that it is not so: but equally it cannot be shown that it is. This will not, however, discourage the scientist who, in the field of human behaviour, as elsewhere, will continue to formulate theories and test them by the facts. And in this he is justified. For since he has no reason *a priori* to admit that there is a limit to what he can discover, the fact that he also cannot be sure that there is no limit does not make it unreasonable for him to devise theories, nor, having devised them, to try constantly to improve them.

But now suppose it to be claimed that, so far as men's actions are concerned, there is a limit: and that this limit is set by the fact of human freedom. An obvious objection is that in many cases in which a person feels himself to be free to do, or not to do, a certain action, we are even now able to explain, in causal terms, why it is that he acts as he does. But it might be argued that even if men are sometimes mistaken in believing that they act freely, it does not follow that they are always so mistaken. For it is not always the case that when a man believes that he has acted freely we are in fact able to account for his action in causal terms. A determinist would say that we should be able to account for it if we had more knowledge of the circumstances, and had been able to discover the appropriate natural laws. But until those discoveries have been made, this remains only a pious hope. And may it not be true that, in some cases at least, the reason why we can give no causal explanation is that no causal explanation is available; and that this is because the agent's choice was literally free, as he himself felt it to be?

The answer is that this may indeed be true, inasmuch as it is open to anyone to hold that no explanation is possible until some explanation is actually found. But even so it does not give the moralist what he wants. For he is anxious to show that men are capable of acting freely in order to infer that they can be morally responsible for what they do. But if it is a matter of pure chance that a man should act in one way rather than another, he may be free but he can hardly be responsible. And indeed when a man's actions seem to us quite unpredictable, when, as we say, there is no knowing what he will do, we do not look upon him as a moral agent. We look upon him rather as a lunatic.

To this it may be objected that we are not dealing fairly with the moralist. For when he makes it a condition of my being morally responsible that I should act freely, he does not wish to imply that it is purely a matter of chance that I act as I do. What he wishes to imply is that my actions are the result of my own free choice: and it is because they are the result of my own free choice that I am held to be morally responsible for them.

But now we must ask how it is that I come to make my choice. Either it is an accident that I choose to act as I do or it is not. If it is an accident, then it is merely a matter of chance that I did not choose otherwise; and if it is merely a matter of chance that I did not choose otherwise, it is surely irrational to hold me morally responsible for choosing as I did. But if it is not an accident that I choose to do one thing rather than another, then presumably there is some causal explanation of my choice: and in that case we are led back to determinism.

Again, the objection may be raised that we are not doing justice to the moralist's case. His view is not that it is a matter of chance that I choose to act as I do, but rather that my choice depends upon my character. Nevertheless he holds that I can still be free in the sense that he requires; for it is I who am responsible for my character. But in what way am I responsible for my character? Only, surely, in the sense that there is a causal connection between what I do now and what I have done in the past. It is only this that justifies the statement that I have made myself what I am: and even so this is an over-simplification, since it takes no account of the external influences to which I have been subjected. But, ignoring the external influences, let us assume that it is in fact the case that I have made myself what I am. Then it is still legitimate to ask how it is that I have come to make myself one sort of person rather than another. And if it be answered that it is a matter of my strength of will, we can put the same question in another form by asking how it is that my will has the strength that it has and not some other degree of strength. Once more, either it is an accident or it is not. If it is an accident, then by the same argument as before, I am not morally responsible, and if it is not an accident we are led back to determinism.

Furthermore, to say that my actions proceed from my character or, more colloquially, that I act in character, is to say that my behaviour is consistent and to that extent predictable: and since it is, above all, for the actions that I perform in character that I am held to be morally responsible, it looks as if the admission of moral responsibility, so far from being incompatible with determinism, tends rather to presuppose it. But how can this be so if it is a necessary condition of moral responsibility that the person who is held responsible should have acted freely? It seems that if we are to retain this idea of moral responsibility, we must either show that men can be held responsible for actions which they do not do freely, or else find some way of reconciling determinism with the freedom of the will.

It is no doubt with the object of effecting this reconciliation that some philosophers have defined freedom as the consciousness of necessity. And by so doing they are able to say not only that a man can be acting freely when his action is causally determined, but even that his action must be causally determined for it to be possible for him to be acting freely. Nevertheless this definition has the serious disadvantage that it gives to the word 'freedom' a meaning quite different from any that it ordinarily bears. It is indeed obvious that if we are allowed to give the word 'freedom' any meaning that we please, we can find a meaning that will reconcile it with determinism: but this is no more a solution of our present problem than the fact that the word 'horse' could be arbitrarily used to mean what is ordinarily meant by 'sparrow' is a proof that horses have wings. For suppose that I am compelled by another person to do something 'against my will'. In that case, as the word 'freedom' is ordinarily used, I should not be said to be acting freely: and the fact that I am fully aware of the constraint to which I am subjected makes no difference to the matter. I do not become free by becoming conscious that I am not. It may, indeed, be possible to show that my being aware that my action is causally determined is not incompatible with my acting freely: but it by no means follows that it is in this that my freedom consists. Moreover, I suspect that one of the reasons why people are inclined to define freedom as the consciousness of necessity is that they think that if one is conscious of necessity one may somehow be able to master it. But this is a fallacy. It is like someone's saying that he wishes he could see into the future, because if he did he would know what calamities lay in wait for him and so would be able to avoid them. But if he avoids the calamities then they don't lie in the future and it is not true that he foresees them. And similarly if I am able to master necessity, in the sense of escaping the operation of a necessary law, then the law in question is not necessary. And if the law is not necessary, then neither my freedom nor anything else can consist in my knowing that it is.

Let it be granted, then, that when we speak of reconciling freedom with determinism we are using the word 'freedom' in an ordinary sense. It still remains for us to make this usage clear: and perhaps the best way to make it clear is to show what it is that freedom, in this sense, is contrasted with. Now we began with the assumption that freedom is contrasted with causality: so that a man cannot be said to be acting freely if his action is causally determined. But this assumption has led us into difficulties and I now wish to suggest that it is mistaken. For it is not, I think, causality that freedom is to be contrasted with, but constraint. And while it is true that being constrained to do an action entails being caused to do it, I shall try to show that the converse does not hold. I shall try to show that from the fact that my action is causally determined it does not necessarily follow that I am constrained to do it: and this is equivalent to saying that it does not necessarily follow that I am not free.

If I am constrained, I do not act freely. But in what circumstances can I legitimately be said to be constrained? An obvious instance is the case in which I am compelled by another person to do what he wants. In a case of this sort the compulsion need not be such as to deprive one of the power of choice. It is not required that the other person should have hypnotized me, or that he should make it physically impossible for me to go against his will. It is enough that he should induce me to do what he wants by making it clear to me that, if I do not, he will bring about some situation that I regard as even more undesirable than the consequences of the action that he wishes me to do. Thus, if the man points a pistol at my head I may still choose to disobey him: but this does not prevent its being true that if I do fall in with his wishes he can legitimately be said to have compelled me. And if the circumstances are such that no reasonable person would be expected to choose the other alternative, then the action that I am made to do is not one for which I am held to be morally responsible.

*   *   *

If this is correct, to say that I could have acted otherwise is to say, first, that I should have acted otherwise if I had so chosen; secondly, that my action was voluntary in the sense in which the actions, say, of the kleptomaniac are not; and thirdly, that nobody compelled me to choose as I did: and these three conditions may very well be fulfilled. When they are fulfilled, I may be said to have acted freely. But this is not to say that it was a matter of chance that I acted as I did, or, in other words, that my action could not be explained. And that my actions should be capable of being explained is all that is required by the postulate of determinism.

If more than this seems to be required it is, I think, because the use of the very word 'determinism' is in some degree misleading. For it tends to suggest that one event is somehow in the power of another, whereas the truth is merely that they are factually correlated. And the same applies to the use, in this context, of the word 'necessity' and even of the word 'cause' itself. Moreover, there are various reasons for this. One is the tendency to confuse causal with logical necessitation, and so to infer mistakenly that the effect is contained in the cause. Another is the uncritical use of a concept of force which is derived from primitive experiences of pushing and striking. A third is the survival of an animistic conception of causality, in which all causal relationships are modelled on the example of one person's exercising authority over another. As a result we tend to form an imaginative picture of an unhappy effect trying vainly to escape from the clutches of an overmastering cause. But, I repeat, the fact is simply that when an event of one type occurs, an event of another type occurs also, in a certain temporal or spatio-temporal relation to the first. The rest is only metaphor. And it is because of the metaphor, and not because of the fact, that we come to think that there is an antithesis between causality and freedom.

Nevertheless, it may be said, if the postulate of determinism is valid, then the future can be explained in terms of the past: and this means that if one knew enough about the past one would be able to predict the future. But in that case what will happen in the future is already decided. And how then can I be said to be free? What is going to happen is going to happen and nothing that I do can prevent it. If the determinist is right, I am the helpless prisoner of fate.

But what is meant by saying that the future course of events is already decided? If the implication is that some person has arranged it, then the proposition is false. But if all that is meant is that it is possible, in principle, to deduce it from a set of particular facts about the past, together with the appropriate general laws, then, even if this is true, it does not in the least entail that I am the helpless prisoner of fate. It does not even entail that my actions make no difference to the future: for they are causes as well as effects; so that if they were different their consequences would be different also. What it does entail is that my behaviour can be predicted: but to say that my behaviour can be predicted is not to say that I am acting under constraint. It is indeed true that I cannot escape my destiny if this is taken to mean no more than that I shall do what I shall do. But this is a tautology, just as it is a tautology that what is going to happen is going to happen. And such tautologies as these prove nothing whatsoever about the freedom of the will.

7

Philosophical defence of freedom

C. Arthur Campbell

C.A. Campbell, unlike A.J. Ayer, regards the human character as the situation for human action rather than its cause. He goes on to say that the situation within which any decision takes place does indeed furnish a broad basis for prediction, but when a man's formed character differs from his moral ideal, there can be no prediction as to how he will act.

Professor Campbell thinks, moreover, that those who refuse to distinguish self from character are falling into the objectification-scheme and thereby viewing human choosing from an external standpoint.

The author faces the problem posed by a *self*-determination that is determined by something other than the self's character. But he believes that the moral experience shows over and over that free action is not the fruit of character. This is somehow bound up with the fact that human freedom functions as creativity, and if it does, then it cannot be viewed extrinsically.

. . . The problem of free will get its urgency for the ordinary educated man by reason of its close connection with the conception of moral responsibility. When we regard a man as morally responsible for an act, we regard him as a legitimate object of moral praise or blame in respect of it. But it seems plain that a man cannot be a legitimate object of moral praise or blame for an act unless in willing the act he is in some important sense a "free" agent. Evidently free will in some sense, therefore, is a precondition of moral responsibility. Without doubt it is the realisation that any threat to freedom is thus a threat to moral responsibility — with all that that implies — combined with the knowledge that there are a variety of considerations, philosophic, scientific, and theological, tending to place freedom in jeopardy, that gives to the problem of free will its perennial and universal appeal. And it is therefore in close connection with the question of the conditions of moral responsibility that any discussion of the problem must proceed, if it is not to be academic in the worst sense of the term.

We raise the question at once, therefore, what are the conditions, in respect of freedom, which must attach to an act in order to make it a morally responsible act? It seems to me that the fundamental conditions are two. . . .

The first condition is the universally recognised one that the act must be *self*-caused, *self*-determined. But it is important to accept this condition in its full rigour. The agent must be not merely *a* cause but the *sole* cause of that for which he is deemed morally responsible. If entities other than the self have also a causal influence upon an act, then that act is not one for which we can say without qualification that the *self* is morally responsible. If in respect of it we hold the self responsible at all, it can only be for some feature of the act — assuming the possibility of disengaging such a feature — of which the self *is* the sole cause. I do not see how this conclusion can be evaded. But it has awkward implications

From C. Arthur Campbell, *A Defence of Free Will* (Glasgow: Jackson, Sons & Company, 1938). Inaugural Address, University of Glasgow, 1938. Reprinted by permission.

which have led not a few people to abandon the notion of individual moral responsibility altogether.

This first condition, however, is quite clearly not sufficient. ·It is possible to conceive an act of which the agent is the sole cause, but which is at the same time an act *necessitated* by the agent's nature. ... In the case of such an act, where the agent could not do otherwise than he did, we must all agree, I think, that it would be inept to say that he *ought* to have done otherwise and is thus morally blameworthy, or *ought not* to have done otherwise and is thus morally praiseworthy. It is perfectly true that we do sometimes hold a person morally responsible for an act, even when we believe that he, being what he now is, virtually could not do otherwise. But underlying that judgement is always the assumption that the person has *come* to be what he now is in virtue of past acts of will in which he *was* confronted by real alternatives, by genuinely open possibilities: and, strictly speaking, it is in respect of these *past* acts of his that we praise or blame the agent *now*. For ultimate analysis, the agent's power of alternative action would seem to be an inexpugnable condition of his liability to moral praise or blame, i.e. of his moral responsibility.

We may lay down, therefore, that an act is a "free" act in the sense required for moral responsibility only if the agent (a) is the sole cause of the act; and (b) could exert his causality in alternative ways. ... The doctrine which demands, and asserts, the fulfilment of both conditions is the doctrine we call "Libertarianism." ...

And now, the conditions of free will being defined in these general terms, we have to ask whether human beings are in fact capable of performing free acts; and if so, where precisely such acts are to be found. In order to prepare the way for an answer, it is desirable, I think, that we should get clear at once about the significance of a certain very familiar, but none the less formidable, criticism of free will which ... the Libertarian has to meet. This is the criticism which bases itself upon the facts of heredity on the one hand and of environment on the other. I may briefly summarise the criticism as follows.

Every historic self has an hereditary nature consisting of a group of inborn propensities, in range more or less common to the race, but specific to the individual in their respective strengths. With this equipment the self just *happens* to be born. Strictly speaking, it antedates the existence of the self proper, i.e. the existence of the self-conscious subject, and it is itself the effect of a series of causes leading back to indefinitely remote antiquity. It follows, therefore, that any of the self's choices that manifests the influence of his hereditary nature is not a choice of which *he*, the actual historic self, is the sole cause. The choice is determined, at least in part, by factors external to the self. The same thing holds good of "environment." Every self is born and bred in a particular physical and social environment, not of his own choosing, which plays upon him in innumerable ways, encouraging this propensity, discouraging that, and so on. Clearly any of the self's choices that manifests the influence of environmental factors is likewise a choice which is determined, at least in part, by factors external to the self. But if we thus grant, as seems inevitable, that heredity and environment are external influences, where shall we find a choice in the whole history of a self that is not subject to external influence? Surely we must admit that every particular act of choice bears the marks of the agent's hereditary nature and environmental nurture; in which case a free act, in the sense of an act determined solely by the self, must be dismissed as a mere chimaera. . . .

The externality of these influences is taken for granted in our reflective practical judgements upon persons. On those occasions when we are in real earnest about giving a critical and considered estimate of a man's moral calibre — as, e.g. in any serious biographical study — we impose upon ourselves as a matter of course the duty of enquiring with scrupulous care into his hereditary propensities and environmental circumstances, with a view to discovering how far his conduct is influenced by these factors. And having traced these influences, we certainly do not regard the result as having no bearing on the question of the man's moral responsibility for his conduct. On the contrary, the very purpose of the enquiry is to enable us, by due appreciation of the *external* influences that affect his conduct, to gain as accurate a view as possible of that which can justly be attributed to the man's own *self*-determination. The allowances that we all of us do in practice make for hereditary and environmental influences in passing judgement on our fellows would be meaningless if we did not suppose these influences to be in a real sense "external" to the self

We know now that condition (a) is not fulfilled by any act in respect of which inheritance or environment exerts a causal influence. For that type of influence has been shown to be in a real sense external to the self. The free act of which we are in search has therefore got to be one into which influences of this kind do not enter at all. . . .

. . . Our reflective practical judgements on persons, while fully recognizing the externality of the influence of heredity and environment, do nevertheless presuppose throughout that there is *something* in conduct which is genuinely self-determined; something which the agent contributes solely on his own initiative, unaffected by external influences; something for which, accordingly, he may justly be held morally responsible. That conviction may, of course, be a false one. But the fact of its wide-spread existence can hardly be without significance for our problem.

Let us proceed, then, by following up this clue. Let us ask, why do human beings so obstinately persist in believing that here is an indissoluble core of purely *self*-originated activity which even heredity and environment are powerless to affect? There can be little doubt, I think, of the answer in general terms. They do so, at bottom, because they feel certain of the existence of such activity from their immediate practical experience of themselves. Nor can there be in the end much doubt, I think, in what function of the self that activity is to be located. There seems to me to be one, and only one, function of the self with respect to which the agent can even pretend to have an assurance of that absolute self-origination which is here at issue. But to render precise the nature of that function is obviously of quite paramount importance: and we can do so, I think, only by way of a somewhat thorough analysis — which I now propose to attempt — of the experiential situation in which it occurs, *viz.* the situation of "moral temptation."

It is characteristic of that situation that in it I am aware of an end A which I believe to be morally right, and also of an end B, incompatible with A, towards which, in virtue of that system of conative dispositions which constitutes my "character" as so far formed, I entertain a strong desire. There may be, and perhaps must be, desiring elements in my nature which are directed to A also. But what gives to the situation its specific character as one of moral temptation is that the urge of our desiring nature towards the right end, A, is felt to be *relatively* weak. We are sure that if our desiring nature is permitted to issue directly in action, it is end B that we shall choose. That is what is meant by saying, as William James does, that end B is "in the line of least resistance" relatively to our conative dispositions. The expression is, of course, a metaphorical one, but it serves to describe, graphically enough, a situation of which we all have frequent experience, *viz.* where we recognize a specific end as that towards which the "set" of our desiring nature most strongly inclines us, and which we shall indubitably choose if no inhibiting factor intervenes.

But inhibiting factors, we should most of us say, *may* intervene: and that in two totally different ways which it is vital to distinguish clearly. The inhibiting factor may be of the nature of another desire (or aversion), which operates by changing the balance of the desiring situation. Though at one stage I desire B, which I believe to be wrong, more strongly than I desire A, which I believe to be right, it may happen that before action is taken I become aware of certain hitherto undiscerned consequences of A which I strongly desire, and the result may be that now not B but A presents itself to me as the end in the line of least resistance. Moral temptation is here overcome by the simple process of ceasing to be a moral temptation.

That is one way, and probably by far the commoner way, in which an inhibiting factor intervenes. But it is certainly not regarded by the self who is confronted by moral temptation as the *only* way. In such situations we all believe, rightly or wrongly, that even although B *continues* to be in the line of least resistance, even although, in other words, the situation remains one with the characteristic marks of moral temptation, we *can* nevertheless align ourselves with A. We can do so, we believe, because we have the power to introduce a new energy, to make what we call an "effort of will," whereby we are able to act contrary to the felt balance of mere desire, and to achieve the higher end despite the fact that it continues to be in the line of greater resistance relatively to our desiring nature. The self in practice believes that it has this power; and believes, moreover, that the decision rests solely with its self, here and now, whether this power be exerted or not.

Now the objective validity or otherwise of this belief is not at the moment in question. I am here merely pointing to its existence as a psychological fact. No amount of introspective analysis, so far as I can see, even tends to disprove that we do as a matter of fact believe, in situations of moral temptation, that it rests with our self absolutely to decide whether we exert the effort of will which will enable us to rise to duty, or whether we shall allow our desiring nature to take its course.

I have now to point out, further, how this act of moral decision, at least in the significance which it has for the agent himself, fulfils in full the two conditions which we found it necessary to lay down at the beginning for the kind of "free" act which moral responsibility presupposes.

For obviously it is, in the first place, an act which the agent believes he could perform in alternative ways. He believes that it is genuinely open to him to put forth effort – in varying degrees, if the situation admits of that – or withhold it altogether. And when he *has* decided – in whatever way — he remains convinced that these alternative courses were really open to him.

It is perhaps a little less obvious, but, I think, equally certain, that the agent believes the second condition to be fulfilled likewise, i.e. that the act of decision is determined *solely* by his self. It appears less obvious, because we all realise that formed character has a great deal to do with the choices that we make; and formed character is, without a doubt, partly dependent on the external factors of heredity and environment. But it is crucial here that we should not misunderstand the precise nature of the influence which formed character brings to bear upon the choices that constitute conduct. No one denies that it determines, at least largely, what things we desire, and again how greatly we desire them. It may thus fairly be said to determine the felt balance of desires in the situation of moral temptation. But all that that amounts to is that formed character prescribes the nature of the situation *within* which the act of moral decision takes place. It does not in the least follow that it has any influence whatsoever in determining the act of decision itself — the decision as to whether we shall exert effort or take the easy course of following the bent of our desiring nature: take, that is to say, the course which, in virtue of the determining influence of our character as so far formed, we feel to be in the line of least resistance.

When one appreciates this, one is perhaps better prepared to recognise the fact that the agent himself in the situation of moral temptation does not, and indeed could not, regard his formed character as having any influence whatever upon his act of decision as such. For the very nature of that decision, as it presents itself to him, is as to whether he will or will not permit his formed character to dictate his action. In other words, the agent distinguishes sharply between the self which makes the decision, and the self which, as formed character, determines not the decision but the situation within which the decision takes place. Rightly or wrongly, the agent believes that through his act of decision he can oppose and transcend his own formed character in the interest of duty. We are therefore obliged to say, I think, that the agent *cannot* regard his formed character as in any sense a determinant of the act of decision as such. The act is felt to be a genuinely creative act, originated by the self *ad hoc*, and by the self alone. . . .

Now in considering the claim to truth of this belief of our practical consciousness, we should begin by noting that the onus of proof rests upon the critic who rejects this belief. Until cogent evidence to the contrary is adduced, we are entitled to put our trust in a belief which is so deeply embedded in our experience as practical beings as to be, I venture to say, ineradicable from it. Anyone who doubts whether it is ineradicable may be invited to think himself imaginatively into a situation of moral temptation as we have above described it, and then to ask himself whether in that situation he finds it possible to *disbelieve* that his act of decision has the characteristics in question. I have no misgivings about the answer. It is possible to disbelieve only when we are thinking abstractly about the situation; not when we are living through it, either actually or in imagination. This fact certainly establishes a strong *prima facie* presumption in favour of the Libertarian position. Nevertheless I agree that we shall have to weigh carefully several criticisms of high authority before we can feel justified in asserting free will as an ultimate and unqualified truth. . . .

I shall begin with one which, though it is a simple matter to show its irrelevance to the Libertarian doctrine as I have stated it, is so extremely popular that it cannot safely be ignored.

The charge made is that the Libertarian view is incompatible with the *predictability* of human conduct. For we do make rough predictions of people's conduct, on the basis of what we know of their character, every day of our lives, and there can be no doubt that the practice, within certain limits, is amply justified by results. Indeed if it were not so, social life would be reduced to sheer chaos. The close relationship between character and conduct which prediction postulates really seems to be about as certain as anything can be. But the Libertarian view, it is urged, by ascribing to the self a mysterious power of decision uncontrolled by character, and capable of issuing in acts inconsistent with character, denies that continuity between character and conduct upon which prediction depends. If Libertarianism is true, prediction is impossible. But prediction *is* possible, therefore Libertarianism is untrue.

My answer is that the Libertarian view is perfectly compatible with prediction within certain limits, and that there is no empirical evidence at all that prediction is in fact possible beyond these limits. The following considerations will, I think, make the point abundantly clear.

(1) There is no question, on our view, of a free will that can will just anything at all. The range of possible choices is limited by the agent's character in every case; for nothing can be an object of possible choice which is not suggested by either the agent's desires or his moral ideals, and

these depend on "character" for us just as much as for our opponents. We have, indeed explicitly recognised at an earlier stage that character determines the situation within which the act of moral decision takes place, although not the act of moral decision itself. This consideration obviously furnishes a broad basis for at least approximate predictions.

(2) There is *one* experiential situation, and *one only*, on our view, in which there is any possibility of the act of will not being in accordance with character; *viz*. the situation in which the course which formed character prescribes is a course in conflict with the agent's moral ideal: in other words, the situation of moral temptation. Now this is a situation of comparative rarity. Yet with respect to all other situations in life we are in full agreement with those who hold that conduct is the response of the agent's formed character to the given situation. Why should it not be so? There could be no reason, on our view any more than on another, for the agent even to consider deviating from the course which his formed character prescribes and he most strongly desires, *unless* that course is believed by him to be incompatible with what is right.

(3) Even within that one situation which is relevant to free will, our view can still recognize a certain basis for prediction. In that situation our character as so far formed prescribes a course opposed to duty, and an effort of will is required if we are to deviate from that course. But of course we are all aware that a greater effort of will is required in proportion to the degree in which we have to transcend our formed character in order to will the right. Such action is, as we say, "harder." But if action is "harder" in proportion as it involves deviation from formed character, it seems reasonable to suppose that, on the whole, action will be of rarer occurrence in that same proportion: though perhaps we may not say that at any level of deviation it becomes flatly impossible. It follows that even with respect to situations of moral temptation we may usefully employ our knowledge of the agent's character as a clue to prediction. It will be a clue of limited, but of by no means negligible, value. It will warrant us in predicting, e.g., of a person who has become enslaved to alcohol, that he is unlikely, even if fully aware of the moral evil of such slavery, to be successful immediately and completely in throwing off its shackles. Predictions of this kind we all make often enough in practice. And there seems no reason at all why a Libertarian doctrine should wish to question their validity.

Now when these three considerations are borne in mind, it becomes quite clear that the doctrine we are defending is compatible with a very substantial measure of predictability indeed. And I submit that there is not a jot of empirical evidence that any larger measure than this obtains in fact.

Let us pass on then to consider a much more interesting and, I think, more plausible criticism. It is constantly objected against the Libertarian doctrine that it is fundamentally *unintelligible*. Libertarianism holds that the act of moral decision is the *self's* act, and yet insists at the same time that it is not influenced by any of those determinate features in the self's nature which go to constitute its "character." But, it is asked, do not these two propositions contradict one another? Surely a *self*-determination which is determination by something other than the self's *character* is a contradiction in terms? What meaning is there in the conception of a "self" in abstraction from its "character"? If you really wish to maintain, it is urged, that the act of decision is not determined by the self's character, you ought to admit frankly that it is not determined by the *self* at all. But in that case, of course, you will not be advocating a freedom which lends any kind of support to moral responsibility; indeed very much the reverse.

Now this criticism, and all of its kind, seem to me to be the product of a simple, but extraordinarily pervasive, error: the error of confining one's self to the categories of the external observer in dealing with the actions of human agents. Let me explain.

It is perfectly true that the stand-point of the external observer, which we are obliged to adopt in dealing with physical processes, does not furnish us with even a glimmering of a notion of what can be meant by an entity which acts causally and yet not through any of the determinate features of its character. So far as we confine ourselves to external observation, I agree that this notion must seem to us pure nonsense. But then we are *not* obliged to confine ourselves to external observation in dealing with the human agent. Here, though here alone, we have the inestimable advantage of being able to apprehend operations from the *inside*, from the stand-point of *living* experience. But if we do adopt this internal stand-point — surely a proper stand-point, and one which we should be only too glad to adopt if we could in the case of other entities — the situation is entirely changed. We find that we not merely can, but constantly do, attach meaning to a causation which is the self's causation but is yet not exercised by the self's character. We have seen as much already in our analysis of the situation of moral temptation. When confronted by such a situation, we saw, we are certain that it lies with our *self* to decide whether we shall let our character as so far formed dictate our action or whether we shall by effort oppose its dictates and rise to duty. We are certain, in other words, that the act is *not* determined by our *character*, while we remain equally certain that the act *is* determined by our *self*.

Or look, for a further illustration . . . to the experience of effortful willing itself, where the act of decision has found expression in the will to rise to duty. In such an experience we are certain that it is our self which makes the effort. But we are equally certain that the effort does not flow from that system of conative dispositions which we call our formed character; for the very function that the effort has for us is to enable us to act against the "line of least resistance," i.e. to act in a way *contrary* to that to which our formed character inclines us.

I conclude, therefore, that those who find the Libertarian doctrine of the self's causality in moral decision inherently unintelligible find it so simply because they restrict themselves, quite arbitrarily, to an inadequate stand-point: a stand-point from which, indeed, a genuinely creative activity, if it existed, never *could* be apprehended. . . .

8

Freedom and reason

Richard M. Hare

Professor Hare argues that the forming of opinions about
moral questions is a rational activity. He believes that moral
philosophers are drawn up along two hard and fast lines, one
side trying to preserve reason and thinking they must let
freedom go, the other side anxious to preserve freedom but
feeling that they therefore must forgo reason. Those who let
reason go are called subjectivists or emotivists; those who let
freedom go are called descriptivists or naturalists. Professor
Hare sees the task of moral philosophy to be that of
reconciling these apparently opposed positions and thereby
resolving the antinomy between freedom and reason.

'OUGHT' AND 'CAN'

5.1. The ethical theory which has been briefly set out in the preceding chapters is a type of prescriptivism, in that it maintains that it is one of the characteristics of moral terms, and one which is a sufficiently essential characteristic for us to call it part of the meaning of these terms, that judgements containing them are, as typically used, intended as guides to conduct. Now there is one objection to all kinds of prescriptivism which is so commonly made, and is of such intrinsic interest, that it requires a chapter to itself. This is the objection that, if moral judgements were prescriptive, then it would be impossible to accept some moral judgement and yet act contrary to it. But, it is maintained (in Hume's words), "'tis one thing to know virtue, and another to conform the will to it';[1] people are constantly doing what they think they ought not to be doing; therefore prescriptivism must be wrong.

There are two points from the preceding chapter which are relevant to a consideration of this objection. The first is that, there too, we saw that there was a problem for prescriptivists where there ought to be no problem for descriptivists — namely the problem raised by our feeling that 'ought' implies 'can'. We saw that if 'ought' were always, as it is sometimes, purely descriptive, there would be no question of 'ought' implying 'can', and therefore no problem; the problem arises because of the fact that in some, and those the typical and central, of their uses moral judgements have that affinity with imperatives which makes me call both prescriptive. To this extent, the very existence of the problem — the fact that ordinary people feel that 'ought' implies 'can' and that it is obvious that whether I shall land in France is out of my control; then, if I ask 'Shall I land in France?' this cannot be understood as a practical question, but only as a request for a prediction, equivalent to 'Am I as a matter of fact going to land in France?' Sometimes the very form of words makes it

From *Freedom and Reason* by R.M. Hare. © Oxford University Press 1963. Reprinted by permission. Pp. 67-85.

[1] *Treatise*, iii, I. i. For a recent development of this objection, see A.C. Ewing, *Second Thoughts in Moral Philosophy*, ch. 1.

impossible to understand a question as a practical one; for example, it is clear that 'Shall I *be driven* on the French shore?' could not be a practical question. The reason is that the event referred to is described in such a way that it could not be the subject of a decision, order, request, or piece of advice, and therefore could not, either, be the subject of a question which asks for these things. Similar questions are 'Shall I fall downstairs by accident?' and 'Shall I go to the wrong room by mistake?' We cannot ask these questions comprehensibly, because the answers to them would be incomprehensible. If somebody said 'Fall down the stairs by accident' or 'Go to the wrong room by mistake', we should be at a loss to know what he was telling us to do, and should have to look for peculiar senses in which to take his words (as, e.g., by understanding 'by mistake' to mean '*pretending* to have made a mistake').

These illustrations could also be used to show that, in similar circumstances, an 'Ought I?' question would be equally incomprehensible, provided that 'ought' was alleged to be being used with its full force. When the word is being so used, it is impossible to understand what a man could be asking if he says 'Ought I to be driven on shore by the gale?' or 'Ought I to fall downstairs by accident?' or 'Ought I to go to the wrong room by mistake?' Here again, there are contrived interpretations that would make sense of these utterances; for example, the man might mean 'Ought I to be the sort of man who makes this kind of mistake; ought I not rather to take a course in Pelmanism to correct my absent-mindedness?'; but this need not concern us. It seems to be true in general that if a description of an action is such as to rule out a practical 'Shall I?' question, then it will also rule out, for the same reason, the corresponding universally prescriptive 'Ought I?' question. It is, in fact, the impossibility of deliberating, or wondering, whether *to* do a thing which rules out asking whether one *ought* to do it.

4.6. I am not so ambitious as to hope, in this short chapter, to solve any of the tangle of problems that go under the name of 'the problem of free will'. Anyone who thinks that he can clear up these problems in less than a complete closely reasoned book shows himself unaware of their complexity. My aim is the more modest one of showing how the fact of moral freedom is what gives moral language one of its characteristic logical properties; it is because we have to make decisions that we have a use for this sort of language. Nevertheless, what has been said so far does perhaps suggest a useful approach to the traditional problem, which it will be worth a digression to explain.

It is commonly thought that if human actions can be predicted, and especially if they can be predicted by means of 'causal' laws, then it is impossible to make moral judgements about them. This, indeed, is one of the chief sources of philosophical perplexity about free will. The perplexity might perhaps be lessened if we could establish that it is only in a certain class of cases that predictability rules out moral judgement, and that the mistake is to assimilate all cases to these. If we had a clear way to distinguish these different cases from one another, the problem would become easier. And it is possible that such a criterion is provided by the test 'Does the question "What shall I do?" arise for the agent?'

This test serves, at any rate, to distinguish from each other the clear cases, in which nearly all of us would be inclined to say, either that predictability ruled out moral judgement, or that it did not. In the case just described of the man who is wrecked on the French coast, we have a clear case where the predictability of the event makes it impossible to ask a prescriptive moral question. Let us contrast this case with another in which this seems not to be so. Suppose that there are two cashiers, one of unexampled probity and the other the reverse, and that the dishonest one says to the honest one, 'You need some money for your holiday; why not take it out of the till?' Now it might be possible for someone who knew this honest man to predict with certainty that he would reject the suggestion — with as much certainty, that is to say, as any contingent event can be predicted. We may even suppose that, with advances in neurology, it may become possible to examine such a man's brain with an encephalograph and predict on the basis of an assured scientific law that nobody with a brain so formed will ever steal money from the till in this man's circumstances. But this does not make me want to stop saying that the man does as he ought — and I must ask the reader whether he does not agree with me. The reason why this case is different from the 'gale' case seems to be the following. In the 'gale' case there was no question of the man asking himself 'Shall I be wrecked?' or 'Ought I to be wrecked?' if these are understood prescriptively. But in the 'cashier' case these questions not only arise — what the man does depends on what answers he gives to them. He actually considers the question 'Shall I take the money?' — he must consider it, since he understands the other man's suggestion, and rejects it; one cannot even reject a suggestion that one has not, at any rate for a moment, considered. And *if* he were to answer, 'Yes, I'll take the money', then he would take the money; only it is predictable that he will not give this answer.

The same can be said about the 'ought'-question. The question 'Ought I to take the money?' certainly arises for him; only he unhesitatingly and predictably answers, 'No, I ought not'; and it is because he gives this answer that he acts as he does. It would be absurd to say that because it was predictable that these questions would arise for him and that he would answer them in a certain way and act accordingly, therefore the questions did not really arise; this contains a manifest contradiction.

There are those who say that if, with the progress of science, we come to be able in principle to predict any action, we shall have to give up making moral judgements. We may suggest that they have perhaps been misled by the apparent analogy between cases of the 'gale' type and cases of the 'cashier' type. The real difficulties of the subject, however, arise when we take what seem to be intermediate cases, and try to decide to which of the two extreme cases, if either, they are to be assimilated. There is a great variety of cases which seem to be like neither of these — both cases which occur normally, and cases, such as those which are the result of post-hypnotic suggestion or brain-surgery or mental disease, where there are abnormal factors at work. So various are these cases, even within a single class (e.g. the hypnotic), that the proper discussion of them would take us too far away from our subject. I am reasonably sure, however, that if we are clear about the extreme cases, and are not misled by the analogy between them into espousing the naive kind of determinism which says 'All is predictable; therefore moral judgements are out of place', we shall be able to avoid the more elementary confusions.

4.7. The absurdity of what I have called the naive determinist view can be seen if we ask what a person who accepted it could possibly do about it — how it could affect his actual behaviour, linguistic and other. This question is best examined in the context of moral education, which so often illuminates questions in moral philosophy. Even if naive determinism were true, it would not alter the position that we find ourselves in when we are trying to bring up our children. So long as people go on having to make up their minds what to do, they will have need of principles (including moral principles) to help them to do it. So long, therefore, as we know that our children will have in the course of their lives to make up their minds on questions which make a great difference to their own and other people's futures, we shall seek to give them, during their upbringing, something by way of a moral outlook which will help them in making these choices. The fact that the whole process was predictable — or even, for that matter, actually predicted by some clever psychologist, provided that he kept quiet about his predictions — would make no difference to our situation. If a naive determinist were to come to us and say that we need not take any trouble with our children's education, because what they are going to do in the course of their lives is in principle predictable, we should be unlikely to take his advice. For even if our children's actions are in principle predictable, *we* do not know what they are going to be (if we did know, we might change our methods of education, and thus falsify the prediction).

If it is suggested that, because naive determinism is true, we cannot but educate them as we are going to, then it must be answered that in that case the acceptance of naive determinism can make no difference to us in any case. But it is to be doubted whether this follows from the doctrine; for according to it, presumably, the acceptance of determinism is as capable of determining our behaviour as any other stimulus. Let us therefore suppose that, as is manifestly the case, we are left, by the acceptance of the determinist doctrine, in the position of having to decide how to bring up our children; and let us ask what changes in our methods we might be led to introduce.

I have said that, even if our children's futures are in principle predictable, *we* do not know what they are going to be. But whatever they are going to be, one of the causes of their being as they are will be the sort of education which we provide. If the determinist were able to produce, at birth, a kind of horoscope predicting all a child's future conduct, then we might give up the task of educating the child. But this is in principle impossible, since one class of data which the determinist requires in order to compile his predictions consists in the environmental influences which affect the child in its formative years. If, therefore, on his advice, we were to abandon or alter the child's education, this part of the data would be altered, and the predictions would then be based on false data and therefore themselves possibly false.

We may conclude that that very large part of morality which is concerned with the education of children would not be rendered futile, though its content and methods might be altered, by any logically possible advances in the predictive power of psychology. But education is continued by self-education (*LM*$_4$.$_3$). It would therefore seem that, if a person is trying to build up for himself a body of moral principles which becomes more solid as his experience of life increases, his endeavour is no more rendered futile by advances in psychology than is that of a parent who is helping his children along the earlier stages of the same process. For example, suppose that I am devoting thought to the question of whether one ought ever, through the possession of inherited wealth, to take for oneself advantages which the less fortunate cannot have (a serious enough question, partly similar to one which we know occurred to Wittgenstein, and which he answered in the negative); even if somebody else can predict what conclusion I shall come to, and on what principle I shall act (whether I shall give all my money away or not), this does not in the least absolve me from considering the question and making up my mind about it. For I have to act in *some* way, and therefore have to answer the question, 'What shall I do?'; and since predictability does not stop me doing this, neither does it stop me asking the question of principle, 'What *ought* one to do in a case like this?'

So the essential part of moral thought, that which consists in trying to form for oneself and others principles of conduct, is not made futile by any advance in our powers of prediction that could possibly take place. The ability to predict and explain will not curtail the freedom which engenders moral thought, though it will, by increasing our knowledge and power, greatly increase both the potential effectiveness and the burdensomeness of that thought. It may also make us more charitable; but charity and the making of moral judgements are not incompatible.

Part **III**

CONTEMPORARY VIEWS ON THE MEANING OF FREEDOM

9

Freedom as a problem

John Dewey

For the American Naturalists, the human intelligence has evolved out of mankind's earlier efforts to cope with the circumstances encountered. The intellect will continue to develop like any living thing through interaction with its environment. Value judgments are therefore made by man as he faces in his experience a conflict of claims for his allegiance. Thinking or experimental intelligence is the organism's effort to adjust to environment, most often by changing some of the incompatible elements in experience. In this process of creating a more valuable world, a man must often set aside what is immediately prized or desired. Therefore, a moral good is that which is to be done here and now in this situation.

It is obvious that Dewey tried to bridge the dualism between knowledge and values by making inquiry instrumental in solving problems, so that an answer is worked out by human behavior in the transformation of reality. The idea that is a satisfactory hypothesis for this transformation is *true* if the transformation succeeds. Success is a social success directed towards individual self-realization.

Thus Dewey restores freedom to a political framework while
he stresses its setting within his consistent position of a man as
an organism, developing by interaction. With regard to
freedom this becomes a relationship between raw human
nature and culture, and thus the process of freedom's growth
is education.

What is freedom and why is it prized? Is desire for freedom
inherent in human nature or is it a product of special circumstances? Is it
wanted as an end or as a means of getting other things? Does its possession
entail responsibilities, and are these responsibilities so onerous that the
mass of men will readily surrender liberty for the sake of greater ease? Is
the struggle for liberty so arduous that most men are easily distracted from
the endeavor to achieve and maintain it? Does freedom in itself and in the
things it brings with it seem as important as security of livelihood; as food,
shelter, clothing, or even as having a good time? Did man ever care as
much for it as we in this country have been taught to believe? Is there any
truth in the old notion that the driving force in political history has been
the effort of the common man to achieve freedom? Was our own struggle
for political independence in any genuine sense animated by desire for
freedom, or were there a number of discomforts that our ancestors wanted
to get rid of, things having nothing in common save that they were felt to
be troublesome?

Is love of liberty ever anything more than a desire to be liberated
from some special restriction? And when it is got rid of does the desire for
liberty die down until something else feels intolerable? Again, how does
the desire for freedom compare in intensity with the desire to feel equal
with others, especially with those who have previously been called
superiors? How do the fruits of liberty compare with the enjoyments that
spring from a feeling of union, of solidarity, with others? Will men
surrender their liberties if they believe that by so doing they will obtain
the satisfaction that comes from a sense of fusion with others and that

Reprinted by permission of G.P. Putnam's Sons from FREEDOM AND CULTURE,
John Dewey. Copyright 1939 by John Dewey. Pp. 359-363, 365-371, 373-374.

respect by others which is the product of the strength furnished by solidarity?

The present state of the world is putting questions like these to citizens of all democratic countries. It is putting them with special force to us in a country where democratic institutions have been bound up with a certain tradition, the "ideology" of which the Declaration of Independence is the classic expression. This tradition has taught us that attainment of freedom is the goal of political history; that self-government is the inherent right of free men and is that which, when it is achieved, men prize above all else. Yet as we look at the world we see supposedly free institutions in many countries not so much overthrown as abandoned willingly, apparently with enthusiasm. We may infer that what has happened is proof they never existed in reality but only in name. Or we may console ourselves with a belief that unusual conditions, such as national frustration and humiliation, have led men to welcome any kind of government that promised to restore national self-respect. But conditions in our country as well as the eclipse of democracy in other countries compel us to ask questions about the career and fate of free societies, even our own.

There perhaps was a time when the questions asked would have seemed to be mainly or exclusively political. Now we know better. For we know that a large part of the causes which have produced the conditions that are expressed in the questions is the dependence of politics upon other forces, notably the economic. The problem of the constitution of human nature is involved, since it is part of our tradition that love of freedom is inherent in its make-up. Is the popular psychology of democracy a myth? The old doctrine about human nature was also tied up with the ethical belief that political democracy is a moral right and that the laws upon which it is based are fundamental moral laws which every form of social organization should obey. If belief in natural rights and natural laws as the foundation of free government is surrendered, does the latter have any other moral basis? For while it would be foolish to believe that the American Colonies fought the battles that secured their independence and that they built their government consciously and deliberately upon a foundation of psychological and moral theories, yet the democratic tradition, call it dream or call it penetrating vision, was so closely allied with beliefs about human nature and about the moral ends which political institutions should serve, that a rude shock occurs when these affiliations break down. Is there anything to take their place, anything that will give the kind of support they once gave?

The problems behind the questions asked, the forces which give the questions their urgency, go beyond the particular beliefs which formed the early psychological and moral foundation of democracy. After retiring from public office, Thomas Jefferson in his old age carried on a friendly philosophical correspondence with John Adams. In one of his letters he made a statement about existing American conditions and expressed a hope about their future estate: "The advance of liberalism encourages a hope that the human mind will some day get back to the freedom it enjoyed two thousand years ago. This country, which has given to the world the example of physical liberty, owes to it that of moral emancipation also, for as yet it is but nominal with us. The inquisition of public opinion overwhelms in practice the freedom asserted by the laws in theory." The situation that has developed since his time may well lead us to reverse the ideas he expressed, and inquire whether political freedom can be maintained without that freedom of culture which he expected to be the final result of political freedom. It is no longer easy to entertain the hope that given political freedom as the one thing necessary all other things will in time be added to it — and so to us. For we now know that the relations which exist between persons, outside of political institutions, relations of industry, of communication, of science, art, and religion, affect daily associations, and thereby deeply affect the attitudes and habits expressed in government and rules of law. If it is true that the political and legal react to shape the other things, it is even more true that political institutions are an effect, not a cause.

It is this knowledge that sets the theme to be discussed. For this complex of conditions which taxes the terms upon which human beings associate and live together is summed up in the word "culture." The problem is to know what kind of culture is so free in itself that it conceives and begets political freedom as its accompaniment and consequence. What about the state of science and knowledge; of the arts, fine and technological; of friendships and family life; of business and finance; of the attitudes and dispositions created in the give and take of ordinary day-by-day associations? No matter what is the native make-up of human nature, its working activities, those which respond to institutions and rules and which finally shape the pattern of the latter, are created by the whole body of occupations, interests, skills, beliefs, that constitute a given culture. As the latter changes, especially as it grows complex and intricate in the way in which American life has changed since our political organization took shape, new problems take the place of those governing the earlier formation and distribution of political powers. The view that love of freedom is so inherent in man that, if it only has a chance given it by abolition of oppressions exercised by Church and State, it will produce and maintain free institutions is no longer adequate. The idea naturally arose when settlers in a new country felt that the distance they had put between themselves and the forces that oppressed them effectively symbolized everything that stood between them and permanent achievement of freedom. We are now forced to see that positive conditions, forming the prevailing state of culture, are required. Release from oppressions and repressions which previously existed marked a necessary transition, but transitions are but bridges to something different.

Early republicans were obliged even in their own time to note that general conditions, such as are summed up under the name of culture, had a good deal to do with political institutions. For they held that oppressions of State and Church had exercised a corrupting influence upon human nature, so that the original impulse to liberty had either been lost or warped out of shape. This was a virtual admission that surrounding conditions may be stronger than native tendencies. It proved a degree of plasticity in human nature that required exercise of continual solicitude. The Founding Fathers were aware that love of power is a trait of human nature, so strong a one that definite barriers had to be erected to keep persons who get into positions of official authority from encroachments that undermine free institutions. Admission that men may be brought by long habit to hug their chains implies a belief that second or acquired nature is stronger than original nature.

Jefferson at least went further than this. For his fear of the growth of manufacturing and trade and his preference for agrarian pursuits amounted to acceptance of the idea that interests bred by certain pursuits may fundamentally alter original human nature and the institutions that are congenial to it. That the development Jefferson dreaded has come about and to a much greater degree than he could have anticipated is an obvious fact. We face today the consequences of the fact that an agricultural and rural people has become an urban industrial population.

Proof is decisive that economic factors are an intrinsic part of the culture that determines the actual turn taken by political measures and rules, no matter what verbal beliefs are held. Although it later became the fashion to blur the connection which exists between economics and politics, and even to reprove those who called attention to it, Madison as well as Jefferson was quite aware of the connection and of its bearing upon democracy. Knowledge that the connection demanded a general distribution of property and the prevention of rise of the extremely poor and the extremely rich was however different from explicit recognition of a relation between culture and nature so intimate that the former may shape the patterns of thought and action.

*   *   *

Finally, the moral factor is an intrinsic part of the complex of social forces called culture. For no matter whether or not one shares the view, now held on different grounds by different groups, that there is no scientific ground or warrant for moral conviction and judgments, it is certain that human beings hold some things dearer than they do others, and that they struggle for the things they prize, spending time and energy in their behalf: doing so indeed to such an extent that the best measure we have of what is valued is the effort spent in its behalf. Not only so, but for a number of persons to form anything that can be called a community in its pregnant sense there must be values prized in common. Without them, any so-called social group, class, people, nation, tends to fall apart into molecules having but mechanically enforced connections with one another. For the present at least we do not have to ask whether values are moral, having a kind of life and potency of their own, or are but by-products of the working of other conditions, biological, economic, or whatever.

The qualification will indeed seem quite superfluous to most, so habituated have most persons become to believing, at least nominally, that moral forces are the ultimate determinants of the rise and fall of all human societies — while religion has taught many to believe that cosmic as well as social forces are regulated in behalf of moral ends. The qualification is introduced, nevertheless, because of the existence of a school of philosophy holding that opinions about the values which move conduct are lacking in any scientific standing, since (according to them) the only things that can be *known* are physical events. The denial that values have any influence in the long run on the course of events is also characteristic of the Marxist belief that forces of production ultimately control every human relationship. The idea of the impossibility of intellectual regulation of ideas and judgments about values is shared by a number of intellectuals who have been dazzled by the success of mathematical and physical science. These last remarks suggest that there is at least one other factor in culture which needs some attention: namely, the existence of schools of social philosophy, of competing ideologies.

The intent of the previous discussion should be obvious. The problem of freedom and of democratic institutions is tied up with the question of what kind of culture exists; with the necessity of free culture for free political institutions. The import of this conclusion extends far beyond its contrast with the simpler faith of those who formulated the democratic tradition. The question of human psychology, of the make-up of human nature in its original state, is involved. It is involved not just in a general way but with respect to its special constituents and their significance in their relations to one another. For every social and political philosophy currently professed will be found upon examination to involve a certain view about the constitution of human nature: in itself and in its relation to physical nature. What is true of this factor is true of every factor in culture, so that they need not here be listed again, although it is necessary to bear them all in mind if we are to appreciate the variety of factors involved in the problem of human freedom.

Running through the problem of the relation of this and that constituent of culture to social institutions in general and political democracy in particular is a question rarely asked. Yet it so underlies any critical consideration of the principles of each of them that some conclusion on the matter ultimately decides the position taken on each special issue. The question is whether any one of the factors is so predominant that it is *the* causal force, so that other factors are secondary and derived effects. Some kind of answer in what philosophers call a *monistic* direction has been usually given. The most obvious present example is the belief that economic conditions are ultimately the controlling forces in human relationships. It is perhaps significant that this view is comparatively recent. At the height of the eighteenth century, Enlightenment, the prevailing view, gave final supremacy to reason, to the advance of science and to education. Even during the last century, a view was held which is expressed in the motto of a certain school of historians: "History is past politics and politics is present history."

Because of the present fashion of economic explanation, this political view may now seem to have been the crotchet of a particular set of historical scholars. But, after all, it only formulated an idea consistently acted upon during the period of the formation of national states. It is possible to regard the present emphasis upon economic factors as a sort of intellectual revenge taken upon its earlier all but total neglect. The very word "political economy" suggests how completely economic considerations were once subordinated to political. The book that was influential in putting an end to this subjection, Adam Smith's *Wealth of Nations*, continued in its title, though not its contents, the older tradition. In the Greek period, we find that Aristotle makes the political factor so controlling that all normal economic activities are relegated to the household, so that all morally justifiable economic practice is literally domestic economy. And in spite of the recent vogue of the Marxist theory, Oppenheim has produced a considerable body of evidence in support of the thesis that political states are the result of military conquests in which defeated people have become subjects of their conquerors, who, by assuming rule over the conquered, begot the first political states.

The rise of totalitarian states cannot, because of the bare fact of their totalitarianism, be regarded as mere reversions to the earlier theory of supremacy of the political institutional factor. Yet as compared with theories that had subordinated the political to the economic, whether in the Marxist form or in that of the British classical school, it marks reversion to ideas and still more to practices which it was supposed had disappeared forever from the conduct of any modern state. And the practices have been revived and extended with the benefit of scientific technique of control of industry, finance, and commerce in ways which show the earlier governmental officials who adopted "mercantile" economics in the interest of government were the veriest bunglers at their professed job.

The idea that morals ought to be, even if they are not, the supreme regulator of social affairs is not so widely entertained as it once was, and there are circumstances which support the conclusion that when moral forces were as influential as they were supposed to be it was because morals were identical with customs which happened in fact to regulate the relations of human beings with one another. However, the idea is still advanced by sermons from the pulpit and editorials from the press that adoption of, say, the Golden Rule would speedily do away with all social discord and trouble; and as I write the newspapers report the progress of a campaign for something called "moral rearmament." Upon a deeper level, the point made about the alleged identity of ethics with established customs raises the question whether the effect of the disintegration of customs that for a long time held men together in social groups can be overcome save by development of new generally accepted traditions and customs. This development, upon this view, would be equivalent to the creation of a new ethics.

However, such questions are here brought up for the sake of the emphasis they place upon the question already raised: Is there any one factor or phase of culture which is dominant, or which tends to produce and regulate others, or are economics, morals, art, science, and so on only so many aspects of the interaction of a number of factors, each of which acts upon and is acted upon by the others? In the professional language of philosophy: Shall our point of view be monistic or pluralistic? The same question recurs moreover about each one of the factors listed — about economics, about politics, about science, about art. I shall here illustrate the point by reference not to any of these things but to theories that have at various times been influential about the make-up of human nature. For these psychological theories have been marked by serious attempts to make some one constituent of human nature *the* source of motivation of action; or at least to reduce all conduct to the action of a small number of alleged native "forces." A comparatively recent example was the adoption by the classic school of economic theory of self-interest as the main motivating force of human behavior; an idea linked up on its technical side with the notion that pleasure and pain are the causes and the ends in view of all conscious human conduct, in desire to obtain one and avoid the other. Then there was a view that self-interest and sympathy are the two components of human nature, as opposed and balanced centrifugal and centripetal tendencies are the moving forces of celestial nature.

Just now the favorite ideological psychological candidate for control of human activity is love of power. Reasons for its selection are not far to seek. Success of search for economic profit turned out to be largely conditioned in fact upon possession of superior power while success reacted to increase power. Then the rise of national states has been attended by such vast and flagrant organization of military and naval force that politics have become more and more markedly power politics, leading to the conclusion that there is not any other kind, although in the past the power element has been more decently and decorously covered up. One

interpretation of the Darwinian struggle for existence and survival of the
fittest was used as ideological support; and some writers, notably
Nietzsche (though not in the crude form often alleged), proposed an ethics
of power in opposition to the supposed Christian ethics of sacrifice.

Because human nature is the factor which in one way or another is
always interacting with environing conditions in production of culture, the
theme receives special attention elsewhere. But the shift that has occurred
from time to time in theories that have gained currency about the "ruling
motive" in human nature suggests a question which is seldom asked. It is
the question whether these psychologies have not in fact taken the cart to
be the horse. Have they not gathered their notion as to the ruling element
in human nature from observation of tendencies that are marked in
contemporary collective life, and then bunched these tendencies together
in some alleged psychological "force" as their cause? It is significant that
human nature was taken to be strongly moved by an inherent love of
freedom at the time when there was a struggle for representative
government; that the motive of self-interest appeared when conditions in
England enlarged the role of money, because of new methods of industrial
production; that the growth of organized philanthropic activities brought
sympathy into the psychological picture; and that events today are readily
converted into love of power as the mainspring of human action.

In any case, the idea of culture that has been made familiar by the
work of anthropological students points to the conclusion that whatever
are the native constituents of human nature, the culture of a period and
group is the determining influence in their arrangement; it is that which
determines the patterns of behavior that mark out the activities of any
group, family, clan, people, sect, faction, class. It is at least as true that the
state of culture determines the order and arrangement of native tendencies
as that human nature produces any particular set or system of social
phenomena so as to obtain satisfaction for itself. The problem is to find
out the way in which the elements of a culture interact with each other
and the way in which the elements of human nature are caused to interact
with one another under conditions set by their interaction with the
existing environment. For example, if our American culture is largely a
pecuniary culture, it is not because the original or innate structure of
human nature tends of itself to obtaining pecuniary profit. It is rather that
a certain complex culture stimulates, promotes, and consolidates native
tendencies so as to produce a certain pattern of desires and purposes. If we

take all the communities, peoples, classes, tribes, and nations that ever existed, we may be sure that since human nature in its native constitution is the relative constant, it cannot be appealed to, in isolation, to account for the multitude of diversities presented by different forms of association.

*   *   *

Tendencies toward sociality, such as sympathy, were admitted. But they were taken to be traits of an individual isolated by nature, quite as much as, say, a tendency to combine with others in order to get protection against something threatening one's own private self. Whether complete identification of human nature with individuality would be desirable or undesirable if it existed is an idle academic question. For it does not exist. Some cultural conditions develop the psychological constituents that lead toward differentiation; others stimulate those which lead in the direction of the solidarity of the beehive or anthill. The human problem is that of securing the development of each constituent so that it serves to release and mature the other. Co-operation – called fraternity in the classic French formula – is as much a part of the democratic ideal as is personal initiative. That cultural conditions were allowed to develop (markedly so in the economic phase) which subordinated co-operativeness to liberty and equality serves to explain the decline in the two latter. Indirectly, this decline is responsible for the present tendency to give a bad name to the very word individualism and to make sociality a term of moral honor beyond criticism. But that association of nullities on even the largest scale would constitute a realization of human nature is as absurd as to suppose that the latter can take place in beings whose only relations to one another are those entered into in behalf of exclusive private advantage.

The problem of freedom of co-operative individualities is then a problem to be viewed in the context of culture. The state of culture is a state of interaction of many factors, the chief of which are law and politics, industry and commerce, science and technology, the arts of expression and communication, and of morals, or the values men prize and the ways in which they evaluate them; and finally, though indirectly, the system of general ideas used by men to justify and to criticize the fundamental conditions under which they live, their social philosophy. We are concerned with the problem of freedom rather than with solutions, in the conviction that solutions are idle until the problem has been placed in the context of the elements that constitute culture as they interact with elements of native human nature. The fundamental postulate of the discussion is that isolation of any one factor, no matter how strong its workings at a given time, is fatal to understanding and to intelligent action. Isolations have abounded, both on the side of taking some one thing in human nature to be a supreme "motive" and in taking some one form of social activity to be supreme. Since the problem is here thought of as that of the ways in which a great number of factors within and without human nature interact, our task is to ask concerning the reciprocal connections raw human nature and culture bear to one another.

10

Freedom and total responsibility

Jean-Paul Sartre

Sartre's identification of man with freedom follows from his separation of all reality into the in-itself and the for-itself. The in-itself is wholly what it is. But of course the for-itself is not; it is open to every possibility within the human situation. Consciousness can never coincide with itself, and to be a for-itself is to be present or conscious.

Freedom reveals itself in dread, a consciousness of the nothingness of a being that is not wholly itself. And since according to Sartre this is what it means for man to be, he can never escape freedom. There is no place for him to look for help with his choices; they are entirely his, without guidance by the past, by law, by knowledge. To be human is to be totally responsible for what one does, and therefore for what other men do. It is up to man to keep himself free and not accept an essence imposed upon him by others where he would become an object in their world. The responsibility Sartre exhorts is responsibility for the world's enhancement, and that is why he claims to be a humanist. But Sartre omits responsibility to someone, which is one of the transcendent elements in human experience.

III. Freedom and Responsibility

Although the considerations which are about to follow are of interest primarily to the ethicist, it may nevertheless be worthwhile after these descriptions and arguments to return to the freedom of the for-itself and to try to understand what the fact of this freedom represents for human destiny.

The essential consequence of our earlier remarks is that man being condemned to be free carries the weight of the whole world on his shoulders; he is responsible for the world and for himself as a way of being. We are taking the word "responsibility" in its ordinary sense as "consciousness (of) being the incontestable author of an event or of an object." In this sense the responsibility of the for-itself is overwhelming since he[1] is the one by whom it happens that there is a world; since he is also the one who makes himself be, then whatever may be the situation in which he finds himself, the for-itself must wholly assume this situation with its peculiar coefficient of adversity, even though it be insupportable. He must assume the situation with the proud consciousness of being the author of it, for the very worst disadvantages or the worst threats which can endanger my person have meaning only in and through my project; and it is on the ground of the engagement which I am that they appear. It is therefore senseless to think of complaining since nothing foreign has decided what we feel, what we live, or what we are.

Furthermore this absolute responsibility is not resignation; it is simply the logical requirement of the consequences of our freedom. What happens to me happens through me, and I can neither affect myself with it nor revolt against it nor resign myself to it. Moreover everything which happens to me is mine. By this we must understand first of all that I am

[1] I am shifting to the personal pronoun here since Sartre is describing the for-itself in concrete personal terms rather than as a metaphysical entity. Strictly speaking, of course, this is his position throughout, and the French "il" is indifferently "he" or "it." Tr.

always equal to what happens to me *qua* man, for what happens to a man through other men and through himself can be only human. The most terrible situations of war, the worst tortures do not create a non-human state of things; there is no non-human situation. It is only through fear, flight, and recourse to magical types of conduct that I shall decide on the non-human, but this decision is human, and I shall carry the entire responsibility for it. But in addition the situation is mine because it is the image of my free choice of myself, and everything which it presents to me is mine in that this represents me and symbolizes me. Is it not I who decide the coefficient of adversity in things and even their unpredictability by deciding myself?

Thus there are no accidents in a life; a community event which suddenly bursts forth and involves me in it does not come from the outside. If I am mobilized in a war, this war is *my* war; it is in my image and I deserve it. I deserve it first because I could always get out of it by suicide or by desertion; these ultimate possibles are those which must always be present for us when there is a question of envisaging a situation. For lack of getting out of it, I have *chosen* it. This can be due to inertia, to cowardice in the face of public opinion, or because I prefer certain other values to the value of the refusal to join in the war (the good opinion of my relatives, the honor of my family, etc.). Anyway you look at it, it is a matter of a choice. This choice will be repeated later on again and again without a break until the end of the war. Therefore we must agree with the statement by J. Romains, "In war there are no innocent victims."[2] If therefore I have preferred war to death or to dishonor, everything takes place as if I bore the entire responsibility for this war. Of course others have declared it, and one might be tempted perhaps to consider me as a simple accomplice. But this notion of complicity has only a juridical sense, and it does not hold here. For it depended on me that for me and by me this war should not exist, and I have decided that it does exist. There was no compulsion here, for the compulsion could have got no hold on a freedom. I did not have any excuse; for as we have said repeatedly in this book, the peculiar character of human-reality is that it is without excuse. Therefore it remains for me only to lay claim to this war.

But in addition the war is *mine* because by the sole fact that it arises in a situation which I cause to be and that I can discover it there only by

---

[2] J. Romains: *Les hommes de bonne volonté;* "Prélude à Verdun."

engaging myself for or against it, I can no longer distinguish at present the choice which I make of myself from the choice which I make of the war. To live this war is to choose myself through it and to choose it through my choice of myself. There can be no question of considering it as "four years of vacation" or as a "reprieve," as a "recess," the essential part of my responsibilities being elsewhere in my married, family, or professional life. In this war which I have chosen I choose myself from day to day, and I make it mine by making myself. If it is going to be four empty years, then it is I who bear the responsibility for this.

Finally, as we pointed out earlier, each person is an absolute choice of self from the standpoint of a world of knowledges and of techniques which this choice both assumes and illumines; each person is an absolute upsurge at an absolute date and is perfectly unthinkable at another date. It is therefore a waste of time to ask what I should have been if this war had not broken out, for I have chosen myself as one of the possible meanings of the epoch which imperceptibly led to war. I am not distinct from this same epoch; I could not be transported to another epoch without contradiction. Thus *I am* this war which restricts and limits and makes comprehensible the period which preceded it. In this sense we may define more precisely the responsibility of the for-itself if to the earlier quoted statement, "There are no innocent victims," we add the words, "We have the war we deserve." Thus, totally free, undistinguishable from the period for which I have chosen to be the meaning, as profoundly responsible for the war as if I had myself declared it, unable to live without integrating it in my situation, engaging myself in it wholly and stamping it with my seal, I must be without remorse or regrets as I am without excuse; for from the instant of my upsurge into being, I carry the weight of the world by myself alone without anything or any person being able to lighten it.

Yet this responsibility is of a very particular type. Someone will say, "I did not ask to be born." This is a naive way of throwing greater emphasis on our facticity. I am responsible for everything, in fact, except for my very responsibility, for I am not the foundation of my being. Therefore everything takes place as if I were compelled to be responsible. I am abandoned in the world, not in the sense that I might remain abandoned and passive in a hostile universe like a board floating on the water, but rather in the sense that I find myself suddenly alone and without help, engaged in a world for which I bear the whole responsibility without being able, whatever I do, to tear myself away from this responsibility for an instant. For I am responsible for my very desire of fleeing responsibilities. To make myself passive in the world, to refuse to act upon things and upon Others is still to choose myself, and suicide is one mode among others of being-in-the-world. Yet I find an absolute responsibility for the fact that my facticity (here the fact of my birth) is directly inapprehensible and even inconceivable, for this fact of my birth never appears as a brute fact but always across a projective reconstruction of my for-itself. I am ashamed of being born or I am astonished at it or I rejoice over it, or in attempting to get rid of my life I affirm that I live and I assume that life as bad. Thus in a certain sense I *choose* being born. This choice itself is integrally affected with facticity since I am not able not to choose, but this facticity in turn will appear only in so far as I surpass it towards my ends. Thus facticity is everywhere but inapprehensible; I never encounter anything except my responsibility. That is why I can not ask, "*Why* was I born?" or curse the day of my birth or declare that I did not ask to be born, for these various attitudes toward my birth — i.e., toward the fact that I realize a presence in the world — are absolutely nothing else but ways of assuming this birth in full responsibility and of making it *mine*. Here again I encounter only myself and my projects so that finally my abandonment — i.e., my facticity — consists simply in the fact that I am condemned to be wholly responsible for myself. I am the being which *is* in such a way that in its being its being is in question. And this "is" of my being *is* as present and inapprehensible.

Under these conditions since every event in the world can be revealed to me only as an *opportunity* (an opportunity made use of, lacked, neglected, etc.), or better yet since everything which happens to us can be considered as a *chance* (i.e., can appear to us only as a way of realizing this being which is in question in our being) and since others as transcendences-transcended are themselves only *opportunities* and *chances*, the responsibility of the for-itself extends to the entire world as a peopled-world. It is precisely thus that the for-itself apprehends itself in anguish; that is, as a being which is neither the foundation of its own being nor of the Other's being nor of the in-itselfs which form the world, but a being which is compelled to decide the meaning of being — within it and everywhere outside of it. The one who realizes in anguish his condition as being thrown into a responsibility which extends to his very abandonment has no longer either remorse or regret or excuse; he is no longer anything but a freedom which perfectly reveals itself and whose being resides in this very revelation. But as we pointed out at the beginning of this work, most of the time we flee anguish in bad faith.

11

Freedom and rebellion

Albert Camus

Like Sartre, Camus expressed his thoughts on freedom in literary works. But Camus was not an existentialist. It is true that he saw man as free to make his own meaning out of himself and the world, but even this meaning was, to him, meaningless or absurd. Radical transcendence is not the root of meaning for Camus; nothingness is the ground of freedom. Man stands at the edge of nothing, looks over and sees the absurdity of acting as he acts for the sake of a more abundant life here and now. The present is all. It requires rebellion so that man can experience himself as freedom. But rebellion signifies that others are there, and hence freedom is the experience that gives rise to the "we." "I rebel," says Camus, "and therefore we are."

In an age when there are increasing threats to man's freedom, Camus exalts the human reality as the free reality, and he declared that revolt gives life its value. The hero in this context is one who faces the absurd and continues to choose.

Now the main thing is done, I hold certain facts from which I cannot separate. What I know, what is certain, what I cannot deny, what I cannot reject — this is what counts. I can negate everything of that part of me that lives on vague nostalgias, except this desire for unity, this longing to solve, this need for clarity and cohesion. I can refute everything in this world surrounding me that offends or enraptures me, except this chaos, this sovereign chance and this divine equivalence which springs from anarchy. I don't know whether this world has a meaning that transcends it. But I know that I do not know that meaning and that it is impossible for me just now to know it. What can a meaning outside my condition mean to me? I can understand only in human terms. What I touch, what resists me — that is what I understand. And these two certainties — my appetite for the absolute and for unity and the impossibility of reducing this world to a rational and reasonable principle — I also know that I cannot reconcile them. What other truth can I admit without lying, without bringing in a hope I lack and which means nothing within the limits of my condition?

If I were a tree among trees, a cat among animals, this life would have a meaning, or rather this problem would not arise, for I should belong to this world. I should *be* this world to which I am now opposed by my whole consciousness and my whole insistence upon familiarity. This ridiculous reason is what sets me in opposition to all creation. I cannot cross it out with a stroke of the pen. What I believe to be true I must therefore preserve. What seems to me so obvious, even against me, I must support. And what constitutes the basis of that conflict, of that break between the world and my mind, but the awareness of it? If therefore I want to preserve it, I can through a constant awareness, ever revived, ever alert. This is what, for the moment, I must remember. At this moment the absurd, so obvious and yet so hard to win, returns to a man's life and finds its home there. At this moment, too, the mind can leave the arid, dried-up path of lucid effort. That path now emerges in daily life. It encounters the world of the anonymous impersonal pronoun "one," but henceforth man enters in with his revolt and his lucidity. He has forgotten how to hope. This hell of the present is his Kingdom at last. All problems recover their sharp edge. Abstract evidence retreats before the poetry of forms and colors. Spiritual conflicts become embodied and return to the abject and magnificent shelter of man's heart. None of them is settled. But all are transfigured. Is one going to die, escape by the leap, rebuild a mansion of ideas and forms to one's own scale? Is one, on the contrary, going to take up the heart-rending and marvelous wager of the absurd? Let's make a final effort in this regard and draw all our conclusions. The body, affection, creation, action, human nobility will then resume their places in this mad world. At last man will again find there the wine of the absurd and the bread of indifference on which he feeds his greatness.

Let us insist again on the method: it is a matter of persisting. At a certain point on his path the absurd man is tempted. History is not lacking in either religions or prophets, even without gods. He is asked to leap. All he can reply is that he doesn't fully understand, that it is not obvious. Indeed, he does not want to do anything but what he fully understands. He is assured that this is the sin of pride, but he does not understand the notion of sin; that perhaps hell is in store, but he has not enough imagination to visualize that strange future; that he is losing immortal life, but that seems to him an idle consideration. An attempt is made to get him to admit his guilt. He feels innocent. To tell the truth, that is all he feels — his irreparable innocence. This is what allows him everything. Hence, what he demands of himself is to live *solely* with what he knows, to accommodate himself to what is, and to bring in nothing that is not certain. He is told that nothing is. But this at least is a certainty. And it is with this that he is concerned: he wants to find out if it is possible to live *without appeal.*

Now I can broach the notion of suicide. It has already been felt what solution might be given. At this point the problem is reversed. It was previously a question of finding out whether or not life had to have a meaning to be lived. It now becomes clear, on the contrary, that it will be lived all the better if it has no meaning. Living an experience, a particular fate, is accepting it fully. Now, no one will live this fate, knowing it to be absurd, unless he does everything to keep before him that absurd brought to light by consciousness. Negating one of the terms of the opposition on which he lives amounts to escaping it. To abolish conscious revolt is to elude the problem. The theme of permanent revolution is thus carried into individual experience. Living is keeping the absurd alive. Keeping it alive is, above all, contemplating it. Unlike Eurydice, the absurd dies only when we turn away from it. One of the only coherent philosophical positions is thus revolt. It is a constant confrontation between man and his own obscurity. It is an insistence upon an impossible transparency. It challenges the world anew every second. Just as danger provided man the unique opportunity of seizing awareness, so metaphysical revolt extends awareness to the whole of experience. It is that constant presence of man in his own eyes. It is not aspiration, for it is devoid of hope. That revolt is the certainty of a crushing fate, without the resignation that ought to accompany it.

This is where it is seen to what a degree absurd experience is remote from suicide. It may be thought that suicide follows revolt — but wrongly. For it does not represent the logical outcome of revolt. It is just the contrary by the consent it presupposes. Suicide, like the leap, is acceptance at its extreme. Everything is over and man returns to his essential history. His future, his unique and dreadful future — he sees and rushes toward it. In its way, suicide settles the absurd. It engulfs the absurd in the same death. But I know that in order to keep alive, the absurd cannot be settled. It escapes suicide to the extent that it is simultaneously awareness and rejection of death. It is, at the extreme limit of the condemned man's last thought, that shoelace that despite everything he sees a few yards away, on the very brink of his dizzying fall. The contrary of suicide, in fact, is the man condemned to death.

That revolt gives life its value. Spread out over the whole length of a life, it restores its majesty to that life. To a man devoid of blinders, there is no finer sight than that of the intelligence at grips with a reality that transcends it. The sight of human pride is unequaled. No disparagement is of any use. That discipline that the mind imposes on itself, that will conjured up out of nothing, that face-to-face struggle have something exceptional about them. To impoverish that reality whose inhumanity constitutes man's majesty is tantamount to impoverishing him himself. I understand then why the doctrines that explain everything to me also debilitate me at the same time. They relieve me of the weight of my own life, and yet I must carry it alone. At this juncture, I cannot conceive that a skeptical metaphysics can be joined to an ethics of renunciation.

Consciousness and revolt, these rejections are the contrary of renunciation. Everything that is indomitable and passionate in a human heart quickens them, on the contrary, with its own life. It is essential to die unreconciled and not of one's own free will. Suicide is a repudiation. The absurd man can only drain everything to the bitter end, and deplete himself. The absurd is his extreme tension, which he maintains constantly by solitary effort, for he knows that in that consciousness and in that day-to-day revolt he gives proof of his only truth, which is defiance. This is a first consequence.

12

Freedom and individualism

Ayn Rand

Ayn Rand looks at freedom of action within a social context, but she defines and defends freedom as a series of individual rights. She sees the right to this kind of freedom as implicit in the right to life and thus considers freedom to be directed towards self-realization. This outlook is widely presented through such novels as *The Fountainhead* and *Atlas Shrugged* as the American concept of freedom — a robust and frank individualism. The American's duty is declared to be that of noninterference with the neighbor's freedom to act, a negative way of insuring that everyone will be free to act in accord with his own choices. Ayn Rand's objectivist philosophy assigns to man only the freedom over his own efforts — in other words, the pursuit of happiness.

MAN'S RIGHTS

If one wishes to advocate a free society — that is, capitalism — one must realize that its indispensable foundation is the principle of individual rights. If one wishes to uphold individual rights, one must realize that capitalism is the only system that can uphold and protect them. And if one wishes to gauge the relationship of freedom to the goals of today's intellectuals, one may gauge it by the fact that the concept of individual rights is evaded, distorted, perverted and seldom discussed, most conspicuously seldom by the so-called "conservatives."

"Rights" are a moral concept — the concept that provides a logical transition from the principles guiding an individual's actions to the principles guiding his relationship with others — the concept that preserves and protects individual morality in a social context — the link between the moral code of a man and the legal code of a society, between ethics and politics. *Individual rights are the means of subordinating society to moral law.*

Every political system is based on some code of ethics. The dominant ethics of mankind's history were variants of the altruist-collectivist doctrine which subordinated the individual to some higher authority, either mystical or social. Consequently, most political systems were variants of the same statist tyranny, differing only in degree, not in basic principle, limited only by the accidents of tradition, of chaos, of bloody strife and periodic collapse. Under all such systems, morality was a code applicable to the individual, but not to society. Society was placed *outside* the moral law, as its embodiment of course or exclusive interpreter — and the inculcation of self-sacrificial devotion to social duty was regarded as the main purpose of ethics in man's earthly existence.

Since there is no such entity as "society," since society is only a number of individual men, this meant, in practice, that the rulers of society were exempt from moral law; subject only to traditional rituals, they held total power and exacted blind obedience – on the implicit principle of: "The good is that which is good for society (or for the tribe, the race, the nation), and the ruler's edicts are its voice on earth."

This was true of all statist systems, under all variants of the altruist-collectivist ethics, mystical or social. "The Divine Right of Kings" summarizes the political theory of the first – "*Vox populi, vox dei*" of the second. As witness: the theocracy of Egypt, with the Pharaoh as an embodied god – the unlimited majority rule or *democracy* of Athens – the welfare state run by the Emperors of Rome – the Inquisition of the late Middle Ages – the absolute monarchy of France – the welfare state of Bismarck's Prussia – the gas chambers of Nazi Germany – the slaughterhouse of the Soviet Union.

All these political systems were expressions of the altruist-collectivist ethics – and their common characteristic is the fact that society stood above the moral law, as an omnipotent, sovereign whim worshiper. Thus, politically, all these systems were variants of an *amoral* society.

The most profoundly revolutionary achievement of the United States of America was *the subordination of society to moral law.*

The principle of man's individual rights represented the extension of morality into the social system – as a limitation on the power of the state, as man's protection against the brute force of the collective, as the subordination of *might* to *right*. The United States was the first *moral* society in history.

All previous systems had regarded man as a sacrificial means to the ends of others, and society as an end in itself. The United States regarded man as an end in himself, and society as a means to the peaceful, orderly, *voluntary* co-existence of individuals. All previous systems had held that man's life belongs to society, that society can dispose of him in any way it pleases, and that any freedom he enjoys is his only by favor, by the *permission* of society, which may be revoked at any time. The United States held that man's life is his by *right* (which means: by moral principle and by his nature), that a right is the property of an individual, that society as such has no rights, and that the only moral purpose of a government is the protection of individual rights.

A "right" is a moral principle defining and sanctioning a man's freedom of action in a social context. There is only *one* fundamental right (all the others are its consequences or corollaries): a man's right to his own life. Life is a process of self-sustaining and self-generated action; the right to life means the right to engage in self-sustaining and self-generated action — which means: the freedom to take all the actions required by the nature of a rational being for the support, the furtherance, the fulfillment and the enjoyment of his own life. (Such is the meaning of the right to life, liberty and the pursuit of happiness.)

The concept of a "right" pertains only to action — specifically, to freedom of action. It means freedom from physical compulsion, coercion or interference by other men.

Thus, for every individual, a right is the moral sanction of a *positive* — of his freedom to act on his own judgment, for his own goals, by his own *voluntary, uncoerced* choice. As to his neighbors, his rights impose no obligations on them except of a *negative* kind: to abstain from violating his rights.

The right to life is the source of all rights — and the right to property is their only implementation. Without property rights, no other rights are possible. Since man has to sustain his life by his own effort, the man who has no right to the product of his effort has no means to sustain his life. The man who produces while others dispose of his product, is a slave.

Bear in mind that the right to property is a right to action, like all the others: it is not the right *to an object*, but to the action and the consequences of producing or earning that object. It is not a guarantee that a man will earn any property, but only a guarantee that he will own it if he earns it. It is the right to gain, to keep, to use and to dispose of material values.

The concept of individual rights is so new in human history that most men have not grasped it fully to this day. In accordance with the two theories of ethics, the mystical or the social, some men assert that rights are a gift of God — others, that rights are a gift of society. But, in fact, the source of rights is man's nature.

The Declaration of Independence stated that men "are endowed by their Creator with certain unalienable rights." Whether one believes that man is the product of a Creator or of nature, the issue of man's origin does not alter the fact that he is an entity of a specific kind — a rational being — that he cannot function successfully under coercion, and that rights are a necessary condition of his particular mode of survival.

"The source of man's rights is not divine law or congressional law, but the law of identity. A is A — and Man is Man. *Rights* are conditions of existence required by man's nature for his proper survival. If man is to live on earth, it is *right* for him to use his mind, it is *right* to act on his own free judgment, it is *right* to work for his values and to keep the product of his work. If life on earth is his purpose, he has a *right* to live as a rational being: nature forbids him the irrational." (*Atlas Shrugged*)

To violate man's rights means to compel him to act against his own judgment, or to expropriate his values. Basically, there is only one way to do it: by the use of physical force. There are two potential violators of man's rights: the criminals and the government. The great achievement of the United States was to draw a distinction between these two — by forbidding to the second the legalized version of the activities of the first.

The Declaration of Independence laid down the principle that "to secure these rights, governments are instituted among men." This provided the only valid justification of a government and defined its only proper purpose: to protect man's rights by protecting him from physical violence.

Thus the government's function was changed from the role of ruler to the role of servant. The government was set to protect man from criminals — and the Constitution was written to protect man from the government. The Bill of Rights was not directed against private citizens, but against the government — as an explicit declaration that individual rights supersede any public or social power.

The result was the pattern of a civilized society which — for the brief span of some hundred and fifty years — America came close to achieving. A civilized society is one in which physical force is banned from human relationships — in which the government, acting as a policeman, may use force *only* in retaliation and *only* against those who initiate its use.

This was the essential meaning and intent of America's political philosophy, implicit in the principle of individual rights. But it was not formulated explicitly, nor fully accepted nor consistently practiced.

America's inner contradiction was the altruist-collectivist ethics. Altruism is incompatible with freedom, with capitalism and with individual rights. One cannot combine the pursuit of happiness with the moral status of a sacrificial animal.

It was the concept of individual rights that had given birth to a free society. It was with the destruction of individual rights that the destruction of freedom had to begin.

A collectivist tyranny dare not enslave a country by an outright confiscation of its values, material or moral. It has to be done by a process of internal corruption. Just as in the material realm the plundering of a country's wealth is accomplished by inflating the currency — so today one may witness the process of inflation being applied to the realm of rights.

The process entails such a growth of newly promulgated "rights" that people do not notice the fact that the meaning of the concept is being reversed. Just as bad money drives out good money, so these "printing-press rights" negate authentic rights.

Consider the curious fact that never has there been such a proliferation, all over the world, of two contradictory phenomena: of alleged new "rights" and of slave-labor camps.

The "gimmick" was the switch of the concept of rights from the political to the economic realm.

The Democratic Party platform of 1960 summarizes the switch boldly and explicitly. It declares that a Democratic Administration "will reaffirm the economic bill of rights which Franklin Roosevelt wrote into our national conscience sixteen years ago."

Bear clearly in mind the meaning of the concept of "rights" when you read the list which that platform offers:

1. The right to a useful and remunerative job in the industries or shops or farms or mines of the nation.
2. The right to earn enough to provide adequate food and clothing and recreation.
3. The right of every farmer to raise and sell his products at a return which will give him and his family a decent living.
4. The right of every businessman, large and small, to trade in an atmosphere of freedom from unfair competition and domination by monopolies at home and abroad.
5. The right of every family to a decent home.
6. The right to adequate medical care and the opportunity to achieve and enjoy good health.
7. The right to adequate protection from the economic fears of old age, sickness, accidents and unemployment.
8. The right to a good education.

A single question added to each of the above eight clauses would make the issue clear: *At whose expense?*

Jobs, food, clothing, recreation (1), homes, medical care, education, etc. do not grow in nature. These are man-made values — goods and services produced by men. *Who* is to provide them?

If some men are entitled by right to the products of the work of others, it means that those others are deprived of rights and condemned to slave labor.

Any alleged "right" of one man, which necessitates the violation of the rights of another, is not and cannot be a right.

No man can have a right to impose an unchosen obligation, an unrewarded duty or an involuntary servitude on another man. There can be no such thing as "the *right to enslave.*"

A right does not include the material implementation of that right by other men; it includes only the freedom to earn that implementation by one's own effort.

Observe, in this context, the intellectual precision of the Founding Fathers: they spoke of the right to *the pursuits* of happiness – *not* of the right to happiness. It means that a man has the right to take the actions he deems necessary to achieve his happiness; it does *not* mean that others must make him happy.

The right to life means that a man has the right to support his life by his own work (on any economic level, as high as his ability will carry him); it does *not* mean that others must provide him with the necessities of life.

The right to property means that a man has the right to take the economic actions necessary to earn property, to use it and to dispose of it; it does *not* mean that others must provide him with property.

The right of free speech means that a man has the right to express his ideas without danger of suppression, interference or punitive action by the government. It does *not* mean that others must provide him with a lecture hall, a radio station or a printing press through which to express his ideas.

Any undertaking that involves more than one man, requires the *voluntary* consent of every participant. Every one of them has the *right* to make his own decision, but none has the right to force his decision on the others.

There is no such thing as "a right to a job" – there is only the right of free trade, that is: a man's right to take a job if another man chooses to hire him. There is no "right to a home," only the right of free trade: the right to build a home or to buy it. There are no "rights to a 'fair' wage or a 'fair' price" if no one chooses to pay it, to hire a man or to buy his product. There are no "rights of consumers" to milk, shoes, movies or champagne if no producers choose to manufacture such items (there is only the right to manufacture them oneself). There are no "rights" of special groups, there are no "rights of farmers, of workers, of businessmen, of employees, of employers, of the old, of the young, of the unborn." There are only *the Rights of Man* — rights possessed by every individual man and by *all* men as individuals.

Property rights and the right of free trade are man's only "economic rights" (they are, in fact, *political* rights) — and there can be no such thing as "an *economic* bill of rights." But observe that the advocates of the latter have all but destroyed the former.

Remember that rights are moral principles which define and protect a man's freedom of action, but impose no obligations on other men. Private citizens are not a threat to one another's rights or freedom. A private citizen who resorts to physical force and violates the rights of others is a criminal — and men have legal protection against him.

Criminals are a small minority in any age or country. And the harm they have done to mankind is infinitesimal when compared to the horrors — the bloodshed, the wars, the persecutions, the confiscations, the famines, the enslavements, the wholesale destructions — perpetrated by mankind's governments. A government is the most dangerous threat to man's rights: it holds a legal monopoly on the use of physical force against legally disarmed victims. When unlimited and unrestricted by individual rights, a government is men's deadliest enemy. It is not as protection against *private* actions, but against governmental actions that the Bill of Rights was written.

Now observe the process by which that protection is being destroyed.

The process consists of ascribing to private citizens the specific violations constitutionally forbidden to the government (which private citizens have no power to commit) and thus freeing the government from all restrictions. The switch is becoming progressively more obvious in the field of free speech. For years the collectivists have been propagating the notion that a private individual's refusal to finance an opponent is a violation of the opponent's right of free speech and an act of "censorship."

It is "censorship," they claim, if a newspaper refuses to employ or publish writers whose ideas are diametrically opposed to its policy.

It is "censorship," they claim, if businessmen refuse to advertise in a magazine that denounces, insults and smears them.

It is "censorship," they claim, if a TV sponsor objects to some outrage perpetrated on a program he is financing — such as the incident of Alger Hiss being invited to denounce former Vice-President Nixon.

And then there is Newton N. Minow who declares: "There is censorship by ratings, by advertisers, by networks, by affiliates which reject programming offered to their areas." It is the same Mr. Minow who threatens to revoke the license of any station that does not comply with his views on programming — and who claims that *that* is not censorship.

Consider the implications of such a trend.

"Censorship" is a term pertaining only to governmental action. No private action is censorship. No private individual or agency can silence a man or suppress a publication; only the government can do so. The freedom of speech of private individuals includes the right not to agree, not to listen and not to finance one's own antagonists.

But according to such doctrines as the "economic bill of rights," an individual has no right to dispose of his own material means by the guidance of his own convictions — and must hand over his money indiscriminately to any speakers or propagandists, who have a "right" to his property.

This means that the ability to provide the material tools for the expression of ideas deprives a man of the right to hold any ideas. It means that a publisher has to publish books he considers worthless, false or evil — that a TV sponsor has to finance commentators who choose to affront his convictions — that the owner of a newspaper must turn his editorial pages over to any young hooligan who clamors for the enslavement of the press. It means that one group of men acquires the "right" to unlimited license — while another group is reduced to helpless irresponsibility.

But since it is obviously impossible to provide every claimant with a job, a microphone or a newspaper column, *who* will determine the "distribution" of "economic rights" and select the recipients, when the owners' right to choose has been abolished? Well, Mr. Minow has indicated *that* quite clearly.

And if you make the mistake of thinking that this applies only to big property owners, you had better realize that the theory of "economic rights" includes the "right" of every would-be playwright, every beatnik poet, every noise-composer and every nonobjective artist (who have political pull) to the financial support you did not give them when you did not attend their shows. What else is the meaning of the project to spend your tax money on subsidized art?

And while people are clamoring about "economic rights," the concept of political rights is vanishing. It is forgotten that the right of free speech means the freedom to advocate one's views and to bear the possible consequences, including disagreement with others, opposition, unpopularity and lack of support. The political function of "the right of free speech" is to protect dissenters and unpopular minorities from forcible suppression — *not* to guarantee them the support, advantages and rewards of a popularity they have not gained.

The Bill of Rights reads: "Congress shall make no law . . . abridging the freedom of speech, or of the press . . ." It does not demand that private citizens provide a microphone for the man who advocates their destruction, or a passkey for the burglar who seeks to rob them, or a knife for the murderer who wants to cut their throats.

Such is the state of one of today's most crucial issues: political rights versus "economic rights." It's either-or. One destroys the other. But there are, in fact, no "economic rights," no "collective rights," no "public-interest rights." The term "individual rights" is a redundancy: there is no other kind of rights and no one else to possess them.

Those who advocate *laissez-faire* capitalism are the only advocates of man's rights.

Part IV

THE PHENOMENOLOGY OF FREEDOM

13

Freedom and Action

Pierre Thévenaz

Pierre Thévenaz here explains the adequacy of the method of phenomenology for an exploration of human freedom. He does this by discussing the work of Sartre who, as an existentialist, nevertheless avails himself of the method developed by Husserl, although Sartre considerably modifies this method in using it.

After having examined the vast literature of disagreement upon the existence and the nature of human freedom, we are well disposed to admit that the whole reality of freedom should be submitted to a presuppositionless descriptive investigation. The first requirement for this venture is to refuse the restriction of freedom to some special area such as "freedom of the will." The naturally subjective aspect of freedom makes it an especially suitable reality for investigation by a phenomenologist.

Our understanding of freedom has profited from our awareness, stimulated by Brentano and Husserl, of the intentional or relational character of our lived experience. In his most free acts man is related to a future and becomes creative.

149

If consciousness is nothingness and project, it is itself nothing and everything lies in front of it. It can be founded on nothing; it is its own foundation to the extent that it disengages itself from everything that is and from everything that it is in order to recover it in an act of free spontaneity. Nothing is given except that from which it is necessary to tear itself away. Consciousness is never given and human freedom, this agonizing and total freedom, if it is ontological or transcendental, is never an empirical datum at the point of departure. It is, on the contrary, the result of a radical phenomenological reduction. The point of departure is rather the "enmired freedom,"[1] the stuck or ensnared existence of *Nausea*.

Freedom is essentially project, that is to say, task, project *of freeing itself*; it is discovered in action and is identical to it. Sartrian consciousness, instead of *being* (it has no essence), has to *make itself*, create itself, and since it is pure spontaneity, to choose itself and invent itself. And here Sartre's ontology is no longer based solely on the dichotomy of the in-itself and the for-itself. We see now that *being* is only a foil and that *doing* is at least equally important. "Having, doing and being are the cardinal categories of human reality."[2] For the first time phenomenology develops in the direction of a philosophy of doing, of creation, of action, in short of a "pragmatism" in the broad sense.[3] To be is to act. A truce to the traditional quarrels about *operari sequitur esse* or *esse sequitur operari*. Henceforth *operari = esse*.

But to make oneself is "to make oneself other," it is to transform. The nihilating withdrawal of consciousness is not a flight into the contemplative attitude or that of the "disinterested spectator" of Husserl; it is project of recovering and transforming. In Husserl the reduction was the *transformation of intentionality*; in Sartre nihilation is the *intention of*

[1] J.P. Sartre, *Situations*, II, 116.
[2] Sartre, *L'Etre et le Néant*, p. 507, and *Situations*, II, 262.
[3] Sartre, *Situations*, III, 182.

transforming the world (or the intention of *self*-transformation since the I is a part of the world). It sufficed, therefore, to push the phenomenological reduction to the limit, to reduce even the Ego and to arrive at a transcendental nothing-consciousness, in order for the intuitive, contemplative, disclosing philosophy that is phenomenology to transform itself into a "philosophy of revolution."[4] And reciprocally, in Sartre — and this is the originality of his philosophy of action — there is no action that is not disclosure. It is precisely only action which enables us to see, to know. The nihilating withdrawal is a way of becoming unstuck from a situation in order to see it, to understand it, to transform it. All of which comes to one thing: comprehension and action go together.[5]

We also rediscover here the teleology, the finality so important in phenomenology. Consciousness is project: it throws itself ahead of itself into the future; one can understand what it is only by what it will be.[6] The phenomenological reduction signifies for Sartre that man tears himself away from his past and from determinism (from efficient causality, which goes from the past to the present), and projects himself out towards his future. "Try to grasp your consciousness and probe it; you will see that it is hollow; you will find there only the future."[7] But the project is at the same time movement from the future towards the present (final causality). "Man is the being who comes to himself on the basis of the future,"[8] who "defines himself by his goals."[9] The goals which I propose to myself or which I project revert backwards to my present situation to clarify and transform it. And if there can be consciousness of the present, it is because of the distance which separates me from it, which is precisely the dimension of my project towards the future. The phenomenological reduction thus operated is then indeed freedom: a tearing-away from the

[4]*Ibid.* pp. 182, 193. Already in Husserl the notion of constitutive operation or of creation (*Leistung*) took on an ever increasing importance. — The problem of action in the phenomenological perspective remains an open problem. See on this subject, A. De Waelhens, "Vie interieure et vie active," in *Les Droits de l'esprit et les exigences sociales* (Rencontres internationales de Geneve), Neuchatel, 1950, pp. 29-39, and the discussion, pp. 171-172.
[5]Sartre, *Situations*, III, 194.
[6]*Situations*, I, 79.
[7]*Ibid.* Note the reciprocal implication of the notion of nothingness and future in Sartre's conception of consciousness.
[8]*L'Etre et le Neant*, p. 169.
[9]*Ibid.* p. 520

determinism of the past and a returning from the future. We recognize the
two complementary phenomenological movements: putting in parentheses
(of the past) and intentionality, and the definition of consciousness of the
present by this double movement.

But in this perspective of a philosophy of action, it is the present
(and not the future as in Heidegger) that is ultimately most accentuated. [10]
Sartre's teleology here differs from Husserl's. Originally phenomenology,
by its method of disclosing, meant to bring out the hidden *meaning*, in the
double sense of signification and of finality. This is to say that the end *was
already there* in a latent form. Thus, the infinite task of philosophy was
that of becoming conscious of what was not yet given but was already
present in a certain manner: phenomenology presented itself as a
consecration of the already there, as respect for the real.[11]

For Sartre, who seems here to have profited from the Bergsonian
critique of finality, there is no already-there, because reduction goes as far
as "nothingness." Intention aims at the *not-yet*, that which is not; not that
which is latent but that which is future. This is why the
consciousness-project will be able to reveal values only by creating them.
There will be no given or latent values, because value never *is*. Man will
only be what he actually makes himself; he will be the creator of values
and the transformer of the real.

Nevertheless, since freedom is not a given but a project of liberation,
it encounters resistance: not only the limits of a factual situation
(facticity) with its menace of entrapment, but also the temptations of
"bad faith" which incite us to shirk the responsibility and solitude of free
decision. Since all action is transformation, effort, struggle, it comes up
against *adversity* and it is *failure*. The theme of failure takes on a growing
importance in Sartre.[12] Free consciousness is continually enmeshed in the
stickiness from which it is unsticking itself. Its very success is its failure,
for "success comprises a secret failure." [13] "By killing I *gave* myself *a
nature. Before*, I dreamt of proving by my crime that I was escaping from
all essence; *afterwards*, my essence is my crime, it strangles me in its iron

---

[10] *Ibid.*, p. 188.

[11] See above in Part I, pp. 52-53, Cf. Problemes actuels de la phénomenologie, Paris,
1952, pp. 26-27.

[12] Sartre, *L'Etre et le Néant*, p. 561; *Situations*, II, 86, *Saint Genet, comédien et
martyr*, Paris, 1952, pp. 177 ff.

[13] *Saint Genet*, p. 180.

fist." [14] In short, phenomenological reduction, described in the abstract, is performed in an instant. But, interpreted now as free action in the world and society or as liberation, it proves impossible of complete realization or at least it needs to be continually done over. It is here that Sartre's ethics is rooted, the ethics which he announced at the end of *Being and Nothingness*. "Thus any ethics which does not present itself explicitly as *impossible today* contributes to the mystification and alienation of men. The moral "problem" arises from the fact that ethics is *for us* both inevitable and impossible. Action must prescribe its ethical norms within this climate of insurmountable impossibility." [15] The circle which began from Husserl is closed here; Sartre's phenomenological ethics seems to present anew the appearance of the Husserlian method: eternal repetition, infinite and never achieved task. But if the infinite task must mean failure, if such must be the last word of this ethics, the Hydra of Lerna or the rock of Sisyphus emerges on the horizon and Husserl would no longer recognize himself in this distant progeny.

[14] *Ibid.* p. 222.
[15] *Ibid.* p. 177.

14

Phenomenology of freedom

William A. Luijpen

Like all phenomenologists who try to see freedom as it is, Professor Luijpen finds that he cannot isolate it from anything human. Freedom is basic to the lebenswelt, and the lebenswelt evolves out of freedom. Hence freedom does not merely qualify a power or action, but it qualifies human being. The greater future of man hangs in the balance; it will come not to men who are seeking some special goal but to those who are open to it, free to find the greater because they are not seeking the less. Freedom is a form of existence. In this personal existence, my decisions are my own, but my being-in-the-world is not my decision. The first world given to me is that of my body.

The non-absolute character of human freedom flows from this very fact that the phenomenologist cannot discover an "isolated subjectivity." Freedom's relation to the human body, to the world, and to others makes it imperfectly autonomous. Man can never fully say "yes" once and for all while he lives in a time-space world, but he can daily live more personally or decisively. A decision wholly made integrates man who, as temporal being, develops within the horizon of past, present, and future. Authentic human existence is wholeness, for in man Being becomes aware of itself. This common human experience is basic to community.

William Luijpen discusses here what has become "unconcealed" for him through a phenomenology of freedom: freedom not with respect to power or action only but with respect to human being. The non-absolute character of human freedom flows here from the fact that phenomenology does not give us any "isolated subjectivity." Freedom's relation to the human body, to the world, and to others make it imperfectly autonomous. Man can never fully say "yes." What light does this cast on the meaning of freedom on its problematic level? Is freedom another name for the unfinished character of human existence?

PHENOMENOLOGY OF FREEDOM

It is not possible to speak of the meaning of life unless being-man is understood as being-free. If man were a thing and if his life were a thing-like process, the term "meaning" would not make sense. Only on the supposition that being-man is being-free is "meaning" more than an empty sound. By means of an analysis of freedom we will attempt to justify this supposition. We may expect that this analysis will lead us back to the question of the meaning of life.

In the works of contemporary phenomenologists the term "freedom" is used in significations which seem to be widely different.

From EXISTENTIAL PHENOMENOLOGY, by William A. Luijpen, Fifth Impression. Copyright 1960 by Duquesne University. Pp. 265-275.
[1]Above all particular goals, such as science, art, economics, and politics, which give meaning and value to man's being as being-in-the-world, there arises in man by virtue of a natural necessity the question regarding the *meaning and value of his being as a whole*, i.e., the question, What am I? whence do I come? what is the ultimate destiny of my life?" Dondeyne, "Belang voor de metaphysica van een accurate bestaansbeschrijving van de mens als kennend wezen," *Kenler en Metaphysiek (Verslag v. d. XIIe alg. verg. der ver. v. Thomistische Wijsb. en v. d. 3de studiedagen v. h. Wijsgerig Gezelschap te Leuven)*, Nijmegen, 1947, p. 37.

Closer inspection, however, will show that an inner dialectics can be discerned in these different significations, that they evoke and complement one another, and are internally coherent. We will endeavor to let these meanings present themselves in their inner coherence, starting from the "lived" experience of the freedom which is our own.[2]

a. To be subject is to be free

Whoever gives a real meaning to the term "freedom" uses it to express negatively a certain absence of necessity and positively a certain autonomy.[3] This use of the term points immediately to man as distinct from a mere thing.

The being of a thing. What a thing is finds its full explanation in its antecedents. A thing is nothing else than the result of processes and forces; the being of a thing is to be a result. Once the processes and forces which causally influence a thing are fully known, the thing itself is wholly known. A thing is only a pause in the endless evolution of the cosmos. It is not something new with respect to the forces and processes causing it.[4] A thing, then, is essentially relative, merely a *part* of the material cosmos, and not *itself* something transcending its antecedents.[5] The being of a thing is nothing else than its pertaining to the material cosmos.

The statement that the being of a thing is nothing else than being-a-result means the same as the assertion that the being of a thing is a being-necessitated, because the world of things is ruled by determinism. Cosmic forces act of necessity and give to processes the constancy which the physical sciences express in their laws. If in individual cases the physicists

---

[2] "Like every human concept, our concept of freedom is drawn from experience and must remain in contact with that experience; otherwise it will end up by standing for an abstract and empty freedom which no longer has anything to do with true human freedom." Dondeyne, "Truth and Freedom," *Truth and Freedom*, Pittsburgh, 1954, p. 30.

[3] Cf. Dondeyne, *ibid.*

[4] Cf. A. de Waelhens, "Linéaments d'une interprétation phénoménologique de la liberté," *Liberté (Actes du IVe Congrès des Sociétès de Philosphie de langue francaise.)* Neuchâtel, 1949, p. 82.

[5] Cf. D.M. de Petter, "Personne et Personnalisation," *Divus Thomas* (Piac.), 1949, p. 164.

notice that their laws do not apply, then they know that other forces must be at work which likewise act of necessity.

The necessary forces of the cosmos are "blind" forces. This term expresses that these forces do not know themselves as forces and their results as results. The world of things is struck with "blindness." Things are utterly "prostrated," they are not for themselves and are not for other things.

The question could be asked how such a statement can be made. The assertions that things are not for themselves and are not for other things, that things have no meaning for themselves and no meaning for other things can be made only if the totality of reality is not identical with the totality of things. If there were nothing else than things, processes, and forces, there would be no meaning, nothing would make sense. But there is meaning. To express it paradoxically, if there were nothing else than things, processes, and forces, nothing would *be* in the only meaning which the term "to be" can assume — namely, to-be-for-man. But there is something. There are things, processes, and forces.

Man is not a mere thing. Once these ideas have been thoroughly understood, it will be impossible to call the *totality* of manhood, i.e., *all that man is*, the result of processes and forces. If man were such a result, he would be a thing and, therefore, to express it again in terms of the above-mentioned paradox, nothing would *be* in the strict sense of the term. But something is — thanks to the fact that man reveals reality. The being of man, therefore, cannot be called in its totality "being a result." Likewise, it cannot be called in its entirety a mere part of the material cosmos. Although man is *also* a result, although he is *also* necessitated, *also* a part of the cosmos, he cannot be wholly result, entirely necessitated, merely a part, for otherwise nothing would be.

In the world of things there is absolute darkness. A thing is not a light for itself or a light for something else in such a way that something would be for a thing. The being of a thing is blindness.

With the appearance of subjectivity in the endless evolution of the cosmos, the darkness is pierced. Man as subject is a "natural light," the light through which something is in the only possible sense of this term.[6] Accordingly, it is through the being of man as subject that are transcended

[6]Cf. Heidegger, *Von Wesen der Wahrheit*, pp. 14-17.

the being-a-result, being-merely-a-part, being-necessitated, which have to be predicated *also* of man.

Being man is being free. Whoever attaches a real meaning to the term "freedom" negatively expresses a .certain absence of necessity. It is evident, therefore, that being subject must be called being free, for it is through his freedom that man transcends necessity. No matter how many aspects there are in man under which he must be considered the necessary result of processes and forces, they cannot be the totality of man's being, for it is only through man's subjectivity that there are necessity, results, processes and forces.[7] The being of man as subject is being free as the "letting be" (*Seinlassen*) of the cosmos.[8]

It should be evident that there is no question here of freedom as the property of an action or of a power. Freedom here is concerned with the *being* of man on the proper level of his manhood. The being of man as subject is being free. It is only in the light of this fundamental freedom that the freedom of human action can be understood and that the many meanings which the term "freedom" has in the philosophical literature of our time become transparent.[9] Before considering these meanings, we must endeavor to express the positive content of being-free in the above-mentioned sense.

The freedom of man as subject implies a certain autonomy.[10] Not everything which man is results from processes and forces, but the being of

[7]"En effet, si la condition de l'homme est de découvrir et d'établir des significations, l'idée que le determinisme pourrait s'appliquer à l'homme devient simplement absurde." de Waelhens, *op. cit.*, p. 83.

[8]"Die Freiheit zum Offenbaren eines Offenen lässt das jeweiligie Seiende das Sciende sein, das es ist. Freiheit entuhllt sich jetzt als das Seinlassen von Seindem." Heidegger, *op. cit.*, p. 15.

[9]Affirmer qu'ontologiquement l'homme est libre par définition et, encore, que la liberté est pour lui la condition de la vérité puisqu'un être non-libre ne pourrait dire ce que les choses sont, n'équivaut naturellement pas à résoudre tous les problèmes que l'existence de la liberté peut poser, ni même à nier que la liberté, relativement à l'homme, peut s'entendre en bien des manières. On pense pourtant que cette affirmation de principe permet seule de comprendre la portée exacte de ces difficultés ultérieures et le sens que l'idée de liberté devra revêtir lorsqu'on l'envisage dans les divers domaines de la philosophie et notamment, sur le plan psychologique, moral, social, religieux." de Waelhens, *op. cit.*, p. 83.

[10]In general philosophers approach the autonomy of being proper to man as subject from the autonomy of human activity. By virtue of the principle "action follows being" they conclude from man's self-acting to his self-being. Cf. De Petter, *op. cit.*, p. 170.

man as subject is a *self*-being. Man cannot be fully explained by his antecedents, but the being of man as subject is a being-of-himself (*aus-sich-sein*). Man's being is not merely being a part of the cosmos, it is not solely a pertaining to the cosmos, but as subject, man is subsistent and belongs to himself.[11] As subject, man is an "I," a "selfhood," a person. [12] The freedom of man as subject, therefore, should be understood positively as a certain autonomy of being, a certain independence of being, a belonging-to-oneself on the ground of a "to be" which is his own and thus also non-generated.[13] Scholastic philosophy uses the term "subsistence" for the ontological autonomy of man as subject.[14] As subject, as person, man "subsists."[15]

Man's ontological superiority constitutes at the same time his rationality. Boethius' famous definition of person as "an individual substance of a rational nature"[16] clearly emphasizes this. The being of man as I means his ontological superiority over the things of the cosmos. But this I, as ontological superiority, is the "natural light" through which man is a rational being. If it were not for man's subjectivity, there would be nothing but darkness. Man's ontological superiority as subject is the light through which there is meaning. To be subject, as being free, means to be rational.[17]

b. Freedom as "distance," as "having to be," and as "project"

No absolute freedom. If being subject means to be free, then the way of conceiving this subject is decisive for the content of the freedom attributed to *man*. If the subject which man is is described as an

---

[11] Cf. H.D. Robert, "Phénoménologie existentielle et Morale thomiste," *Morale Chrétienne et Requêtes contemporaines*, Tournai-Paris, 1954, pp. 208-209.

[12] Cf. de Petter, *op. cit.*, pp. 170-171.

[13] Cf. de Petter, *op. cit.*, p. 171.

[14] Cf. de Raeymaeker, *The Philosophy of Being*, p. 241.

[15] Cf. de Petter, "Het Persoon-zijn onder thomistisch-metaphysiche belichting," *De Persoon (Verslag v. d. XIIIe alg. verg. der ver. v. Thomistische Wijsb. en van de 4de studiedagen v. h. Wijsgerig Gezelschap te Leuven)*, Nijmegen, 1948, pp. 45-46.

[16] *De daubus naturis*, c. III.

[17] It is important to draw explicitly attention to the fact that in the case of a person, the concept "rational nature" is not related to "subsistence" or "supposit" as an extrinsic difference but expresses that rationality means a higher perfection of subsistence itself. Moreover, it is only in the case of a rational nature that there can be question of subsistence in the strict and proper sense. Cf. de Petter, *op. cit.*, pp. 45-46.

isolated subjectivity, his freedom must evidently be called absolute. As a matter of fact, there are a few contemporary phenomenologists who do this.[18] Their views, however, mean that they have given up the phenomenological way of thinking on this particular point.

There is no absolute freedom in human beings, because the subject which man is, is not an isolated subjectivity.[19] The self occurs only as involved in the density of reality, in the facticity of body and world, with which it is not identical. The self posits itself only in relativity, it exists, it is intentional, and situated.[20] The ontological autonomy, therefore, which man is, is very relative, for it is not what it is without the body and the world. The freedom which is proper to man because of his being-subject is at the same time immediately a bond, and this bond must be conceived as a kind of "powerlessness." Freedom is not an "acosmic liberty," not the *perfectly autonomous* source of reality's meaning, for without this reality subjectivity is not what it is. On the other hand, man is not merely a phase of the material cosmos, for without man there would not even be a cosmos.

The self as non-distant from reality. If attention is paid to the meaning of manhood, understood as "engaged" subjectivity, as situated freedom, one sees that the envolvement of the subject in reality implies a "distance which is at the same time zero and infinite."[21] Reality is conceived here as the facticity of the world and of being corporeal in the broad sense, i.e., the facticity of what with Strasser we have called the "quasi-objective ego."[22] That there is a "zero distance" between the self and reality means that the self as conscious "I," as self-affirmation, simply does not occur except in fusion with consciousness of reality, in fusion with the affirmation of bodily being and the world. Accordingly, the "zero distance" is nothing else than what we have previously called "intentionality."

[18] Cf. Robert, *op. cit.*, p. 202-204.
[19] "Im Ich-sagen spricht sich das Dasein als In-der-Welt-sein aus." Heidegger, *Sein und Zeit*, p. 321.
[20] "Si le sujet est en situation ... c'est qu'il ne réalise son ipséité qu'en étant effectivement corps et en entrant par ce corps dans le monde." Merleau-Ponty, *Phénoménologie de la perception*, p. 467.
[21] Cf. de Waelhens, *op. cit.*, p. 81.
[22] Cf. above, pp. 114 f.

The self-affirmation of the I, however, lies on a two-fold level, just as the affirmation of the reality in which the self is involved by virtue of its intentionality. It lies, first of all, on the cognitive level, the level on which the self is *recognized* as self and reality as reality.[23] The ontological superiority of the self, as "natural light," i.e., the rationality of subjectivity, constitutes at the same time the rationality of reality by "letting it be."[24] Secondly, the self-affirmation of the I and the affirmation of reality which is fused with this self-affirmation by virtue of intentionality lie on the affective level. The subject is not only a *Cogito*, but also a *Volo* (I will). The affective aspect of subjectivity is distinct from the cognitive level. The self-affirmation of the I contains not only a *recognition* of the self as self and of reality as reality, but also a *consent* of the self to the self and, fused into one with it, a consent to reality. The taste of the first cigarette after breakfast, the relish of a glass of wine, the joy over a lovely baby, the rapture of the bride over the groom, the happiness over the finding of a long-sought truth, the burst of laughter over an hilarious stroke of wit, the emotion over the sight of the ocean or of mountain scenery – all are examples of being affectively involved in, and of affirming reality. Fused with this consent of the self to reality is the consent of the self to itself. The self-affirmation of the I on the affective level means a certain plenitude of being, a certain fulfilment and satisfaction, a kind of rest and peace, which may be called "happiness."

The self as infinitely distant from reality. The involvement of the self in reality, however, may not simply be called "zero distance," for it is just as immediately "infinitely distance," on the cognitive as well as the affective level. What is meant by this infinite distance?

It implies that the positivity of the self-affirmation which the I is, is not simply what it is without negativity, without self-negation. At the same time negativity affects the affirmation of reality which is fused into one with self-affirmation by virtue of intentionality.

As self-affirmation, the I is positivity of being. On the cognitive level, however, the recognition of the self as self implies a negation –

---

[23] "C'est en communiquant avec le monde que nous communiquons indubitablement avec nous-mêmes." Merleau-Ponty, *op. cit.*, p. 485.
[24] "On ne peut dire ni que l'homme libre veut la liberté pour dévoiler l'être ni le dévoilement de l'être pour la liberté; ce sont là deux aspects d'une seule réalité." S. de Beauvoir, *Pour une morale de l'ambiquité*, Paris, 1947, p. 99.

namely, the denial that the self is identical with any reality whatsoever, conceived as the facticity of my bodily being and my world. The ontological positivity of the I, therefore, as cognitive self-affirmation, is not what it is without ontological negativity: the self is not the All, but a finite positivity of being. Likewise, the cognitive affirmation of reality which is fused with the self-affirmation of the I by virtue of intentionality implies a negation — namely, the negation that the reality of bodily being and world are identical with the self, and the negation that any reality is identical with any other reality whatsoever. No single reality is the All, but every reality is a finite positivity of being.

The positivity of being-for-itself. The well-informed reader will recognize a Sartrian thought in the foregoing remarks, although there is a difference insofar as we conceive the self and intentionality primarily as positivities. Sartre's "for-itself" is pure nihilation. This is not correct. While the "for-itself" is *also* nihilation, it is not nothing but nihilation. The subject-I, therefore, is not pure nothingness, but a positivity of being which is affected by negativity and consequently finite. Sartre considers the negativity of intentionality in *Being and Nothingness* especially from the cognitive level. In his literary works, mainly in *Nausea*, he is primarily concerned with the affective level. On this level he likewise absolutizes negativity: for Sartre, the affective involvement of the subject in reality is pure nausea. This, too, is not correct.

Nevertheless, in the affective self-affirmation of the subject and in the affirmation of reality which is fused into one with this self-affirmation by virtue of intentionality there is an aspect of negativity, an affective "no." The consent to reality is never a consent without reservation. The subject which man is, is never capable of a perfect "yes" to reality. [25] Money, sex, bodily health, power, revolution — nothing fully satisfies man.[26] The subject's affective "yes" to reality includes an affective "no." The same applies to the affective self-affirmation, the consent of the subject to itself. All fullness of being is at the same time emptiness, all fulfilment and satisfaction is affected by unfulfilment and dissatisfaction, all rest, peace, and happiness are permeated with unrest, lack of peace, and unhappiness.

[25] "Il manque a son assentiment quelque chose de massif et de charnel." Merleau-Ponty, *Eloge de la philosophie*, p. 81.
[26] S. de Beauvoir, *op. cit.*, pp. 65-75.

"Man is a being which in its being is concerned with its being." It is
not at all a purely imaginary danger that the details which had to be
mentioned in considering the subject's involvement in reality may have
obscured somewhat the view of man's being in its totality. Nevertheless,
these details were necessary to prevent certain aspects from being
emphasized at the expense of others, as is done in Sartre's works. To
counteract the danger, let us endeavor to see man again in his totality. We
will do so by means of an expression used by Heidegger. When the German
philosopher wants to explain that man is not a thing among things, that he
is a subject, a person, he calls man a "being which in its being is concerned
with its being."[27] A thing "is not concerned with what it is," for it lies
"prostrated in what it is."[28] A man is not bald in the same way as a
billiard ball is smooth, he is not sick in the same way as a cabbage is
spoiled, he is not hunchbacked as a willow tree is gnarled, for "man is
concerned with" his bald pate, with the disintegration of his organism,
with his deformity. He has a relationship to what he is — bald, sick,
hunchbacked, etc. — namely, as a subject. Heidegger expresses this idea by
saying that man's being, *Dasein*, possesses a relationship to being
(*Seinsverhaltnis*) which is an understanding of being (*Seinsverstandnis*). [29]
This understanding relationship is what distinguishes the being of man
from the being of a thing. For this reason Heidegger says that man "in his
being" is concerned with what he is, thus excluding that there would be
question only of something accidental to man's being.[30] In the
relationship of man as subject to what he is lie the positive and negative
aspects on both the cognitive and the affective levels which were spoken of
above. All this is lacking in a thing. A thing is not related to its own being,
but is compact density, it is "prostrated in what it is," so that there is no
possibility that it will raise questions, be astonished, bored, glad, sad,
anxious, hopeful, or desperate.

---

[27] "Das Dasein ist ein Seiendes, das nicht nur unter anderem Seienden verkommt. Es
ist vielmehr dadurch ontisch ausgezeichnet, dasz es diesem Seiendem in seinem Sein
um dieses Sein selbst geht. Zu dieser Seinsverfassung des Daseins gehört aber dann,
dasz es in seinen Sein zu diesem Sein ein Seinsverhältnis hat." Heidegger, *op.cit.*,p.12.
[28] Heidegger's idea is taken over by Sartre when he sais: "L'être de la conscience est
un être, pour lequel il est dans son être question de son être." *L'être et le néant*, p.
116.
[29] Cf. Heidegger, *Sein und Zeit*, pp. 12-15.
[30] The old philosophers expressed this in the definition: man is a rational animal.

"Situated" freedom and distance. As was stated above, being-subject is being-free, and this freedom manifests itself as a superiority of being with respect to the being of things. The subject, however, is not a human subject without being involved in reality. Freedom is not acosmic freedom but a situated freedom. When one considers this freedom, it is seen to include a "distance which is at the same time zero and infinite." Such an assertion can be made only on the basis of being-subject. A thing is not a subject and, therefore, is not at a distance from what it is; a thing is not concerned with what it is, for it is compact density and lies "prostrated in what it is."[31] Because being-subject is being-free, it is readily understood why several phenomenologists use the term "freedom" for the distance itself which characterizes man on the ground of his being-subject as situated subjectivity. They use this term in this sense even without first drawing attention to the ontological superiority, the subsistence, of the subject.[32]

That there is justification for the use of the term "freedom" for the distance which, as pointed out, is implied in the subject's involvement in reality can, of course, be seen fully only when being-subject is conceived as being-free. About the same has to be said regarding a third meaning of the term "freedom" — namely, *zu sein, avoir à être,* or "having to be." These meanings likewise are intelligible only through a more profound penetration of freedom as distance.

Man as a "natural desire." The effective distance of the subject from reality, as an infinite distance, is invincible. Although there is an unmistakable consent of the subject to reality, the reservation, the negativity, which affects this consent cannot be eliminated. No value-experience is such that man's "yes" is definitive and not permeated with "no." This applies to every level of intentionality, to man's existence in the technical, economic, political, social, medical, pedagogical, artistic,

---

[31] "Mais si nous supposons une affirmation dans laquelle l'affirmé vient remplir l'affirmant et se confond avec lui, cette affirmation ne peut s'affirmer par trop de plénitude. . . . Tout se passe comme si pour libérer l'affirmation *de* soi du sein de l'etre il fallait une décompression d'être." Sartre, *op. cit.*, p. 32.

[32] "La liberté est échappement à un engagement dans l'être, elle est néantisation d'un être qu'elle est. . . . Simplement le surgissement de la liberté se fait par la double néantisation de l'être qu'elle est et de l'être au milieu duquel elle est." Sartre, *op. cit.*, p. 566. See also de Waehlens, *op. cit.*, p. 81.

and intellectual realms. Insofar as an economic, social, or political order has a certain value, man is capable of consenting to it and to himself as an economist, a sociologist, or a politician. The same applies to the arts, sciences, education, etc. However, there is never a consent that is not affected by negativity. For this reason man cannot stand still, but has to go forward. He is never *"finished,"* whether as economist, artist, philosopher, physician, or anything else. The same applies to his world. Because man "is bored by what is established,"[33] because his "yes" can never be definitive, he is constantly urged on. Man as subject is not only a "natural light," but also a "natural desire."

To understand this characteristic of man, it is necessary that in considering freedom as infinite distance emphasis be placed on affective "nihilation." It is in this sense that certain expressions of Sartre must be taken to be fully understood. Thus, for instance, one may say that "nothingness haunts being,"[34] for all affirmation is affected by an invincible "nihilation." Or "nothingness lies in the very heart of being as a worm,"[35] which expresses that the affective "yes" is never "massive" and definitive. Affective nihilation always means a certain distance of subjectivity from reality, a not-being-attached-to-it, a certain reservation and affective non-immersion in facticity which are never overcome.

Terms such as "nihilating rupture,"[36] "nothingness of being,"[37] "hole of being,"[38] "decompression of being,"[39] are synonyms which may be used to express that the affective involvement of subjectivity in reality can never mean a definitive consent.

Man as a task-in-the-world. What we have actually explicitated here is what phenomenology means when it calls man's being a *zu sein, avoir à*

---

[33] Cf. Merleau-Ponty, *Eloge de la philosophie*, p. 79.

[34] "La condition nécessaire pour qu'il soit possible de dire non, c'est que le non-être soit une présence perpétuelle, en nous et en dehors de nous, c'est que le néant hante l'être." Sartre, *op. cit.*, p. 47.

[35] "Le néant ne peut se néantiser que sur le fond d'être; si du néant peut être donné, ce n'est ni avant ni après l'être, ni d'une maniere générale, en dehors de l'être, mais c'est au sein même de l'être, en son coeur, comme un yer." Sartre, *op. cit.*, p. 57.

[36] Sartre, *L'être et le néant*, p. 514.

[37] *Ibid.*, p. 516.

[38] *Ibid.*, p. 121.

[39] *Ibid.*, p. 116.

être, of "having to be." Man is a task, a task-in-the-world. As long as man is man, his being is a task, and essentially a task. Man is never "finished." A task which is "finished" is no longer a task. A human being which is "finished" is no longer a human being. Man, of course, may fail to see the task-like character of his being in the world, but then he fails to see himself as he is, as man. In doing so, he gives himself the mode of being of a thing, for a thing "is not concerned with what it is." For a thing being is not a task, because a thing is not a subject, not free.

15

Cosmic freedom

Pierre Teilhard de Chardin

In a living conception of the world — which is that of Pierre
Teilhard de Chardin — there would have to be wide room for
freedom, and freedom as wide and deep as the cosmos. Cosmic
freedom, as described in a variety of places in Teilhard's
writings, apparently includes many factors of freedom that
have been stressed in the past but very often isolated from one
another. Cosmic freedom implies man's immersion in and
direction of an evolutionary process, man's relation to a
transcendent point of personal attraction, the individual man's
differentiation from others — above all in his exercise of free
choice — and finally, the person's convergence with others,
center to center, for an exuberant growth in freedom.

Thus the concept of cosmic freedom embraces man's earthly
rootedness, his infinite longings, his vocation to community.
Real freedom, in this perspective, requires that the choice that
accompanies a too rugged individualism be unmasked as a
fradulent form of freedom.

Because the world is more cosmogenesis than cosmos, cosmic
freedom is dynamic; because the universe, according to

Teilhard, is personalized, cosmic freedom is personal and
therefore transcendental; because the cosmos is striving
towards community, freedom must be both individual and
universal. Whereas the personalists insist upon man as
conscious life, the life of decision, and social naturalists like
Dewey underscore man in society, while metaphysicians tend
to teach that goodness in itself really is, Teilhard developed his
cosmic personalism upon reflection on man's earth-rootedness,
his aspirations, his solidarity with others, his future
possibilities. Whoever, then, is responsible for the evolution of
the cosmos is responsible for the state of freedom today.
Teilhard teaches that the future evolution of the human world
is man's radical responsibility. How to increase freedom — this
is man's problem.

The Higher Freedom

At the beginning we seemed to see around us nothing but a
disconnected and disordered humanity: the crowd, the mass, in which, it
may be, we saw only brutality and ugliness. I have tried, fortified by the
most generally accepted and solid conclusions of science, to take the
reader above this scene of turmoil; and as we have risen higher so has the
prospect acquired a more ordered shape. Like the petals of a gigantic lotus
at the end of the day, we have seen human petals of planetary dimensions
slowly closing in upon themselves. And at the heart of this huge calyx,
beneath the pressure of its in-folding, a centre of power has been revealed
where spiritual energy, gradually released by a vast totalitarian mechanism,
then concentrated by heredity within a sort of super-brain, has little by
little been transformed into a common vision growing ever more intense.
In this spectacle of tranquility and intensity, where the anomalies of

detail, so disconcerting on our individual scale, vanish to give place to a vast, serene and irresistible movement from the heart, everything is contained and everything harmonised in accord with the rest of the universe. Life and consciousness are no longer chance anomalies in Nature; rather we find in biology a complement to the physics of matter. On the one hand, I repeat, the stuff of the world dispersing through the radiation of its elemental energy; and on the other hand the same stuff re-converging through the radiation of thought. The fantastic at either end: but surely the one is necessary to balance the other? Thus harmony is achieved in the ultimate perspective, and, furthermore, a programme for the future: for if this view is accepted we see a splendid goal before us, and a clear line of progress. Coherence and fecundity, the two criteria of truth.

Is this all illusion, or is it reality? It is for the reader to decide. But to those who hesitate, or who refuse to commit themselves, I would say: 'Have you anything else, anything better to suggest that will account scientifically for the phenomenon of man considered as a whole, in the light of his past development and present progress?

You may reply to me that this is all very well, but is there not something lacking, an essential element, in this system which I claim to be so coherent? Within that grandiose machine-in-motion which I visualize, what becomes of that pearl beyond price, our personal being? What remains of our freedom of choice and action?

But do you not see that from the standpoint I have adopted it appears everywhere — and is everywhere heightened?

I know very well that by a kind of innate obsession we cannot rid ourselves of the idea that we become most masters of ourselves by being as isolated as possible. But is not this the reverse of the truth? We must not forget that in each of us, by our very nature, everything is in an elemental state, including our freedom of action. We can only achieve a wider degree of freedom by joining and associating with others in an appropriate way. This is, to be sure, a dangerous operation, since, whether it be a case of disorderly intermingling, or of some simple form of co-ordination, like the meshing of gear-wheels, our activities tend to cancel one another out or to become mechanical — we find this only too often in practice. Yet it is also salutary, since the approach of spirit to spirit in a common vision or a shared passion undoubtedly enriches all; in the case of a team, for example, or of two lovers. Achieved with sympathy, union does not restrict but exalts the possibilities of our being. We see this everywhere and every day on a limited scale. Why should it not be worth correspondingly more on a vast and all-embracing scale, if the law applies to the very structure of things? It is simply a question of tension within the field that polarises and attracts. In the case of a blind aggregation, some form of unification brought about by purely mechanical means, the principle of large numbers comes into play. That is true: but where it is a matter of unanimity realised from *within* the effect is to personalize our activities, and I will add, to make them unerring. A single freedom, taken in isolation, is weak and uncertain and may easily lose itself in mere groping. But a totality of freedom, freely operating, will always end by finding its road. And this incidentally is why throughout this paper, without seeking to minimise the uncertainties inherent in Man's freedom of choice in relation to the world, I have been able implicitly to maintain that we are moving both freely and ineluctably in the direction of concentration by way of planetisation. One might put it that determinism appears at either end of the process of cosmic evolution, but in antithetically opposed forms: at the lower end it is forced along the line of the most probable *for lack of freedom*; at the upper end it is an ascent into the improbable through the *triumph of freedom*.

We may be reassured. The vast industrial and social system by which we are enveloped does not threaten to crush us, neither does it seek to rob us of our soul. The energy emanating from it is free not only in the sense that it represents forces that can be used: it is moreover free because, in the Whole no less than in the least of its elements, it arises out of a state that grows ever more spiritualized. A thinker such as Cournot, *Considerations sur la Marche des idées et des Evenements dans les Temps modernes* (Réédition Mentre. Vol. II, p. 178) might still be able to suppose that the socialised group degrades itself biologically in terms of the individuals which comprise it. Only by reaching to the heart of the Noosphere can we hope, and indeed be sure, of finding, all of us together and each of us separately, the fullness of our humanity.

*   *   *

Conditions of Freedom

If it is true that, bound by the collective interaction of its liberties, the human social group cannot escape from certain irreversible laws of evolution, does this mean that, observed along its axis of 'greatest complexity' (i.e. increasing liberty) the World is coiling upon itself with as much sureness as it is in other respects radiating outwards and explosively expanding? In other words, because certain unalterable factors compel us to advance, with no possibility of return, in the direction of increasing hominisation, must we conclude that biological evolution on Earth will easily achieve its purpose — that Thought will necessarily succeed in so shaping itself that in the end it will comprehend everything.

By no means; and for a series of reasons (or conditions to be fulfilled) which I must now set forth, from the most superficial to the most profound. First, conditions of survival, then, conditions of health, and finally, above all, conditions of synthesis.

a. *Conditions of Survival.*   I am not thinking particularly of the possibility of a cosmic catastrophe which might render the earth prematurely uninhabitable. The presumed duration of the whole human development (a few million years) is so trifling compared with the extent of astronomic time, even at the lowest estimate, that the chance of a variation of the solar equilibrium while the anthropogenesis is in process may be ignored. Nor do I propose to dwell upon the truly negligible possibility of some rash or criminal experiment blowing up the world or even some infectious disease causing the total elimination of an animal group as far-sighted progressive and ubiquitous as Mankind in the adult state. But on the other hand, I think we must pay serious attention to warnings such as that recently uttered by Mr. Fairfield Osborn in his book *Our Plundered Planet.*

In our hurry to advance are we not squandering our reserves to such an extent that our progress may be brought to a halt for lack of supplies? Where physical energy and even inorganic substances are concerned, science can foresee and indeed already possesses inexhaustible substitutes for coal, petroleum and certain metals. But foodstuffs are another matter. How long will it take chemical science to find ways of feeding us by the direct conversion of carbon, nitrogen and other simple elements? The population graph is rising almost vertically, while arable land in every continent is being ruined for lack of proper husbandry. We must take care: we still have feet of clay.

b. *Conditions of Health.*   I am thinking less of hygiene and physical culture, to which sufficient thought is devoted already, than of the vital problems posed by genetics, which are wilfully ignored. After rising slowly until the 17th century, when it reached about 400 millions, the earth's population began to shoot up in an alarming fashion. It was 800 millions by the end of the eighteenth century, 1,600 millions by 1900 and over 2000 millions by 1940. At the present rate of increase, regardless of war and famine, we must expect a further 500 millions in the next 25 years. This demographic explosion, so closely connected with the development of a relatively unified and industrialised Earth, clearly gives rise to entirely new necessities and problems, both quantitative and qualitative. From the palaeolithic age onwards, and still more after the neolithic age, Man has always lived in a sate of expansion: to him progress and increase have been one and the same thing. But now we see the saturation point ahead of us, and approaching at a dizzy speed. How are we to prevent this compression of Mankind on the closed surface of the planet (a thing that is good in itself, as we have seen, since it promotes social unification) from passing that critical point beyond which any increase in numbers will mean famine and suffocation? Above all, how are we to ensure that the maximum population, when it is reached, shall be composed only of elements harmonious in themselves and blended as harmoniously as possible together? Individual eugenics and racial eugenics ... present apparently insuperable difficulties, administrative and psychological. But this does not alter the fact that the problem of building a healthy Mankind already stares us in the face and is growing more acute every day. With the help of science, and sustained by a renewed sense of our species, shall we be able to round this dangerous corner?

c. *Conditions of synthesis.*   What does the term mean? Cosmically speaking ... Man is collectively immersed in a vortex of organization which, operating above the level of the individual, gathers and lifts individuals as a whole towards the heightening of their power of reflection by means of a surplus of technical complexity. But, given the nature of the *reflexive* phenomenon, what rule must this evolutionary process observe if it is to fulfil its purpose? Essentially the following: that within the compressive arrangement which gathers them into a single complex centre of vision, the individual elements must group and tighten not merely without becoming distorted in the process, but with an enhancement of their 'centric' qualities, i.e., their personality: a delicate operation and one which, biologically, it would seem to be impossible to carry out except in an atmosphere of unanimity or mutual attraction. Recent totalitarian experiments seem to furnish material for a positive judgment on this last point: the individual outwardly bound to his fellows by coercion and solely in terms of function, deteriorates and retrogresses: he becomes mechanized. To repeat what I have already said, under these purely enforced conditions the centre of consciousness cannot achieve its natural growth rising out of the technical centre of social organisation. Only union *through* love and *in* love (using the word 'love' in its widest and most real sense of 'mutual internal affinity'), because it brings individuals together, not superficially and tangentially but centre to centre, can physically possess the property of not merely differentiating but also personalizing the elements which comprise it. Even under the irresistible compulsion of the pressures causing it to unite, Mankind will only find and shape itself if men can learn to love one another in the very act of drawing closer.

But how is this warming of hearts to be realized? In my paper on the formation of the Noosphere I suggested that the very excess of external compression to which we are subjected by the relative contraction of our planet may one day cause us to breach that mysterious wall of growing repulsion which, more often than not, sets the human molecules in opposition to one another, and enter the powerful, still unknown field of our basic affinities. In other words, attraction will one day be born of enforced nearness. I am very much less disposed to believe today that the tightening of the human mass will *of itself* suffice to warm the human heart. But I continue to believe, if anything more strongly, in the hidden existence and eventual release of forces of attraction between men which are as powerful in their own way as nuclear energy appears to be, at the other end of the spectrum of complexity. And surely it is this kind of attraction, the necessary condition of our unity, which must be linked at its root with the radiations of some ultimate Centre (at once transcendent and immanent) of psychic congregation: the same Centre as that whose existence, opening for human endeavor a door to the Irreversible, seems indispensable for the preservation of the *will* to advance, in defiance of death, upon an evolutionary path become reflective, conscious of the future . . .

If this is true, is it not apparent that the success of Anthropogenesis, ultimately dependent upon achieving contact with the supracosmic, must, despite the rigours of its external conditioning, essentially contain an irreducible element of indeterminacy and uncertainty?

All things taken into account, where does the balance lie between these diverse influences, 'for and against'? Faced by the biological dilemma confronting our zoological group (unite or perish) which are we to accept, which way rather than another, as the direction in which the indeterminacy essential to the human adventure is most likely to be resolved?

As I have said elsewhere, the more we study the past, noting the steady rise of Life over millions of years, and observing the ever-growing multitude of reflective elements engaged in the construction of the Noosphere; the more must we be convinced that by a sort of 'infallibility of large numbers' Mankind, the present crest of the evolutionary wave, cannot fail in the course of its guided probings to find the right road and an outlet for its highest ascent. Far from being stultified by overcrowding, the cells of individual freedom, in a concerted action growing more powerful as they increase in numbers, will rectify and redress themselves when they begin to move in the direction towards which they are inwardly polarised. It is reasoned calculation, not speculation, which makes me ready to lay odds on the ultimate triumph of hominization over all the vicissitudes threatening its progress.

*   *   *

The Omega

By its structure Omega, in its ultimate principle, can only be a distinct *Centre radiating at the core of a system of centres*; a grouping in which personalization of the All and personalizations of the elements reach their maximum, simultaneously and without merging, under the influence of a supremely autonomous focus of union. That is the only picture which emerges when we try to apply the notion of collectivity with remorseless logic to a granular whole of thoughts.

And at this point we begin to see the motives for the fervour and the impotence which accompany every egoistic solution of life. Egoism, whether personal or racial, is quite rightly excited by the idea of the element ascending through faithfulness to life, to the extremes of the incommunicable and the exclusive that it holds within it. It *feels* right. Its

From pp. 262-264, 307-310 in THE PHENOMENON OF MAN (hardbound edition) by Pierre Teilhard de Chardin, translated by Bernard Wall. Copyright 1955 by Editions du Seuil. Copyright © 1959 in the English translation by Wm. Collins Sons & Co. Ltd., London and Harper & Row, Publishers, New York. Reprinted by permission of Harper & Row, Publishers, Inc.

only mistake, but a fatal one, is *to confuse individuality with personality* In trying to separate itself as much as possible from others, the element individualizes itself; but in doing so it becomes retrograde and seeks to drag the world backwards towards plurality and into matter. In fact it diminishes itself and loses itself. To be fully ourselves it is in the opposite direction, in the direction of convergence with all the rest, that we must advance — towards the 'other'. The goal of ourselves, the acme of our originality, is not our individuality but our person; and according to the evolutionary structure of the world, we can only find our person by uniting together. There is no mind without synthesis. The same law holds good from top to bottom. The true ego grows in inverse proportion to 'egoism'. Like the Omega which attracts it, the element only becomes personal when it universalizes itself.

There is, however, an obvious and essential proviso to be made. For the human particles to become really personalized under the creative influence of union, they must not — according to the preceding analysis — join up together anyhow. Since it is a question of achieving a synthesis of centres, it is centre to centre that they must make contact and *not otherwise*. Thus, amongst the various forms of psychic inter-activity animating the noosphere, the energies we must identify, harness and develop before all others are those of an 'intercentric' nature, if we want to give effective help to the progress of evolution in ourselves.

Which brings us to the problem of love.

*   *   *

It only remains for me, in bringing this work to a close, to define my opinion on three matters which usually puzzle my readers: (a) what place remains for freedom (and hence for the possibility of a setback in the world)? (b) what value must be given to spirit (as opposed to matter)? and (c) what is the distinction between God and the World in the theory of cosmic involution?

a. As regards the chances of success of cosmogenesis, my contention is that it in no way follows from the position taken up here that the final success of hominization is necessary, inevitable and certain. Without doubt, the 'noogenic' forces of compression, organization and interiorization, under which the biological synthesis of reflection operates, do not at any moment relax their pressures on the stuff of mankind.

Hence the possibility of foreseeing with certainty (*if all goes well*) certain precise directions of the future. But, in virtue of its very nature, . . . the arrangement of great complexes does not operate in the universe except by two related methods: (i) the groping utilization of favourable cases and (ii) in a second phase, reflective invention. And what does that amount to if not that, however persistent and imperious the cosmic energy of involution may be in its activity, it finds itself intrinsically influenced in its effects by two uncertainties related to the double play — the chance at the bottom and freedom at the top? Let me add, however, that in the case of very large numbers the process tends to 'infallibilize' itself, inasmuch as the likelihood of success grows on the lower side (chance) while that of rejection and error diminishes on the other side (freedom) with the multiplication of the elements engaged.

b. As regards the value of the spirit, I would like to say that from the phenomenal point of view, to which I systematically confine myself, matter and spirit do not present themselves as 'things' or 'natures' but as simple related *variables*, of which it behoves us to determine not the secret essence but the curve in function of space and time . . .

c. Lastly, to put an end once and for all to the fears of 'pantheism', . . . how can we fail to see that, in the case of a *converging universe* such as I have delineated, far from being born from the fusion and confusion of the elemental centres it assembles, the universal centre of unification (precisely to fulfil its motive, collective and stabilizing function) must be conceived as pre-existing and transcendent. A very real 'pantheism' if you like but an absolutely legitimate pentheism — for if, in the last resort, the reflective centres of the world are effectively no more than 'one with God' this state is obtained not by identification (God becoming all) but by the differentiating and communicating action of love (God all *in everyone*).

Church thought everything was god
& God was all was a kind
of Xtian pantheism

Part V

THE PHILOSOPHY OF FREEDOM

THE PHILOSOPHICAL
INTERPRETATIONS OF FREEDOM

16

Freedom and society

Karl Jaspers

Karl Jaspers notes the bipolar character of man's participation in society. On the one hand, man develops power by participation in technological society, thus altering his relationship to nature, making him transcend and dominate it. On the other, he grows personally by participating creatively in community, thus altering his relation to his fellow men and simultaneously his relation to the Transcendent.

Jaspers suggests that unless power receives its direction from man-in-community, power becomes meaningless or corruptive. He points out that modern society now makes available for men an organized freedom, but only an ordered freedom will make the whole of life meaningful. Technology is a new value, community an old one. For real freedom to exist in the modern world, these values must converge.

To say that in order for freedom to be real there must be community is to say that individual choice is related to the happiness of other men, and no society, however well organized, can substitute for a freely created community.

For as a result of technology, community itself is with us in a new form. The encompassing community, which used to move as one, is now split — a split we have become aware of as the gulf between community and society. That substantial community was historic, unique in each instance, borne by an unfathomable past to which it listened, which was handed down by word of mouth and in books, manners, customs, habits, and proprieties, above all by the family and by a common faith. It had grown and could not be planned; it was maintained but could not be organized. The technical collective of society, on the other hand, belongs to the moment, can be transferred at random and identically repeated, has no past to remember, is thoroughly planned, and can be surveyed and organized. It can replace every individual without changing itself; it treats them as mere means, as parts, and as functions. It has no future other than the unfelt, unsubstantial one of quantitative increase, mechanical improvement, and replacement of worn-out men and materials.

Today this gulf yawns as if substantial community and technical society were mutually exclusive. But it has always existed in the tension between traditional repetition and rational change, between technically thoughtless compliance and methodically improving thought. Viewed as a whole, it is an essentially human polarity. If one side outweighs the other, both fall short. Pure substance becomes meager as a reality in the world; it remains helpless and impotent in nature. Pure planning does indeed give immense power, but with a tendency to crush the human being, to whom this power would be significant. When the member of the substantial community feels lost and helpless before nature, when he is in want or exhausted by toil, he will turn enthusiastically to the technical world. At first, he will see nothing but deliverance in the mechanical collective. But when he feels it grinding him down, when he cannot breathe any more, he will yearn for the substantial community.

We have seen, in greatly simplified form, that man belongs to two polarities: first to that of individual and collective, and then, within the

From Karl Jaspers, *Philosophy and the Modern World* (Chicago: Henry Regnery Company, 1963), pp. 59-67. Reprinted by permission.

collective, to that of substantial community and technically planning society.

The essence of man grows with the wealth of substance that is present in community — a substance represented, among other things, by the creative personality which recognizes itself in the communal echo. The power of man, on the other hand, grows with the control he obtains of nature, by the cooperation of all, in producing his technical environment. Yet man's essence and his power do not coincide. The essence derives its strength in the world from the power, while the power depends on the essence for its meaning and its satisfaction.

Today the two polarities seem to be moving in the direction of the one technical apparatus overshadowing everything else. The specific features which distinguish modern technology from any previous one cannot be incidentally discussed; it must suffice us to know that something entirely new in history has been brought forth here over the past two hundred years — slowly at first, swiftly in the past hundred years, by leaps and bounds for some eighty. It was this new phenomenon that severed the two polarities, of individual and community and of community and society.

In extreme cases, communtiy will vanish altogether behind the machinery that overpowers but does not animate all. Of the rich, living collective in which man found himself, nothing remains but a bustle in which he is a function, interchangeable and superfluous as himself. Loss of self and loss of community go together where the technical apparatus creates a relentless organization of labor simultaneously with chaos in the human soul.

The extremes show this most clearly. On one side, forced laborers condemned to murderous exploitation are degraded in concentration camps to the inhuman existence of mere beasts; on the other side, workmen freed by protective legislation and shortened hours are at a loss — without community, they can no longer be themselves and thus do not know what to do with themselves. It takes the collective organization of leisure to redeem them from their empty freedom. From the bustle of work they drift into a bustle of pleasure.

Such descriptions are imaginary; reality goes so far only in borderline cases. As with everything we have said, these constructions are merely contemplative. We are observing what happens. But there is a limit to this cognitive attitude, and it is reached at the point where we ourselves are the object of cognition. We do not know ourselves like natural events, which happen no matter whether or not we know them; how we know our existence will affect events and us. We are always more than we know about ourselves, and the surplus is not a dark background, not a dim unconscious. It is our freedom, the brightest part of ourselves, although objectively we do not know it at all. What we do is up to us.

If we equate self-knowledge with a knowledge of nature, it tends to guide our dealings with ourselves from an imaginary point outside, a supposed knowledge of what will necessarily happen to us. In fact, however, its purpose is to try to absolve us from action, to let us give up real action, to deliver us from freedom to an allegedly known necessity.

As a result we shall either — from this imaginary outside point — proclaim our omnipotence, or else — from an inner point of view — we shall proclaim our impotence. Whatever is taken for knowledge in a relative sense — we already mentioned a few patterns, such as the technological bustle which consumes the individual and what used to be state, family, political freedom — will serve, then, to furnish the desperate with arguments for crippling their own possible initiative, for giving up on themselves in the expectation of the seemingly inevitable.

For salvation, we are offered modern myths which transfigure the horror and make it look glorious.

We are shown a new, impersonal man, one who bears the stamp of the idea of technological existence. This man knows himself as a type, not as an individual; as supremely skilled and sure of functioning; as obedient, because he has no desire for private existence; as great and superior to anything personal, because the fact of being interchangeable with others boosts his consciousness. He despises solitude, lives with open doors, knows no place of his own. He is ever available, ever at work, and ever true to type. Though lost when he is alone, left to himself, he is indestructible because his replacements keep growing after him. Personality is an old-fashioned and now ridiculous concept. Being a type gives strength, contentment, and the consciousness of perfection.

There are other modern myths which make the surrender of self seem like a great moral act — the myth of the progressive movement of history, for example. To sacrifice ourselves unconditionally to its inexorable necessity is called the greatest happiness in existence, because it is the only meaningful action. The individual, in this view, is worthless except in the service of history; any resistance to its colossal march means liquidation as a sick person. This march of history may be conceived as the economic process of toil for the perfect universal order, which will now maintain itself — or as the racial evolution of the pure, healthy, perfect breed — or as the life of the nation, whose gain is the absolute standard for achieving the goal of one single chosen people, which will assimilate or govern all the rest.

Here lies the great choice for every individual. Those myths are false myths, without transcendental reality, will-o'-the-wisps on the road to the temporal and eternal ruin of man. They conceal reality by creating transient realities in the form of totalitarian state structures which seem grand but fade into nothing. These myths are false because they keep man from the requisites of his realization — from clear thinking, from rational inquiry, from a responsible way to the future. There is something frightening about men who follow those myths. They do not really look at us; in their piercing gaze, or nongaze, we see empty eyes. They themselves are not there at all. They do not speak; it speaks through them. They run amuck without question, or they smile from habit. The comradeship they offer is exchangeable at any time and personally quite untrustworthy. There is terrorized submission to the commands of a "line," or conformist submission to what everybody else does and seems to believe.

The conclusion that those myths are false is compelling in so far as they pretend to be knowledge. But their character as symbols of Being — the true reality by which we live — can be accepted or rejected only in an individual existential decision. One man feels instantly that to believe in them would put him on the road of evil; another may be as thrilled as if the myths were his true life. The choice is whether the individual gives up on himself or wants to be himself. It is a fight for existence, spiritual at first, and later violent. The carriers of those myths are willing to resort to force from the start.

On one side we see a world which on principle absorbs the individual in a collective subject to total planning, to a myth garbed as a pseudoscience. On the other side we have a world whose course cannot be foreseen, and thus can never be taken in hand by total planning. On principle, this world leaves the individual free to unfold spontaneously. And it depends upon the initiative of individuals — on those rare, perceptive, trustworthy, responsible ones who get their chance precisely because political freedom should come to be a general condition.

Then the conduct of the majority may bring powerful pressures to bear on the course of events, but the decision at any time will still come from a few men. There is no telling what one man can do if he stands at the helm. War and peace and the course of things, all this can be essentially up to him — though only by way of his grasping what masses want if they are told, and if they come to see.

The same applies on a small scale as on a large one. The elite of the past carried a connotation of status; today it is a sociologically undefinable selection of self-chosen individuals. Everyone, for instance, can take marriage and family seriously; everyone can find fidelity and responsibility in them, the happiness of being sheltered in his background, the authority for telling right from wrong — despite the statistics about the decay of the family and the tales of its disintegration. If the Kinsey Report shows that seventy-five per cent of American males desire extra-marital sexual intercourse and that fifty per cent practice it, the statistical figures are neither expressions of a permissible norm nor statements of man's "natural" behavior.

If political decisions are made by the ballot, the majority is not the voice of God; it is a technical means to determine the collective will of the moment, open to future correction. Respect for minorities is the hallmark of democracy. It is not rare for the best of men to be in a minority. Mankind always lives by the fact that a minority of higher-ranking norms and realities will serve as a model for others. Men who do right, and who are right, exert an influence that waxes greater for being unintended.

In the great trend of our time, in this absorption of the old polarities of individual and community, substantial community and rational society, the great summons is therefore addressed to the individual. For in all destruction there remains the chance of man himself. Whether in public life or in obscurity, the reformation of real community which may some day reanimate the world of technical bustle can come only from individuals.

It is not true that the individual has vanished. Nor is it true that under the worst conditions he must necessarily be altogether lost. It has been shown that in the world of totalitarianism individuals can don an inner armor, can refuse to yield to the deceptions, and can make a secret but resolute judgment not to believe in the false gods.

Yet even there the individual will not be himself without another. Out of a collective that has deteriorated into a gigantic engine of terror he can turn into a new source of true community. It is when we are lost that Nietzsche's word applies: "Truth begins with two." It is no longer parties

– they have become mere wraiths – which face each other, but substance and unsubstantiality. An extraordinary burden has been placed upon the individual; it is only in the utmost obscurity that the bearer of the future, the man who now feels the eternity of truth in his own being, is still alive.

Today the threat of doom overshadows every human problem. For the end of the world, which Jesus and the first Christians wrongly expected, has now become the real perspective of the self-destruction of mankind – not by bringing the world to an end, but by exterminating life on earth. It looks as if the potentialities of man's technological creation were slipping out of his calculating grasp. The present step of technology recalls one taken at the very beginning, when the way to make fire was found. But a conflagration, however destructive in the particular, did not annihilate the whole. An atomic holocaust would mean total annihilation.

Some react thoughtlessly, as if it were no concern of theirs. Others give themselves up to lamentation.

It will be very important, of course, to make agreements and arrangements to keep the worst from happening. Some day, however, all this will fail just the same, unless there are men whose sense of responsibility checks the course of events.

If the course of events is not controlled by all, or by many, or by a few individuals whose existence sets an example, the end will certainly come in a few decades. But if man preserves himself as an individual, he may, with the revival of his community, hope to resist the doom of mankind – if only, perhaps, by a moral-political change in him that would amount to a self-reversal.

17

Freedom in the personal nexus

John Macmurray

John Macmurray points to the problem of freedom as a problem not of language, as the linguistic analysts would have it, but of life. He sees its locus to be not in the individual alone, as does Ayn Rand, nor in the relation between nature and man, as does John Dewey, but in the relation between person and person.

Here there is no question of any abstract opposition between necessity and freedom. It is rather a case of necessary conditions for freedom to be real. Constraint is indeed opposed to freedom if freedom is defined as the absence of constraint; this constitutes a kind of logical opposition, if you will. But for the absence of that constraint which is *really* opposed to freedom, man must be among friends.

Friendship is therefore the matrix or the formative milieu for the existence and growth of human freedom.

Now human strife arises more from the conflict of intentions than from differences in opinion. If my freedom is the ground of my possibilities, as it is so often put today, then the existence of your freedom can also be the source of impossibilities for me. Another's refusal to cooperate with me is an enslaving action. It wounds me in my freedom. Such a refusal can disable someone from having what is psychological-ly desired by that person and objectively possible to attain. We regret but do not complain about a lack of power. It is different when we are deprived of our power. The mere piling up of power does not, in fact, insure freedom. MacMurray cogently argues that only when good personal relationships exist will the increase of power mean an increase of freedom, since the increase of one's possibilities for acting without the conditions for effective action only diminishes freedom. Such conditions are neither noninterference, nor natural or cultural ones, but personal conditions — those of friendly cooperation.

Community, not merely society, is the essential condition for freedom. That is why freedom can be described as an interpersonal reality.

The traditional formulations of the problem of human freedom are so abstract that they have neither substance nor meaning. Or perhaps it would be more appropriate to say that they have substance and meaning only as it is lent to them by the personal interests and assumptions of individuals, so that they change from generation to generation, from country to country, from circumstance to circumstance. If the issue is to be put in the way of solution we must begin by determining what we are discussing when we discuss freedom. This cannot be done by any mere definition of terms, which would carry no further than the use of the word in the present context. We must determine the locus of the problem in universal human experience. We must discover the center of disturbance. We must put our finger upon the concrete origin of the question, if it is to be real and not artificial; a problem of life and not of language.

The traditional dilemma of free will or determinism is entirely artificial, like most exclusive alternatives of a high order of abstraction. If a rigid determinism obtained in the field of human behavior there could, of course, be no choice; and equally if a rigid freedom of will prevailed there could be no choice either, since both alternatives would be equally open. But it would be a waste of energy to pursue an abstract argument when it is easy to see by inspection that the debate is artificial. We need only suppose that we have accepted either alternative, and ask what difference it makes in concrete experience. If everything is determined, it still remains unquestionable that a man is freer out of prison than in it; freer in America at peace than in Germany at war; freer in health than in sickness; freer when he has money in his pocket than when he is penniless. If man possesses freedom of will equally these variations in freedom remain unaffected. The locus of the real problem lies in these variations of human freedom under varying conditions. The question is not, "Are we free?" but "How free are we?" It is not, "Have we freedom of will?" but "Under what conditions have we most freedom of will?"

Men have craved for freedom, demanded freedom, and fought for freedom. This proves that they have meant by "freedom" something that could be achieved by human effort; and not something that we either have or lack. If the free-will controversy were no more than a scholastic wrangle, nothing could be done about freedom, whichever of the two alternatives were correct. This fact throws a curious light upon the metaphysical controversy itself. If we can increase freedom by taking the appropriate action, then freedom must be conditioned. It is only by altering its conditions that we can increase or diminish freedom. . . .

. . . Real freedom depends upon the character of the nexus of personal relations in which we are involved. This is the thesis which I wish to expound. It can be expressed and understood best by drawing attention to the kind of experience of freedom and constraint which it makes the center of the problem. If I am in the company of strangers whose good will is important to me, and cannot be depended on, my conversation with them and my behavior towards them suffer from constraint. I cannot express myself spontaneously. I must think carefully before I speak, and seek to make a good impression. I must act a part; I cannot "be myself." If I leave this company and join a number of intimate friends whom I know and trust, this constraint disappears and is replaced by freedom. I can now allow my whole self to appear. I can say what comes into my mind. I can behave "naturally." I need not fear criticism, and so I can be spontaneous, speaking and acting without an eye upon effects. Here then is one familiar type of experience in which the contrast between "freedom" and "constraint" appears. My thesis is that this contrast is the central one; and that when we wish to go to the root of the problem of freedom, this is precisely the sort of case which we should accept as a type instance, and have in mind as an example. My reason for saying this is not that there are no other types of cases which are important, such as those which form the stock in trade of all discussions of political liberty. It is that the type of experience I have chosen involves, in principle, all the others; that if it is understood, then all the others are, in principle, understood; if it is solved, then all the others are soluble. The understanding of other types, on the other hand, is not possible, or at least cannot be complete, unless this type of case is understood; nor can the problem be solved in the other types of instances unless it is solved in this type. I believe, in other words, that the problem of freedom appears at different levels of experience, and that its solution at the upper levels depends upon its solution on the basic level. And I believe that if we consider the problem as it appears in the nexus of direct personal relationships, we are attacking it at ground level; we are laying bare its foundations. Only if we do this is it possible to envisage a radical solution. Even if such a radical solution is impracticable, it will still enable us to understand what partial solutions are possible and practicable at other levels, such as the political or the economic; and it will prevent us from expecting too much from reforms that do not go to the root of the trouble.

In our effort to determine the general field in which the real problem of freedom arises, we noticed that it was not the mere absence of power that created the problem, but the absence of power relative to a real desire. We noticed further that a real desire — the kind of desire that can give rise to deliberate action — depends upon a belief in the possibility of its satisfaction. This involved a curious paradox. It would seem that we can only experience a real loss of freedom in the presence of an impossible possibility. I do not mean by this that we must believe something to be possible which is in fact impossible; for this is the situation in which we enjoy a freedom which is objectively illusory. We must find ourselves in a situation in which a real possibility is actually impossible to realize; in

which we believe, and believe rightly, that what we desire to achieve can
be achieved and at the same time cannot be achieved. For it is only in such
conditions that we can experience a real frustration of our will. It is only
then that we feel, and rightly feel, that we are *prevented* from realizing our
intentions, that we are *deprived* of our freedom.

How can such a situation arise? Surely any action that I propose is
either possible or impossible. At most, it would seem, I may be mistaken
in thinking it possible when it is impossible, or impossible when it is not.
Surely it cannot both *be* possible and impossible at the same time.
Logically, of course, it cannot. But logic does not have the last word.

For our logical judgments depend upon the distinction between
subjective and objective, which holds in the field of reflection but not in
the field of action. In reflection about the nature of the objective world
we are guided by the postulate that all unreason falls into the subjective
field; so that if any illogicality comes to light it must belong to the
processes of thinking, and not to what is the object of our thought. But in
action the unreason of the subjective field is carried over into the
objective, and our mistakes are objectively revealed and have an objective
embodiment. If two of us differ in our conclusions about an objective
question, then the disagreement makes no difference to the fact; it merely
shows that one of us at least is mistaken, and ought to change his mind.
The error of another cannot here by its mere existence destroy the
correctness of my own judgment. His inability to think logically does not
interfere with the freedom of my own processes of thought. But when we
pass from the sphere of thought to that of action this immunity is left
behind. For in action the irrationality of others can frustrate the
rationality of my intentions, and my irrationality can frustrate theirs. If
our intentions contradict one another, they destroy each other's
possibility. What is objectively . possible becomes actually impossible.
Wherever, indeed, the achievement of an intention depends upon
cooperation, the simplest of objective possibilities may be made impossible
by the unwillingness of those concerned to cooperate; and this
unwillingness may, on occasion, rest upon completely irrational and
totally absurd grounds. The capacity of human beings to "cut off their
noses to spite their faces" is very high, and it is not unusual to find a group
of individuals who refuse to cooperate in the achievement of an objective
which all of them desire, for reasons so irrational that they must conceal
them even from themselves. This is the resolution of the paradox of the

impossible possibility which lies at the root of the problem of freedom. It is the nexus of personal relationship that is responsible for the variation in human freedom. We can prevent one another from achieving our purposes, even when they are objectively possible, and so limit or destroy one another's freedom. Moreover, this is the only way in which real freedom can be limited; for only thus can what is objectively possible be rendered actually impossible. Only persons can limit the freedom of persons. Any limitation of freedom must have its source in us; in the character of our relationships, as personal agents, to one another.

It is the instinctive recognition of this truth that links the experience of a lack of freedom with the idea of oppression and tyranny. When men feel the loss of freedom they behave as though someone were responsible. They instinctively feel that some individual or class is wrongfully depriving them of a freedom which is theirs by natural right. The struggle for freedom is always a struggle against oppression. The oppressors have defended themselves on the plea that the freedom demanded was in the nature of things impossible; that the constraint complained of was in fact illusory. In this instinct there is a core of essential truth, however mistaken the accusation may be in any particular case. If men feel the loss of freedom they are always justified in looking for its source in the personal field. If men are not free, then they are oppressed. Their inability to do what they desire is not a mere lack of power, but a deprivation of power, for which the responsibility rests with their fellows. The fact that we often make mistakes in assigning the responsibility, that often indeed we are satisfied to wreak our vengeance on any available scapegoat, is no argument against this truth; any more than the fact that we often assign the wrong cause for an event suggests that it is causeless. We are therefore at liberty to lay down a principle of far-reaching importance. The solution of any problem of human freedom depends on the alteration of the relationships of persons. The importance of this principle lies in what it denies. It denies that any increase in power can solve the problem of freedom. Indeed, an increase in power which is not accompanied by a change in the nexus of personal relationships must inevitably diminish freedom. For it enlarges the field of objective possibility without altering the conditions of effective action, and so widens the gap between what can be intended and what can be achieved.

Consider two examples of this. The increase of scientific knowledge during the past century has immensely increased the range of human possibility. Much is really possible today that was objectively impossible a hundred years ago. As a result there has been a noticeable diminution of human freedom and an increase of oppression. There is nothing paradoxical about this. It is, in fact, just what must happen provided the character of the personal nexus remains, as it has remained, substantially unaltered. The increase in what is objectively possible cannot be equated with an increase in freedom. It increases the range and variety of the satisfactions that men can reasonably hope to attain. But if it leaves their forms of relationship adjusted to a narrower range of actual achievement only, then the effect is to diminish freedom. The subjective constituent of freedom must not be overlooked. Freedom does not consist in the objective existence of power, but in the possibility of using it for desired ends. If a century of scientific development has made it possible to raise the general standard of living by 20 per cent and it has actually risen only by 10 per cent then in this respect there has been a restriction of freedom by 10 per cent. (The figures, of course, are not to be taken seriously.)

Consider, in the second place, the increase in oppression which reveals itself in modern dictatorship. In olden times a despotic monarch, however arbitrary and cruel, could interfere with the freedom of his subjects only to a quite limited extent. In a modern society with the same type of relationship between ruler and ruled, the enormous increase in the range of human power involves a correspondingly enormous increase in the restriction of freedom. Not only is the tyrant's capacity to interfere with the activities of his subjects vastly increased, but the range of possible satisfactions which he can deny them is also greatly enlarged. Here again we see that an increase in objective possibility involves a decrease of freedom if the character of the personal nexus in society remains unaltered.

It might seem that this leads us to endorse the view, widely held at present, that freedom is a function of the structure of society. This is partly correct, but only partly. The more important corollary, which must be combined with this, is that the structure of society is itself a function of the personal nexus of relationship between its members. There is an ambiguity in our use of the term "society" which is apt to result in a dangerous confusion. In general, the term refers to that nexus of relationship which binds human individuals into a unity. The ultimate fact upon which all society rests is the fact that the behavior of each of us conditions the behavior of the others and is therefore a determinant of their freedom. But the resulting nexus of relationship contains two distinguishable elements in virtue of the types of motive which underlie the active relationships involved. It is of the first importance to recognize, and to bear in mind, that a subjective element necessarily enters into all human behavior, and so into the constitution of all human relationships. The elementary type forms of these contrasted motivations are hunger and love. Hunger is a motive which gives rise to actions designed to appropriate something for one's own use. Love, in contrast, is the motive of actions in which we expend what is ours upon something or someone other than ourselves. Both these types of motive are *necessary* in the sense that they belong universally to the psychological constitution of human nature and are inescapable elements in the determination of human behavior. Both give rise to a nexus of dynamic relationships which bind us together. The first type gives rise to functional co-operation in work, and its basic forms are economic. The second gives rise to the sharing of a common life. Since the term "society" has in our day come to be so closely bound up with discussions of the organized forms of political and economic relationship, we had better specialize it for this use, and distinguish the forms of relationship which spring from the impulse to share a common life by using the term "community" to refer to them. The contrast to which our attention is now directed becomes thus a contrast between society and community.

The exact difference between society and community and the proper relation between them are best recognized by reference to the intentions involved. The intention involved in society lies beyond the nexus of relation which it establishes. In community it does not. If follows that society is a means to an end, while community is an end in itself. This may be stated from another angle by pointing out that a society can always be defined in terms of a common purpose, while a community cannot. Let us look, by way of example, at the simplest possible type of case, in which only two persons are involved. Two men may be associated as partners in a publishing business. They may also be associated as friends. That these two forms of relationship are different, and at least relatively independent, is shown by the fact that they may dissolve the partnership and remain friends; or they may remain in partnership and cease to be friends. Their association as partners is constituted by a cooperation in the achievement of a common purpose. Its form is dictated by this purpose. It involves a plan of cooperation and a division of labor between them. In virtue of this plan each of the two has a function in the business, in performing which he contributes his share of work to the achievement of the common purpose. Success depends on the proper co-ordination of their functions; and if the plan achieves this and each performs his function efficiently the partnership is a satisfactory association. The whole nature of their relationship as business partners is expressible in such functional terms with reference to the common end to which the association is the means.

Now consider their relationship as friends. We are not concerned here merely with their feelings, but with the mind of active relationship which is implied in their being friends. Notice in the first place that this association cannot be defined in terms of a common purpose. We cannot ask, what is the purpose of their friendship? without implying that they are not really friends, but only pretend to be friends from an ulterior motive. A relationship of this type has no purpose beyond itself. Consequently its form is not dictated by a purpose; it does not give rise of necessity to a functional division of labor. For the same reason it cannot be organized. Nevertheless it is not motiveless. Its motive is to be found in the need to share experience and to live a common life of mutual relationship, which is a fundamental constituent of human nature.

We can use the same simple instance to help us to understand the relationship of these two types of association. That they are at least partly independent of one another we have seen, since they may vary independently. But we must now notice that friendship, though it cannot be constituted by cooperation for a common purpose, necessarily generates such cooperation. A friendship which did not result in the formation of common purposes and in cooperation to realize them would be potential only. Indeed the underlying motive of love is precisely to do something for the satisfaction of the other, and its mutuality inevitably leads to functional cooperation. But there are important differences to be noticed. Since the association is not *constituted* by a common purpose, it permits of a change of purposes. In a partnership, if the common purpose is dropped or becomes unrealizable, then the partnership is at an end. Not so with a friendship. If the two friends drop one common purpose for which they cooperate, it is only to find another. In the second place, the common ends which are worked for and the cooperation for their achievement are together means to maintaining and deepening the friendship. From this we must conclude that in the nexus of personal relationship community is capable of generating and containing society within itself, of making the cooperation for the achievement of common ends a means to itself and an expression of itself. Therefore it is clear that if the problem of community is solved the problem of society will be well on the way to solution.

It still remains true that within limits at least society can be independent of community. Our two men can be partners and cooperate in the work of running their business without being friends. The necessity of making a livelihood, the pressure of immediate self-interest, may be sufficient motives to maintain the association. But there are limits to this. In the first place, though their cooperation is theoretically possible in the absence of friendship between them, in practice the absence of friendship limits the possibilities of effective cooperation in many ways; while if strong personal antagonism enters in it may easily render cooperation impossible. It may simplify the issue if we remember that we are using the term friendship to draw attention to the whole range of forms of relationship which depend upon other-regarding motives; that is to say, upon motives which give rise to actions intended to affect the lives and fortunes of others. Such motives range from murderous hate, through a theoretical point of pure indifference, to the love which is ready to sacrifice life itself for the profit of the loved one. If we keep this whole range of behavior in mind it is much less clear that functional cooperation is quite independent of the more personal forms of relationship of which friendship is our example. The more positive the personal interest the easier, *ceteris paribus*, the cooperation must be. The stronger the personal animosities between cooperating individuals the more difficult and inefficient the cooperation is likely to prove. It is only at the theoretical point of complete personal indifference that the cooperation is freed from the influence of the more personal elements in the nexus of relationship. Such an indifference is psychologically impossible between people who are in direct contact with one another. But it is possible and natural in highly organized societies, where very few of the individuals cooperating can know one another personally at all.

In the second place, any social organization is liable to be hampered or even disrupted by the intrusion of personal animosities. The machinery of cooperation seems to work smoothly only if the personal relations of the individuals concerned are kept, as it were, at a level of low tension. The more each one concentrates on doing his own part in the common task the better. The more the relations between them are determined by the common objective and the functional necessities of the plan of cooperation, the more efficient their efforts are likely to be. In all forms of organized cooperation, therefore, there is a tendency to look upon the more personal forms of relationship as a source of possible danger to the unity of the group. There is a latent tension between the two aspects of relationship. Society demands from its members a devotion to a common end which transcends all "private" ends, and a loyalty which is ready to sacrifice both oneself and one's neighbor to accomplish it. But from the standpoint of community, such a demand is absurd and blasphemous. For its values lie within, not beyond, the nexus of relationship; and all cooperation is a means of expressing the common life. Persons, not purposes, are absolute.

It has been necessary to draw the contrast between those two forms of relationship in the personal nexus because it is vital to the problem of freedom.

Probably everyone to whom freedom is a practical issue would agree that it only becomes a real issue when there is oppression; when somebody is putting constraint upon someone else and so infringing his natural liberty. This is to recognize, of course, that the locus of the problem of freedom lies in the personal nexus. From this recognition it is a natural step to the view that the solution of the problem must lie in a reorganization of society which will order the relations of individuals in such a way that the tyranny of one man over another, of one group or class over another, is eliminated. All the great struggles for freedom have taken their stand upon this view. Yet when they have won their victories in the revolt against this tyranny and that and have established the new order for which they strove, the result has always proved a disappointment to the idealists. Freedom remained obstinately unachieved. Constraint and tyranny reappear in forms ever more complicated and more difficult to deal with. Today, after centuries of struggle and effort, it is at least doubtful whether all the progress made has not left the majority of men less free than they were in the days of serfdom and slavery; with a wider gap than ever between their reasonable desires and the satisfactions they can actually attain. This is not to say that there has been no progress. Progress has been immense and in spite of the pessimists is increasing its speed every year. The measure of progress is the increase in the range and complexity of what is objectively possible for man. This has risen so high that it is not absurd to say that already we are in a position to eliminate poverty from the life of mankind. But freedom is measured by the ratio between what is objectively possible and what we can actually achieve. It looks as though that ratio is lower than it has ever been in the history of civilization. Two things seem to be true together in the strange period to which we belong: that man's power of achievement has grown vast beyond belief; and that his capacity to achieve any serious human purpose is diminishing at an alarming rate. It is an age at once of unparalleled effort and unparalleled frustration.

The reason for this paradox seems to me to lie in our failure to distinguish the two aspects of relationship in the personal nexus. Not only do we use the terms "society" and "community" more or less interchangeably, but we tend increasingly to think of the nexus of personal relationship as a nexus of organized cooperation. As a result we are bound to conceive the problem of freedom as a problem of social organization; and, since the central organ of social organization is the State, as a political problem, to be solved by political means. The effort to solve the problem politically can only have the result of producing the organization of tyranny in the totalitarian state.

For consider. If a man is primarily a function in an organized cooperation pursuing a "common" purpose, then he exists for the group, as a means to the achievement of the common purpose. This is equally true of all his fellows. He and they have no more fundamental unity which might determine or modify or in any way challenge the social purpose. It is this purpose which determines them, sets them their places and their functions. Only in virtue of this organizing purpose are they a group. One is inclined to reply at once that this is clearly nonsense; and indeed it is. But we must not locate the "nonsense" in the wrong stage of the argument. If human society were fundamentally a nexus of politico-economic cooperation, as so much of our modern thought and practice asserts or assumes, then any limitation of the claims of the group sovereignty upon the individual would be ridiculous, and any freedom for the individual would be accidental. The theory and practice of the totalitarian state are direct corollaries of this characteristic modern assumption. If, on the other hand, the individual has any ground of claim against the State; if it can treat him unjustly and deprive him of a freedom which is his by right of nature; then he is not primarily a functional element in an organized cooperation. He embodies in himself, as it were, an authority which limits and defines the merely political authority of the organized society. Moreover, it is not as a mere individual that he can claim such an authority; as a mere individual he cannot even exist. It can only be as a member of a more primary nexus of relationships than those of any organized society, and in which the ground of all organized society is to be found. This is the nexus of communal relationship, which we here distinguish from the social nexus. We have thus reached the point at which we can say that freedom can only be maintained in this nexus of human relationship by maintaining the primacy of the personal nexus of community over the functional nexus of organized society. If this is secured, then no doubt a well-organized society will provide greater freedom for its members than an ill-ordered society. But the most perfect organizing of society, if it involves the primacy of the State, as the authority of organized society, must result not in the extension but in the obliteration of freedom.

The problem of human freedom is then the problem of that nexus of human relationships of which friendship is the type. It belongs to the field of our direct personal relationships; not primarily to the world of our indirect, functional, or legal relationships. This was the one point which I set out to maintain. I may well conclude by showing that this means that the basis of freedom is personal equality.

The essence of any friendship consists in the achievement, in it, of a real sharing of life, of an effective mutuality of experience. This involves, of course, material cooperation, as we have seen. It is in this effort to achieve such a nexus of relationship between ourselves and others that we have our most direct experience of freedom and constraint. Freedom is the result in so far as we succeed. Constraint is the penalty, as it is the proof, of failure. Freedom is the product of right personal relations. Constraint in the personal nexus is evidence that there is something wrong with the relationships involved. This "rightness" in such relationships is in fact personal equality. If there is constraint in a personal relationship there is a failure to achieve and maintain equality. Unless people treat one another as equals they are not friends. If one treats the other as an inferior, then he is using him as a means, and the friendship ceases to be a friendship. Thus personal equality is the structural principle of relations which are communal in type, while the experience of freedom in relations is their characteristic expression. What throws the personal nexus out of gear, and so introduces constraint and limits or destroys freedom, is always a failure to achieve or maintain personal equality. In other words, what destroys freedom is the will to power. Where one man seeks power over others, the denial of equality involved creates constraint and limits freedom. And there is no way in which freedom can be restored or increased except by overcoming the desire for power.

The conclusion is a negative one; and not particularly comforting. To all the plans for achieving or defending freedom by political or economic organization it comes as a serious and unwelcome warning. There can be no *technique* for achieving freedom. The field in which freedom has to be won or lost is not the field of economics or politics, of committees and rules. It is rather the field which has hitherto been the undisputed domain of religion. An age that has put religion aside without even recognizing the need to put something in its place has already lost the sense of freedom and is ripe for the organization of tyranny. On the other hand, the will to power, though it may infect an epoch like an epidemic, is still a disease. It is not natural. And it may help us back to health to recognize the disorder from which we suffer.

THE METAPHYSICAL FOUNDATION
OF FREEDOM

18

Incarnation of freedom

Auguste Brunner

The phenomenologists have described man as an embodied spirit. Maurice Merleau Ponty believes that verbalization is necessary for man to become self-present. If thought cannot exist without language, then by speaking we actualize the *transcendental attitude*. This is not a denial of the spiritual elements in our conscious experience but an admission that human history is important for the development of truth. The intersubjective character of human history also tells me that my actions are not wholly mine. What I do is not solely the result of my initiative, since the latter occurs within the horizon of self-developing Being. There are many dimensions to body, and spirit is the highest of those dimensions, so that in its depths the human person is coextensive with all being; interpersonal unity transcends individuality. Much of experience that men share is based upon their intercorporality.

In the passage that follows we face the other side of the intimate relation of all the human dimensions in man's body as Auguste Brunner points out the inevitable limitations of an incarnate freedom. This reflection upon the given conditions for exercising freedom provides a self-awareness that the Eastern sages would find refreshing.

The same relationship between the spirit and the soul animating the body is likewise found in the will. A pure spirit would spring forward at one go towards its end with all its soul and power; it would achieve with one sole movement the totality of the élan which carries a being completely and intensely towards the object of its love. But the body has not the agility characteristic of spirit. It feels the entire weight of its matter — inertia. Living matter is uplifted by life; and animal life ascends to participate in the life of spirit. Of themselves neither matter nor animal life can keep at this level of being but tend to fall to their natural level. We know this phenomenon in what we call the nature of man as opposed to person. When the spiritual will moves this corporeal inertia, it finds itself slowed down and weakened by it. But once the body and all that belongs to it is put into motion, it continues in the given direction and cannot be stopped at will, as when the emotions are aroused. To change this, a new personal effort must be made. The spirit's movement takes on something of the heaviness and the weight of corporeal, material motion. Spiritual energy is only communicated to the body progressively. The person cannot turn instantaneously in any one direction. . . . Spirit in man is no longer a pure liberty but deflected by past corporeal and psychic habits. These influence our will as diagrams determine our knowledge by forcing it into a more or less rigid framework. Passions are situated within this border region between freedom and determinism; hence their often irresistible influence upon freedom — for good or more often for evil. Hence there is the possibility of letting oneself be swept along in more or less conscious bad faith to what fundamentally one does not want, to sins of frailty which a pure spirit cannot commit inasmuch as it always acts with complete lucidity.

Thus our freedom is profoundly penetrated with passivity and, in general we may act by will only after receiving an attraction or repulsion. These involuntary tendencies can be thwarted only through creating

AUGUSTE BRUNNER, LA PERSONNE INCARNÉE — Etude sur la phénoménologie et la philosophie existentialiste. Bibliothèque des Archives de Philosophie — ancienne série. Beauchesne éditeur, Paris. 1947. Pp. 182-202. Translated by M. Clark.

opposed tendencies by education. In M. Sartre's system, education must be purely intellectual, an awareness of the profound direction which absolute freedom gives. Life lets us know, however, that such an enlightened conscience, no matter how useful, is simply not enough.

We must acknowledge common nature and the finite freedom following from it and causing the prevailing uniformity of behavior among men. A pure freedom would be unique, of absolute novelty and radical individuality. A finite but spiritual freedom would also have a pronounced novelty. But matter brings with it a great uniformity and allows exact physical laws to be established. The constant motion of matter can scarcely be called a "becoming" in the sense of novelty. The more matter changes, the more it remains the same. Animal life is found between spirit and matter. So it will exhibit a greater uniformity than do pure spirits, a uniformity which shows up in acquired habits. Without appealing to the matter-form theory, this set-up makes sense of that scholastic theory of every angel constituting a species. The extreme differentiation arising from their freedom would leave few common traits and a character wholly formal. We might express this graded novelty thus: as the hierarchy of being is ascended, each individual existence or personal history is more accentuated than the essence or common nature. Matter is completely dominated and determined by the nature received; man fashions his nature by his free action.

Yet in a created finite being the primacy of existence over nature could never be absolute. For it is received being that is the foundation of everything, limiting the existence of freedom and imposing absolute limits upon its possibilities. A created being, however great and spiritual it is, will always have a past. . . .

The Conquest of Freedom

The living subject is absorbed in the task of conserving life. Nourished by worldly objects, it is not detached from them; it is incapable of retreating. In man these tendencies exist and he tries to put them at the service of the higher self. Ordinarily the self acts as the mixed human self, not a purely spiritual self. Obviously any pure and simple subordination of the person-subject to the living-subject would be immoral, as opposed to their ontological hierarchy. But we should not condemn all concern for life and all such action. Such action is natural to an embodied subject. The person-subject can, by setting up the direction and the initiatives, through these very concerns, fulfil itself, freely accepting them and purifying them of their naturally egotistical tendencies. Thus does it avoid falling under their law and living only as the subject of corporeal life, making the pursuit of pleasure or of power the whole point of existence. Its role as a person takes it beyond this, and thanks to this transcendence, man is man rather than animal. As a person man does not lose himself within the world where he is engaged. But because of embodiment, the person-subject is ever threatened with submersion by the vital level of life where the aim is only this very life. The person needs to defend himself against becoming stuck in matter to safeguard his freedom and to keep intact the very faculty of enjoying objects, a faculty easily compromised by a weakening of personal subjectivity. So man experiences an incessant struggle to hold on to the freedom of an embodied subject. A too relaxed life risks the subject's being bogged down by earthly urgencies and lessens one's power to appropriate things and somehow animate them and personalize them.

Nor is the collective life any less open to that instability which G. Simmel has called "the tragedy of civilization": in multiplying artificial objects, humanity risks being crushed under their weight. A certain asceticism which is only a need to be saved from the tyranny of objects becomes a human fact, and history testifies to its universality. Man cannot feel at ease within nature as the animal can. Yet the goal of asceticism is not to disengage the human person from the world; it is and essentially remains an embodied person. It is merely a question of subordinating the various human levels in accord with the dignity of each one. It is true that the need to dominate can even filter into the efforts at personal liberation and become a new means to acquire power. This is the case with certain forms of the Hindu Yogi. This is likewise the case with those phenomena of *potlatch* so acutely analyzed by M. Sartre. It can also turn into an orgy of destruction for the sake of destruction by which man seeks self-identity through giving in to the pressures of instinct. We may never lose sight of the ambiguity present in all that is human. The noblest élan may become the pretext and mask for the most abject egoism which is taken for the sublime. Yet this danger does not justify the tendency to disparage the reality of all true disinterestedness and to expose vile and contemptible motives in every noble enterprise. Such literature is positively dangerous;

for a man is only too happy to find in everyone's alleged baseness the justification for his own. Besides, this tendency to hypocrisy and bad faith would be meaningless if there were no such things as disinterested motives. In reality man acts from a mixture of disinterested and egotistical motives, and this is to be expected in a being like man. The pure and uniform subjectivity of "idealism" would have to shoulder all these degradations, for they would be inherent to such subjectivity and inseparable from it. It would then be reasonable to see in it as M. Sartre does a radically incurable "decompression of being". But it would be difficult to understand with this hypothesis why the subject makes attempts which must fail and yet renews them to go beyond that "decompression" intimate to it.

The spontaneous movement of life is diametrically opposed to that of the person. Hence in man there is incessant struggle between the personal principle and the vital principle, a struggle not between two things-as-enemies, but between two parts of a divided self. Man has been wounded and this affects his self-awareness. The lower principle desires the spiritual forces to be at its service: it acknowledges the higher value of personal being but so that the latter will relinquish its independence and place itself at the service of the struggle for life, and life will thereby gain through intelligence those means which it itself could never discover. Animal life wishes us to be a personal-slave, a contradiction in terms, a contradiction within man's being, never allowing him to be at peace in any consented descent from personal dignity.

The person experiences the need to liberate itself from life's control. Not that the person is hostile to life, but it cannot allow this life to take the primacy. Hence it tries to put the vital level in its place as a means subordinate to the essential ends of the person. Certainly, life is no pure means inasmuch as it participates somehow in subjectivity. Hence the person cannot simply sacrifice life as one does a thing. But there is the duty of subordinating life to the exigencies of personal being, the right to place life in danger for higher goals without which it would no longer be a personal being.

Matter and individuality

The incarnation of the soul is therefore not the original fall; the fall is seen in the natural insubordination of the vital plane to the personal plane. Still less should one, as certain idealists of romantic tendency do, see in matter the result of this fall or of the lack of charity. According to them, there would be merely an opaque interval separating souls from perfect identity with the Whole. Certainly, as we mentioned, corporeal life renders our being heavier than that of pure spirit, both diminishing our élan and enfeebling our initiatives. But this diminishment takes place only in relation to an unreal ideal which is not an authentic vision of man, or else it is a way of expressing the distance which separates our conceptions from their realizations. This distance partially marks the interval between our two subjectivities. Spiritual being transcends the possibilities of corporeal life. It thus constantly feels itself easily hampered and limited. The schema of limitation taken from fabrication naturally comes to mind here, and corporeal life or matter will function as the principle of limitation, of individuation. This stated theory implies such a conception. Without matter all spirits would coincide in the Whole. Therefore individuality is conceived as a degradation, a sort of non-being. But on the contrary, it is evident that individuality becomes more powerful as the degree of being becomes higher. No being is so much itself and thereby so different from all else than God. As a matter of fact, the common nature is that which has its source in corporeal life and matter, as we noted.

Finally we must add that the diminishment in question is that of our body and not of matter in general. And we have shown that corporeal life may not be conceived as constituted by the spirit in any idealist way. Also, have we understood what happens to matter when interpreted in spiritual or existential terms? It seems to us that this only compounds the mystery. Indeed, is it conceivable that in a universe where there is only the spiritual, a spiritual effect would be hidden from the eyes of this spiritual being, so radically disguised that no one except for a few philosophers would recognize it? Why would it not remain on the spiritual level where spirits are? Better to stop trying to understand where understanding has lost its rights. Such identification at any price is probable only if we consider matter globally and abstractly, the idea of matter rather than matter itself. When we turn to concrete forms, the astronomical worlds and their evolution prior to man's appearance, the diversity of chemical elements, the atomic structure, or even in thinking of mountains or sea, we cannot help wondering how all this variety could be understood as an interval between persons brought about by lack of charity.

What remains objective in the proposed theories is that our attitude influences what we understand of the thing-itself. Man is free to identify his personal center with anyone of the levels constituting his being. The world for him is more or less rich in possibilities, and these possibilities change their character as he utilizes more or less spiritual energy. His initiatives will arise from within as a result of spiritual considerations or he will let himself be passively hindered by the weight of his body and through laziness will renounce his privilege of being a free agent imposing his laws upon events.

Urgencies, like values, are constituted by two factors: by the objective reality and by man's attitude. This is only natural if we do not inject the Cartesian abyss between the body and the spirit, and if we see in the human body that point where freedom is inserted in the material world through the mediation of vital subjectivity. The more this subjectivity yields itself as a docile instrument to personal initiatives, the more the person provides new possibilities for the world.

It is true that what often separates persons and makes them opaque to each other, what prevents their union reaching perfection is matter, not matter in itself, but matter in its quality of artificial object in the broad sense of the word, namely, as an object to possess, as property. If charity were perfect, man would have no need to surround himself with a rampart of possessions, for such goods are at the exclusive disposition of an individual to shelter his freedom from the threats and dangers to which body, accessible to physical constraints, exposes it. Corporeal needs would remain in a human world where there reigns perfect charity — but egoism would no longer transform them into means of domination.

Bracketing Existence

It is now possible for us to justify that particular trait of eidetic reduction which enjoins us to bracket the object's reality. But real life which is influenced by biological life is not interested merely in the idea of something, in knowledge. For it, the idea is interesting only insofar as it prepares us to possess the real. To abstract from existence is to diminish preoccupation with the vital interest in the immediate and tangible profit and thereby to facilitate the disinterested attitude. So this bracketing already constitutes an inhibiting of the vital thrust, a beginning of disinterestedness, a recapturing of the person itself.

But in certain cases this seems to have assumed a character which Husserl because of his idealist inclination did not foresee. Existence is a chief aspect of the real. How can one turn away from it if one wants to know the real precisely as real? In the case of persons, we have seen that such bracketing is even impossible. Phenomenology should also consider existence and its structures as essences. But this it will do in the same disinterested attitude which directs the search for essences. Hence, in phenomenological research, existence will be put into brackets even when it becomes the object of study, but this will then be done in a special way: we shall bracket the relationships of utility, the existing thing's being able to be possessed and utilized, briefly all that which in real existence takes its interest from preoccupation with life — and this will not be existence as such.

These consequences of real existence interest us in ordinary life to such a point that they constitute for us the very reality of things and become the signs which manifest existence. To inhibit the tendency to domination and possession would have on natural attitude the effect of a complete suppression of this existence; for the impossibility of any practical profit makes it resemble ideal existence. The philosopher will therefore try to regard the *given* with a pure gaze like God's own gaze, leaving the given as it is. And precisely by the disinterestedness of this gaze, the philosopher's attitude will also be reminiscent of the artist's. In fact, in the two attitudes, preoccupation with immediate utility is inhibited to leave scope for the one interest in view. What distinguishes the two attitudes from each other is their objects. The artist looks at sensible forms as expressions to draw from them some pure forms of expression. The philosopher searches for the real in itself, such as it is in itself as presented without trying to evaluate or without trying to discover its possible value for me or for another, or for any being wishing to derive some advantage from it. Apparently, these advantages could in turn become the object of a disinterested consideration. We are struck by how this attitude resembles love. Scheler has insisted greatly upon this and perhaps even exaggerated their reduction to each other.

However, the distinterestedness required for the phenomenological epoché concerns only the interests of biological life and whatever is based upon it — domination and possession. Far from being an indifference, this implies the most ardent interest in beings, the only true interest, since the vital interest in beings is really a self-interest, an egotistical interest like the cow's interest in grass, the wolf's in the lamb. But this interest does not affect love; it is purely cognitive, contemplative. It does not mobilize the subject in all its personal reality, but only its knowledge. By this restriction we underscore that the philosophical attitude is not a spontaneous attitude, but an artificial one. This also distinguishes it from asceticism. It does not intend like asceticism the real transformation of the whole man but is content to be a purely cognitive attitude which has not necessarily any repercussions on action nor even upon the non-philosophic knowledge of the subject.

We know that Plato closely related philosophy and asceticism, the art of knowing well and the art of living well. The two tendencies certainly spring from the same profound source. But their link is not as close as Platonism suggests, for Platonism has ever been led to make of philosophy a kind of religion where mind finds salvation through an essentially intellectual ascent.

This would also explain and justify Scheler's opinion that it is love's amplitude which in a given epoch determines the possible amplitude of its understanding of the real and thereby affects all domains of human action. In fact, if detached and disinterested knowledge constitutes a first element of love which is detached from it only by force, this isolated element could not transcend its first amplitude. This evidently implies that wherever such basic relationships are, the subordinate elements of the higher and first unity can appear in a detached and isolated way only in the measure that their terrain is, so to speak, open by this first unity.

Freedom's Limits

After all these analyses what remains of M. Sartre's thesis that consciousness is an absolute, that it is absolute freedom and only that? It is evident that it is nothing of the kind; and M. Sartre only apparently holds this opinion. In reality his description indicates many essential limits of human consciousness. The past which determines the margin of our possibilities, the very contingency of this liberty and its facticity, what are these except limits? What gives M. Sartre's thesis an apparent truth is the badly defined and changing sense of the word absolute. We can truly say that our will never wills anything situated beyond the horizons of possibilities characterizing it at any given moment. This horizon determines the possibility of willing. This fact may be expressed by the formula that I never will anything that I do not will; and in this sense I am absolutely free. But everyone sees that it is only by this play on words that we succeed in affirming an absolute freedom in an absolute sense. A freedom always moves within its possibilities: these are limited by its being. But if this being is a limited being, its freedom will also be limited, and it will really be incapable of willing anything situated beyond the limits set up by its being. Thus freedom along with existence of which it is only an aspect participates in the privilege of being present in man before his free acts, and in being neither willed nor imposed, for one only imposes something upon a being which already exists and already enjoys freedom. The concepts in question apply to freedom as little as the concepts of sight and blindness apply to matter. We may not conclude from the fact that I have willed neither my existence nor my freedom that they have been imposed upon me. The acceptance of freedom as of existence would presuppose the two, as would the refusal of them. It is the same with existence's or freedom's self-limitation: metaphysically, if not temporally, they would precede this limitation, i.e. they would be infinite; but neither their infinite existence nor such a freedom could ever be limited. A being is therefore free within the limits of its being; and since it can never go outside its being, its freedom can assure for it a certain absolute character. The impossibility at stake here is strikingly evident in the impossibility everyone experiences of willing to be an "I" other than the one it is. The "I" can certainly desire to possess such or such a quality, to enjoy some situation enjoyed by another subject, but these very things are desired as embellishments of its own "I"; the *I* itself wants to enjoy them. Nothing would be gained if the desired change achieved any pure and simple disappearance of personal identity, for then it would cease to exist and another would enjoy the desired privileges — which is already the case.

The absolute freedom attributed by M. Sartre to consciousness is no true freedom but rather what the scholastics used to call "freedom from constraint": whatever does not possess an immediate and interior influence upon the subject's being cannot directly limit his freedom but only indirectly through external pressures upon his body. It is this inaccessibility to all direct manipulation by any created being which accounts for the dignity of the person. But it is far from constituting a freedom which interiorly by its very being would be unlimited. Man can indeed modify his being, but this modification has not unlimited possibilities. What M. Sartre really has proven is that a subject may be limited only by himself, and therefore nothing which is metaphysically or temporally subsequent to his being and his freedom can impose any limitation. For this freedom is one with his being. Because we must distinguish them we come to imagine a freedom external to the subject's being — able to be limited while leaving this being intact. When this attempt fails we wrongly conclude to a freedom unlimited except by oneself. No being can limit itself in the strict sense of the word. Whatever in our life may be limited by us already has a certain character of otherness, belonging to the domain of "having" rather than "being" and it lets itself be limited insofar as the reality-in-question belongs to the domain of "having".

Consequently, the only acceptable sense of this formula, "consciousness is an absolute," is this: every subject must itself act. I am not the origin of *your* acts, and as origin no one can replace you. We may be replaced in many functions and especially when the individuality of the result does not count or almost does not, when the results so resemble one another that to our imperfect knowledge they seem just the same. But as subject, no one may replace another. As soon as another replaces me, it will no longer be my acts which are done but his. The means to acquire the knowledge of certain facts can vary and very much vary. I can learn them by myself or by communication from another; in any case it is necessary that I learn. The case of the subject is only the most evident one because we daily experience this according to the most general law: that each one has its own being and cannot exist with another's existence. Existence is incommunicable and along with it whatever is attached to it, above all — actions and their freedom. I cannot be conscious by the consciousness of another, only by mine. And this is still more pronounced in the case of freedom: I am free by my freedom and only by it; I can renounce being free and let myself be freely influenced. But we must pay attention to this: it is a question of influences which by their nature must take place through my freedom. But this impossibility of replacing another as "this individual" is something totally different from a consciousness closed upon itself and drawing from itself all that it knows in the sense that Husserl speaks of experience as Leistung. In reality human consciences are not closed; they communicate with one another, chiefly by language. This communication enters into their very essence. Apparently, this communication has about it nothing of a purely material causality; consciousness may not be submitted to methods which change material things nor grasped as something to be presented to another. To influence consciousness one must have recourse to means on the same level — to reasons, to motives. This is the psychic level, by itself closed and dumb, incapable of opening itself by communication. It is also by communication that the world common to all is constituted. But because of the union of soul and body in the same principle, communication is not accomplished except through the body. Influences striking the body determine the psychic states which in their turn solicit certain acts or attitudes from the person. There is thus a multiple exchange between the subject and the world mediated by the body, and the subject's freedom is found to be limited by this. By its union with the body, the soul is open to influences which come from material things. M. Sartre's word: "It is therefore senseless to dream of complaining since nothing alien has decided what we feel, what we live and what we are," is a half-truth. Nothing conscious occurs without us. But we are not its only causes, nor are we as causes always free to escape such or such experience whose repercussions upon our being we cannot avoid. Doubtless we may still decide the meaning that this repercussion will have in our life, but another experience would have fatally produced another repercussion and opened out other possibilities.

Yet it remains true that a limited or finite consciousness can only perceive its limitation after operating. For if at the moment itself it did so, it would already transcend its limitation. Every consciousness takes itself at each moment for the Whole beyond which, phenomenologically speaking, it is nothing. But if human consciousness succeeds in recognizing its limitation, this is thanks to two facts. The first consists in the limitation of other consciousnesses, manifested by their subjectivity and by their errors. It is with another, indeed, that we first come upon these defects. After doing this apropos of all subjects we encounter, one can scarcely remain convinced that one is an exception. We are always inclined to believe ourselves infallible; and this partly comes from discovering the limitations of consciousness first of all in another.

The other fact consists in the discovery of our own ignorance and error. This discovery is usually made after a mistake. It is therefore not the fact of being limited that consciousness can directly grasp, but the fact of having been limited in the past. For this reason the limitation will assume the same character as the past; consciousness is this past without being it, or rather it is it in a special way. This way is like that of the consciousness of death, the supreme limit of temporal life. A consciousness can never realize its limit at the very moment it occurs. For formally a limit is a mental-being, the realization that the being ceases and no longer goes on. It is also this mental-being, this film of non-being which separates us from objects: everyone is himself and thereby not an object. Non-being is not grasped in itself but across another being found in the place of what is expected. Likewise, a limit is established experimentally only through experience of another being found beyond limited being. But consciousness is incapable of establishing at the same moment this beyond of which it is not conscious. The past, the fact of finding oneself at every moment "thrown" into a situated existence is a real limit given not solely by consciousness.

19

Freedom as human creativity

Paul Ricoeur

Paul Ricoeur offers a philosophic interpretation of the coming together of the many factors involved in the experience of willing. Some of these factors have been celebrated by contemporary philosophers whose variety of views was presented in the third section.

Professor Ricoeur moves far in the direction of putting order within freedom taken as a whole. He gives due scope to the independence that asserts itself in effort, consent, and choice. He admits the dependence that comes to the will through the human situation of incarnation. As a closer observer of human conduct, he must conclude that freedom is never pure act, never purely creative. It is created by values, powers, and nature. In each of its moments the will is activity and receptivity. The human will is not an absolute but only an image of the absolute. Ricoeur suggests that human freedom is closer to absolute freedom when it consents to being highly motivated rather than when it functions independently of motivation.

As a function of human existence that is received existence, human freedom is most creative when it is highly receptive.

The adequacy of the human response to any transaction is in proportion to man's attentiveness to the situation. If the situation is interpreted inadequately, the response will be less real. The interpretation is not adequate if the presence of Transcendence is not acknowledged; only when the other is seen within the horizon of Absolute Being is the freedom of man fully responsive.

At the conclusion of this reflection on the voluntary and the involuntary it might appear that the dualism, which we attacked, has found refuge in a more subtle and radical duality at the very center of the subject, with the aspects or moments of willing.

Freedom of choice is distinct from freedom of motion, it might seem. Liberty of consent is different from liberty which commands an event and imposes its plans on things through bodily effort.

Our reflection on consent progressed, and the difference seemed to grow as we advanced away from a liberty which inaugurates being, which proceeds from possibility to existence. Finally we reached a liberty which surpasses necessity, yielding to the initiative of things. This liberty, it might seem, dares nothing more; it consents; it surrenders.

We would do well to pause at this discrepancy, before going on to the radical paradox of human liberty.

It is hardly possible to accentuate, at the expense of one or the other, either the moment of choice and effort or the moment of consent. In our century knowledge itself is ultimately paradoxical. A call to boldness and risk, an ethic of responsibility and involvement find their limit in a peaceful reconciliation with the incoercible exigencies of our corporeal and earthly condition.

But mediation with an unbendable necessity has its own limit in a 'sursum' of liberty, an acceptance of responsibility by which I proclaim: this body which upholds and betrays me; it is I who move it. This world which gives me life according to the flesh: it is I who change it. Through choice I create existence both within and outside me.

From PHILOSOPHIE DE LA VOLONTÉ by Paul Ricoeur, Paris, Aubier, 1950; pp. 453-456; by permission. Translated by C. Nolan.

Descartes summarized the diversity of knowledge for Princess Elizabeth in three maxims transposed for her from the three precepts of his *Discours de la Methode*. Here one can read a testimony to the three virtues of decision, effort and consent. "The first (rule) is to try always to use intelligence to the best of one's ability to understand what one should or should not do in all circumstances of life. The second is to have a firm and constant resolution to carry out all that reason counsels without being waylaid by passions or appetites. The third is to consider that while one acts in this way, as far as possible according to reason, all the goods he does not possess are beyond his power; in this way he learns not to desire them, for desire, regret and repentance are the only things which can keep us from happiness."

But we can hardly stop at this contrast which threatens to harden into an abstract distinction and compartmentalize the will into several acts. For in a unique, intentional way each of the moments of liberty, deciding, moving, consenting, unites action and passion, initiative and receptivity.

The analysis of consent only illuminates more brightly the meaning of choice. ... You will remember that we could not resolve either to reduce the ferment of choice to impulses or even to rational motives, or to sacrifice the attention which we give to apparent good to the 'fiat' of choice.

Choice appeared as a paradox of initiative and receptivity, of spontaneity and reason. In certain respects choice is absolute, the absolute of an impulse. In other respects it is relative, relative to motives and values in general, to motives and values in particular. The grandeur and the poverty of human liberty were joined in a sort of dependent-independence. This independence of will is present in effort, consent and choice. Similarly, the will's dependence changes only in direction when it progresses from a value offered in motivation, an organ spontaneously offered, and a necessity imposed by character, the unconscious and life.

Thus paradox occurs not so much among the moments of the will, since these are only distinct because of their aim, as between the triple form of initiative and the triple form of receptivity.

This is why we can interchange the expressions appropriate to these different moments and say that the will, which surrenders to motives, consents to the reasons of its choice. Conversely, consent, which affirms non-willed existence — its limits, shadows and contingencies — is like a choice of self, a choice of necessity, like the 'amor fati' of Nietzsche.

Boldness and patience are continuously uniting at the center of the will. Liberty is not pure act; in each of its moments it is activity and receptivity. It is created by welcoming that which it does not create: values, powers, and pure nature.

In this respect our liberty is *only* human; it comes to understand itself only in relation to certain limiting-concepts, which we realize to be abstractions, like Kantian ideas, regulatory and non-constitutive, like ideal essences determining the limit of the essences of consciousness (which, we have seen, have an already limited purity in relation to error).

1. The idea of God as a Kantian idea is the limit of a liberty which is not creative. Liberty is, we might say, like God in its independence from the object, its limitless and yet self-determining being. But we conceive of a liberty which is no longer receptive with regard to motives in general (of powers and of nature), a liberty which would not create itself by accepting, by arousing a spontaneity, by acquiescing to necessity, but which could decree itself. Would we say that this liberty creates good or that it is the good? This distinction, capital from many points of view, has little bearing on our proposal: this liberty would no longer be a motivated liberty, in the human sense of a liberty receptive to values and ultimately dependent on a body. It would no longer be an incarnate liberty; it would no longer be a contingent liberty. A motivated, incarnate and contingent liberty is thus an image of the absolute in its indetermination capable of determining itself, but it is distinct from the absolute in ITS RECEPTIVITY.

This first concept governs a flood of subordinate ideas whose very sequence constitutes a difficult problem.

2. Next I imagine a motivated liberty like that of man, but motivated in an exhaustive way, transparent, absolutely rational. We have often referred to this ideal of perfectly enlightened liberty; my type of temporality, which derives from my temporal situation, separates me from this end. In the three analyses of indecision, duration and choice, we insisted on the link between human temporality and the confusion of motives which spring from the body. First of all I am a liberty who continually emerges from indecision because values always appear to me in an apparent good manifested to me by affectivity. Affectivity has a problematic nature, calling for endless clarification. It is comparable in the practical order to the inadequacy of perception by touch, outline, profile. Only time

clarifies, as we have stated. Secondly, our liberty is an art of continuity. Certainly as far as we are the ones who conduct this continuity, our control is not an imperfection but a perfection, or an image of perfection. But, since the clarification of motives is always incomplete, decision always hurried by urgency, and information always limited, this liberty of attention remains one with the limits of corporeal existence. It can perceive only apparent goods, it is capable only of inadequate reading of values. The nature of human choice is thus, thirdly, to proceed from risk and not from decree. This risk is a perfection only if one considers the independence of an attention which ceases. But for a motivated, non-creative liberty risk is only a caricature of a free divine decree and remains a weakness in relation to it. Ultimately the arbitrary case of attention bears less resemblance to a free decree of God than does a less bold but more reasoned choice, where the conviction of good is united with the spontaneity of regard. This perfectly motivated liberty would be the highest approximation of divine liberty compatible with motivated liberty.

3. Again, I conceive an incarnate liberty, like that of man, but whose body would be absolutely docile, a gracious liberty, whose corporeal spontaneity would cooperate fully with the initiative which moved it. The athlete and the dancer sometimes communicate to me both an image and a nostalgia for this.

4. Finally, I conceive in the abstract a liberty which would be the very measure of man, without natural limitations, whose motives would be absolutely transparent and whose contingency would be subordinate to its own initiative. But this last Utopia of liberty reveals that the whole cycle of these ideals centers around a creative liberty.

The only purpose of these ideas is to demonstrate by contrast the reciprocity of voluntary and involuntary. They do not constitute a transcendence of subjectivity, for true Transcendence is more than an ideal; it is a presence which inaugurates a revolution in the theory of subjectivity and introduces a radically new dimension – the dimension of poetry.

At least these ideals succeed in determining the position of a liberty which is human and not divine, a liberty which does not assert itself absolutely because it is not Transcendence.

To will does not mean to create.

20

Freedom and existence

Joseph de Finance

Joseph de Finance presents here a metaphysical interpretation
of human freedom in the manner to be expected: by relating
his analysis of freedom to an analysis of human existence.
Although contemporary man has distanced himself from
nature and is aware that a person is in himself a totality, it is
also apparent that this totality is not the whole of existence.
The destiny of the individual person cannot be separated from
the global destiny of mankind. There is an echo here of that
yearning for unity that grounded the work of liberation
undertaken by the sages of the East. Eastern thinkers have
long felt that Western man has neglected the energies of the
spirit, that he has developed the intellect at the expense of the
soul. Professor de Finance insists that the physical is the organ
of the spiritual. He also suggests that every aspect of freedom
that has been isolated and cherished by any writer is
nevertheless rooted in man's basic drive toward unity, and
therefore all the aspects of freedom can be harmonized. This is
done, he thinks, not by compromising or limiting any one of
them, but by insuring that each is itself when freedom is well
understood. His analysis shows that a finite subject cannot
attain   perfect   freedom,   authentic   autonomy,   or   real

self-mastery except in the measure that, instead of closing in on himself, he opens and gives himself. Here an examination of the conditions for obtaining the fullest form of freedom establishes the existence of transcendence; however, the argument shows that the presence of Transcendence does not release man from using choice and control for the progress of people but requires creative concern for the human community by the improvement of material and social conditions.

1.   The dynamic threefold sign of unity

Liberty, we have said, is not only man's way of realizing himself; already present on the path of our destiny, it also awaits us at the conclusion. God is not the Lord of the dead but of the living. He has created beings for existence; and only those exist, in the full sense of the word, who are capable of assuming themselves, of containing within themselves the principle of their action, of determining the meaning and direction of their own being. Creation will attain its goal in the measure that the spirit, by which creation is accomplished, enjoys complete spontaneity, transparence and autonomy, responding on the creature's level to the inalienably Autonomous One. A God-Liberty only finds his glory in creating liberties; and free offerings are the only ones which please him.

But we also saw creation in another light. In so far as it introduces subjects to participation in the original unity — the unity of which liberty is a dynamic expression — we see that creation "converts" subjects to itself, refers them to itself. Thus, by creation, the being is placed for God, toward God, at the same time that he is in and for himself. He has a double center; his end does not consist simply in being himself, by and for himself, in expanding a fully possessed and interiorized existence, but in relating totally to God through love and giving.

From EXISTENCE ET LIBERTÉ by J. de Finance, Lyon, Vitte, 1955, pp. 293-302, 375-383; by permission. Translated by C. Nolan.

This is not all. We showed that, on the creature's level, the unity and self-sufficiency of the first cause are reflected, not only in the liberty and interiority of the individual subject, but in the reciprocal relationships of the elements of the universe. Persons do not escape this law, although it applies to them on a higher level. No doubt a person cannot be considered purely and simply as a part of the universe. He is a totality in himself. But this totality is not the whole of existence. For the person is surrounded by other totalities similar to himself. The unity of the creative act must find itself in their ensemble. The universe, in its fullest meaning, embraces not only the physical but also the spiritual world. And, in fact, the physical is the organ of the spiritual. Thus the destiny of the individual creature cannot be separated from the global destiny of creation. A finite being does not contain his whole meaning; his finality must in one way or another be subordinated to that of the universal community.

The participation of beings in Unity expresses itself in a triple orientation: toward liberty and personal autonomy through self-affirmation; toward union with the Source of being through knowledge and love; and toward effective and practical union with all citizens of the universe. At first sight these three directions appear divergent. Perfect autonomy implies that a being has his law and meaning within himself; it precludes, seemingly, the possibility of finding his meaning in God or in others. Is the spiritual creature condemned to a division whose only solution is radical sacrifice? Since these three tendencies all derive from the same original unity, we presume that their disharmony is only apparent and that it is possible to harmonize them. However, if this harmony consists simply in compromise and mutual limitation, it would remain exterior. True accord must proceed from within. We must show then that the perfect satisfaction of each tendency envelops the satisfaction of the two others. In order to maintain the perspective we set, we must establish that a finite subject cannot attain complete liberty, or true autonomy, cannot take hold of himself fully except in the measure that, instead of closing in on himself, he opens and gives himself.

The method here will be to analyse man's aspiration to liberty, to study its demands, and to determine the conditions of its realization. This analysis and study, however, will not have full meaning unless we keep in mind man's efforts to escape original servitude, and the progressive stages where man imagines he has discovered liberty. Only a critique of pseudo-liberation can reveal the precise shape and presuppositions of authentic liberty.

In the third book of the *Summa Contra Gentiles*, Saint Thomas, having set knowledge of God as the end of the intellect, by means of a metaphysical deduction, suddenly changes his perspective; placing himself at man's angle he goes on to reach the same conclusion, even more precisely, by a concrete analysis of the tendency toward happiness and a criticism of illusory felicity. An analogous process might and should be undertaken here. We already know that the true meaning of liberty is the capacity to give oneself spontaneously to God; but this conclusion, established after consideration of creative action, must be reached again by analysis of the concrete movement of our free will. As you can see, we need nothing less than a phenomenology of human action. The monumental work of Blondel shows that this is not impossible, while at the same time reminding us of our limitations. It suffices for us to establish in the following pages some typical, elementary aspects of man's progress toward liberty. Still, it is appropriate to note that these diverse moments, whose historical sequence we do not pretend to reproduce, are never found in a pure state, and that even the most simple experiential situations derive from their combination and reciprocal reaction.

Let us remember at the offset how the problem of total liberation affects the spiritual creature.

2.   The double poverty of the finite

Self-sufficiency, as Descartes noted, possesses a two-fold identity: negative and positive. On one hand it signifies that the being is not determined from outside or, more profoundly, that nothing, no form, essence or nature, acts as a distinct principle to condition the pure spontaneity of its act. Beyond this it implies that the being contains in and by himself his own determination. In other words, although not determined from without, Being itself is not indeterminate. Though not subordinate to any physical, logical or a priori axiological condition, it is not beyond good and evil, true and false, being and non-being; rather, it possesses within and for itself all essence, truth and value.

The condition of a finite being is very different. First of all, it is dependent being: dependent on the radical principle of existence (this goes without saying); dependent also on other finite beings whose ensemble expresses, without equalling, what his finitude lacks — beings who constitute the universe outside which we could neither exist nor be conceived; dependent, third and most profoundly, on his nature, on structures which he did not create, which he finds within himself from his first moment of existence, which, while making him what he is, nevertheless limit to a certain extent the surge of being within him. The desire for happiness may well reside at the intimate center of our being; it is none the less an initial force expressing nature's desires — and nature is there even without us. While free and even seemingly unconditioned, the will appears submissive to conditions. This is the first radical condition: that the will is not free to be free. Liberty, in its initial form, free will, is a gift; some might say a burden. It leads to the awareness of obligation. We are not meant sincerely to call good that which we see to be evil. Nor are we meant to deny the call to sacrifice — even the sacrifice of life; for we risk losing the very reason for living. Our spontaneity and autonomy are not complete, and, no matter what people claim, we are not creators of value. Ours is not a pure liberty, but a liberty in situation, conditioned liberty. . . . More precisely, it is a liberty which does not contain its own conditions but is ontologically posterior to them.

Interior and exterior dependence prove that the finite being is not self-justifying, that his existence does not explain itself, beginning with itself. In other words, it is contingent. Dependence is not something fortuitous in man; it is his essence to be dependent. His finitude demands that his being be founded outside himself. Man only exists by that which is not himself.

It is not necessary to see in each particular being an arbitrarily isolated fragment of the whole — a being whose very isolation manifests contingence. Such an explanation might stand up in a question of infra-human beings (although contingence would then be treated on the universal level, clearly incapable of sustaining the 'prodigious burden' of self-sufficiency); but it becomes plainly inacceptable in the case of persons. Persons are beings in the fullest sense. Though penetrated with mutual relations, these do not exhaust their reality. Their presence to self, through consciousness and freedom, attests to their ontological solidity; they are, in their own way, absolutes. Even if we admit that the material elements of my being owe their union to the necessary play of natural energy, it nevertheless remains true that I cannot be reduced to a collection of elements. I am I. My character and temperament may well be determined; I am not reducible to either one. I am myself, and the presence of this "I", here and now, is contingent. Nothing can prevent my presence at this moment from offering something surprising. Why am I myself? Why do I have this history, this destiny? Why do I find myself plunged into these circumstances, in this milieu? At the core of our existence there is a state of fact we can do nothing about, except to recognize it. Whether I like it or not, I am from the beginning 'in situation.'

No doubt, the so-called theory of individuation by matter seems, at first sight to declare our astonishment without any purpose. I am necessarily what I am; my personality is linked to the individual character of my organism, which could not be different in given circumstances. But the disquiet of contingence is not dissipated so easily. Considered from outside, my personality can be linked to circumstances which have brought about the apparition of my empirical individuality. But my personality does not allow itself to be known entirely from outside. It has an irreducible interiority. Thus the mystery reappears. As an object, a thing, I can only know that which I am, the place where I am. But why is the ego in some way a thing? Why does thought exist, determined and limited, in the here and now? There is nothing more absurd, seemingly, than the question asked above: Why am I myself? Yet it comes up — so forcefully that many men are bitter about what they are. An illusion proceeding from inadequate understanding? But how can it be that I, a thinking being, have inadequate understanding? This is always to say, in sum: Why am I myself? There is a contingent link between the exigencies of pure spiritual nature and its determinations in me. Beneath its apparent absurdity, the question asked above uncovers another one. This second question can be formulated merely by adding a comma to the first: Why am I, myself? My existence does not have its justification within itself.

This double state of dependence and contingence creates a tension, almost a metaphysical disquiet, in the finite being. Contingence and dependence contradict the necessity and spontaneity appropriate to pure *Esse*, while finitude contradicts its infinity. Is it true that to be finite means not-to-be-fully, and that limit, by distinguishing creatures from the One who fulfills unrestrainedly the potentialities of his radical act, prevents the creature from remaining in himself? If so, then we must also highlight the fact that man's principle and reason for existence lie outside of himselt. The contingent being contains an essential ambiguity. He is himself only by means of that which differentiates, and limits him: his finite nature.

But, interior to his essence, and perfecting it, an act operates which, in its metaphysical purity, transcends all conditioning or limiting determination. It is precisely this ambiguity which, interiorized in the spirit, gives birth to the question: why am I what I am? — a question which is not only speculative but existential, in the full sense of the word. It is a question of salvation.

Man comes only tardily to a lucid realization of the division inherent in the finite spirit — the division which transposes to an interior realm the paradox of the being-who-is-not-Being. This division exists, and through sometimes crude expressions it commands the human being's progress, his constantly renewed effort to liberate himself from internal or external determinations, to affirm his independence from outside influences or pressures (physical, economic, social, political, etc.), from his instincts, passions, prejudices, etc., and even from nature (in attempts to transcend reality, to escape logical, esthetic, axiological structures).

From the creature's point of view, the root of dependence is finitude. The finite being thus tends to free himself by getting out of and going beyond himself. Finitude finds its expression in the other, since the positive reality of the other contributes to what is lacking in the finite being. The creature will try either to destroy, to absorb or to annex the other in order to free himself. We need not think only of temporal moves (political or economic will to power); the most spiritual activity can also be imperialistic and destructive. Consider the lust of the eyes: the egotistical passion for learning — libido sciendi.

In seeking to free himself, the finite spirit also seeks to strengthen himself. While he rejects exterior determinations, he has no intention of remaining in the chaos of the indeterminate. His ambition is to give himself a reason for being, to bypass the void which lies in wait for uncommitted individuals, to procure a value which will justify his existence. In this light, all human activity, and notably the process of acquisition mentioned above, receives a new significance.

Man seeks to surmount both dependence and contingence, (although spiritual deepening frustrates his effort). To imposed situations which appear as limits to freedom, man seeks to substitute situations created by his reason and will. In the depth of the created spirit there lies a permanent temptation: the pretension to autocracy.

We shall try to present briefly the principal steps of man's double effort toward liberation and affirmation.

II.   THE EFFORT OF LIBERATION.

1.   The awakening of liberty

The distinction between free will, as the power to direct onself at the risk of advancing in the wrong direction, and liberty, as exemption from servitude, constraint and imperfection, is a common idea in Christian philosophy. It is significant to note, however, the degrees of free will. One can imagine a freedom of choice such that the subject, already master of himself, has only radically to orientate his being, through a total and decisive option where the direction of his existence would be determined once and for all. (We need not seek such a liberty here, since it certainly does not figure in our experience.) Human liberty, even when understood as the power of option, is not full at the outset. It must grow and deepen. Little by little we take hold of our existence and give it an eternal significance. If free will were not there from the beginning, it would never emerge from amid determinations. At first its presence is so discreet and timid that man seems like a thing, encased in necessity. He is not really. Without man's suspecting it, spiritual spontaneity orientates his animal reactions to surpass the instinctual level. In the daily battle between man's will to live and external pressures, in the growing awareness of limits and constraints on man's 'elan': in these surges up the most rudimentary concept of liberty: to depend only on oneself, to act as one chooses, without clashing with antagonistic powers (forces of nature or other wills).

Liberty is surely exercised in man's expert manoevers to escape the tyranny of the elements, to subdue nature. But this is not where liberty reaches total self-consciousness. It is, rather, in the relationship with other liberties. If love and friendship are privileged experiences, it seems that this consciousness ordinarily forms and grows in conflict. The first form of liberty which man explicitly recognizes is liberty with regard to men. A will which opposes mine and resists my pretensions attests to both my strong personality and my limiting dependence. Hopefully I can progress from the immediate irrational desire to dominate toward the awareness of a liberty which I can protect and encourage.

2.   *Possession of the world*

A.   *Possession of things.*   In his effort to escape exterior constraints, man, a spirit involved and extended in things, necessarily finds support in them. Since his spirituality is not yet unified enough to reveal its authentic exigencies, man proclaims and affirms his liberty objectively by designating a certain zone of things where the I exteriorizes itself and which are its property.

It would be superficial to view property and wealth primarily as possibilities for enjoyment. Exterior possessions are only understood as the outcome and expression of the fundamental having (avoir) which is the subject himself as disponible to himself.

Gabriel Marcel sees the fact of 'having a body' as the prototype of all possession. Only an incarnate spirit can possess, in the strict sense, exterior goods. But we believe further that mastery of self — liberty — is the archetype of possession. Before possessing a body, the subject possesses himself. His first possession, first good, is himself: se habet.

On this level, having is not distinguished from being. The free existent is indivisible possessing-possessed. Contradiction comes outside of pure spiritual interiority, in the realm of incarnate being. The relationship between contradictory terms is reconciled in the free act which gives them immediate unity. The one who possesses is always a free being, a person; and for him possession consists essentially in the power to use objects, to express himself through them in the objective world, without the opposition of a hostile liberty. The link between the object and the liberty can be more or less strict, its disponibility more or less immediate; in any case, the thing possessed is an extension and integration of the subject in so far as the thing belongs directly to him and is immediately available only to him.

Integration and extension are made possible because of the duality in human freedom (and in created liberty in general.) Man comes upon a fact with which he does not coincide. Because of this fact, man (finite spirit) can be said to dispose of himself, to be master of himself, to determine himself, etc. Our liberty is exercised only in a truly a priori nature. It is conquered gradually by our dependence on things. Without this necessary incarnation, man's spirituality would be a nebulous idealism, and his liberty a verbal abstraction. There is no authentic desire without an attempt at realization; no true liberty without some sphere where it can be exercised. Extroverted by nature, I know myself as master of self only when I see myself as master of things. Only an exceptionally well-developed personality manages to affirm his intimate liberty after his exterior independence has been lost. Every slave does not become Epictetus Sparticus.

Property, then, is the 'body' of liberty. Not only does it permit man to preserve relative autonomy with regard to other men, but, by rescuing him from need, it offers him the possibility of giving himself for freely chosen goals.

The soul cannot act without the body; but sometimes it happens that a body excessively hinders the action of the soul. Property offers possibilities of free action; it liberates man from some external constraints; but it accomplishes these by creating a frightening risk of division at the interior of the subject.

By favoring the satisfaction of desires, possession reduces violence and tends to make man more and more captive of his instincts, caprices, passions, and, in this way, to make him a slave to the exterior. If the soul does not already possess interior equilibrium, if it is not already free within, the possession of goods will only aggravate its desire for the things it does not possess.

Furthermore, all too often these goods, which should help the ego to discover and affirm itself, end up substituting for it. Man's personal, spiritual value is eclipsed by their value. He neither sees nor wills himself except in them. This alienation of man by possession, this dialectic reversal by which the possessor becomes the possessed has been described too often to need further insistence.

Property alone cannot liberate man. But it can help condition his liberation. Nothing can be gained until man masters that within him which prevents him from being fully himself.

Private property is not the only issue in question. On the contrary, it is primarily on the collective level that our century is most tragically experiencing man's domination by his possessions. Mystiques of the machine, of technology, work, productivity, etc. − all these ideologies tend to place the end of human activity in the exploitation of the material world. They subordinate man's finality to that of his work, making him the servant of a huge machine whose exigencies impose their rhythm on his life and someday may even govern his education and propagation. These are greater permanent threats to liberty than private property, and they prove that possession of the world does not spell human freedom.

B.   *The possession of subjects.*   In the conflict of liberty, another presents himself as a limit to the subject. The effort of liberation tends to suppress this limit, not in suppressing but in dominating the other. My liberty will be truly free only if other liberties docilely follow its movements.

It is not a question of simple exterior response. If, under hidden or obsequious gestures, the other opposes me by refusal or disdain, then my liberty seems to have failed. This refusal or disdain is a menace. Even a simple silence suffices . . .

Man desires to capture the esteem and love (or at least the fear) of other men, to occupy their heart and spirit, to extend and expand his being in theirs. Here the effort of liberation interferes with the effort of building-up. People who build up a man's self-image, to the point of divinization, give to his existence a fullness and solidity which it would never find within.

The passion for power and glory is deeper than the desire for material goods for themselves and not as instruments. It shows a superior degree of self-transcendence and spiritualization in the subject. His desire to be recognized indicates his awareness of the price of recognition and the value of other subjects. He broadens socially. At the same time he grows deeper. He does not see only the object of his animal desires; the good he desires − the existence he conceives − is immaterial; he becomes conscious of his own spirituality.

And while riches remain irremediably exterior to him, the esteem of others comes to raise him in his own estimation, to help him discover and surpass himself. Man carries these others in himself, just as he lives in them. Their approval, blame (or silence) resound within him. His being grows from these reflections of himself offered by others.

CONCLUSION

Existence et Liberté

We set out at the beginning of this work to further the study of liberty by a metaphysics of the act of being. Our reflection has led us to see the archetype of liberty in the very Act by which Absolute Being exists. The determination of self by self, characteristic of our liberty as creatures, appeared as the reflection of the sovereign Independence of the Existent on dependent being — the Existent in whom act coincides with nature and who manifests his original Liberty by creating subjects capable of determining their own meaning and, in a certain sense, the meaning of being.

This illuminates the tendency — or temptation — of a spiritual creature to dominate his own condition more and more completely. The burgeoning of existence is a burgeoning of liberty; the steps in the ladder of being are degrees of autonomy and self-possession. The direction of the process of being is an ascension toward more total liberation, more perfect interiorization of the principles of personal action and, if possible, existence.

But divine Liberty is not a blind caprice: it coincides with the fullness of Being, Truth and Goodness. A creature's liberty cannot involve a fatal isolation. It is possible only when founded on nature and applied with reason. Moreover, it is only achieved by adherence to the Value, synonymous with Liberty, which is the archetype and efficacious principle of all liberty.

In addition, while the creative act gives reality to beings and autonomy to subjects, it also 'converts' them into itself. Although centered on ourselves, we are also and more radically centered on God. Are these two directions irremediably divergent, leaving man hopelessly sundered or reduced to destruction in order to achieve unity? No. A study of the concrete steps by which man progresses toward perfect liberty indicates that the secret of self-affirmation lies in the complete adhesion of our will to the divine Will. No matter how perfect this adhesion were, however, there would remain an exteriority between God's will and ours, if, by a gratuitous and transcendent initiative, He had not put his own love in us, decentralizing us from ourselves so that we could no longer love or will self except in Him.

By this unforseeable intervention, our liberty was effected, and our existence achieved a new solidity. Thanks to the mediation of love our existence received the infinite possibility of act at the heart of its finitude. To exist fully is to be God. Our nature cannot make any pretences on this subject. It does not and cannot seek to exist except within its own limits. And yet, it is as if an absurd dream haunts man's heart and secretly commands his action: to be God while still remaining man, to be God-man. Without this dream, the serpent's promise would have found no echo. Despite so many calm and wise voices, warning against excess, inviting man to be content with happiness and freedom in proportion to his being, man is not content. His sacrilegious· rages, blasphemies and despair, as well as his Promethian efforts, attest in their own way to man's aspiration to become 'sicut dei.' This aspiration cannot even strictly be called natural, for its metaphysical basis lies deeper than nature in the tension between finite essence and the act of existence, and its effective exercise is closely related to the concrete existential conditions of a humanity historically invited to share in divine privileges.

The deification, impossible in the lines where the creature's pride seeks it, can be achieved only by God, by His free decision, and in ways inconceivable to human reason. It is by the mediation of God made man that it was accomplished. Only man recreated in Christ can be born to true liberty, liberty which gives man to himself without abandoning him to his nothingness. Liberty which, in harmony with its goals, possesses itself and all things by being possessed by God, an immense liberty like that of divine Being, the liberty of a being who, without ceasing to be what he is, no longer acts in himself but in God, the rule and measure of his action. By the perfection of his dependence the creature participates in a new and incomparable way in the sovereign independence of absolute Being.

Thus, the 'malaise' which plagues all finite being is definitively cured; man becomes conscious of his being and his finitude. Here the expressions of Marx come to mind spontaneously, as if they were discovering for the first time their natural habitat; thus, the conflict between essence and existence, objectivity and subjectivity, nature and the ego is resolved. Finite being finds its highest unity, and realizes in itself in an exalted way the synthesis of transcendentals. His supreme truth is not the one he manifests to his consciousness: nor is his supreme value the one which appears to his own eyes. His primary truth is in the sight of God and his authentic value is the one divine love bestowed on him. This liberating intervention grants truth and value before God by making man a participant in divine consciousness. Being, truth and goodness are thus unified at the inaccessible center of natural consciousness. One might say that the flood of transcendent light and love gives rise to a new consciousness, beside which ordinary consciousness seems exterior. The being is thus ready to occupy freely and lucidly the metaphysical site which defines — in him and for God — his condition as creature, and which we have shown to be at the 'interior' of God.

"Tria mirabilia fecit Dominus: res ex nihilo, liberum arbitrium et Hominem-Deun." This text by the young Descartes, which we cited at the beginning of our study, expresses an idea more profound than appears at first sight, whose meaning the author probably did not exhaust. The three miracles mentioned in the fragment of *Cogitationes privatae* have many other links than their common effect on our wonder. Creation, the work of Liberty, finds its meaning only in the existence of subjects freely giving themselves. It is the grace of the Man-God which attained the completion toward which man's illusory plans were leading in vain, and raised man, without destroying him, to the sphere of God.

No doubt some will object that such a reply has little bearing on the concrete problems of mankind. The liberty it promises is an eschatalogical liberty; our contingency and finitude will be healed only in the hereafter. Such a deliverance, foreign to the conditions of present life, the exclusive fruit of an initiative from above, has little effect on our action. The message is merely a huge mystification, whose result will be to dull man's taste for concrete tasks and truly liberating endeavors, as he awaits an illusory liberty.

To say that perfect liberty is a gratuitous gift from God in the hereafter does not diminish the degrees accessible to our own effort. Effort itself is incapable of elevating us beyond our condition but, at the heart of our condition it preserves all its value and constitutes man's most noble aspect. This is not all. The hereafter is prepared in the here and now; glory is present in grace. Perfect liberty is not purely and simply reserved for the next life; it is invisibly present and working in the present. A Christian bears within himself the principle and the pledge. Thus, it is not simply a question of awaiting from prison an ultra-terrestrial deliverance, but of developing and manifesting this already-operating and liberating energy. In the future human effort is going to take on a new meaning. On one hand it will seek to encourage the growth of spiritual liberty, by removing obstacles which risk hindering and even suffocating it. Simultaneously, on the other hand, it will tend to express and outline in the temporal order and in human structures (the social structure, for example) a liberty which is already acquired but still hidden in the secret depths of the spirit.

The Christian attitude does not consist in passive acceptance of all servitude, under the pretext that true liberty is transcendent and cannot be acquired by our own effort. Awareness of spiritual liberty will not make a Christian indifferent to physical, economical and social constraints which limit the exterior practice of freedom. Supposing that his liberty had become strong and lively enough to survive amid the worst tyrannies, he knows that, for most men, liberty perished within when it cannot be exercised outside. Authentic liberty is charity. It seeks to nourish the existence and freedom of others. It would only betray itself if it took refuge in the enjoyment of its autonomy.

The Christian will thus take seriously the diverse economic and political freedoms; he will seek to rise above his narrowness through culture; he will seek to master himself; he will espouse higher values; he will take an interest in his community; he will dedicate himself to building a world where all can be free. But he will not forget that this liberty remains imperfect as long as it is merely man's liberty. A subtle temptation lies in wait for many generous souls. It is very true that the news of the hereafter rings false in many ears, since it does not necessarily proceed from authentic zeal and since, in promising the sky to others, a person is always suspected of keeping for himself the earth and its 'essential' goods. However the zeal for social justice can be equally ambivalent. Instead of a love directed toward the whole man in order to turn him entirely to God, it can betray a neglect of higher values and a sort of deadening of the 'caelestia desideria.' Nothing is more sterile for the Christian than a 'charity' severed from its theological root, which, instead of freeing man leaves him imprisoned in the human. The freedom which truly delivers is divine liberty, which becomes ours by love — a love whose source is God Himself, which frees us by captivating us — a love which, allowing us to love God in his Deity, also teaches us to love others for what they are.

Thus the Christian continues — already liberated at the center of his being, but still partially subservient to vanity, trying to raise himself and others to the kingdom of total love and charity. Although this kingdom will never be achieved in this world where flesh weighs down the soul and prevents perfect communion, nevertheless this world reflects perfect communion and derives its highest value from this reflection.

Liberty by charity in truth: this, as we see it, is the task offered to human effort. The help of all sciences and all skills is not too much to accomplish our task, as far as it is possible here.

Nothing is small if it can help man, incarnate spirit, to attain his spiritual fullness. To consider true freedom as deliverance of self by an invasion of divine charity does not imply any separation from life. It gives direction to human action and, if we seem to promise much less now than the mystics of the here and now, who make heaven descend to earth, at least the fruit we offer does not taste of ashes but of infinite hope.

The whole drama of human history is contained in a question which our era asks with never-before attained lucidity: will man liberate himself − make himself God − in and by God or without and against God? And we know which alternative our century, for the most part, has chosen. Without wanting to play prophet or to explain the Apocalypse, we might say that ours is the century of the Anti-God, man seeking divinity within himself and enclosing himself in the limits of an existence headed toward nothingness rather than acknowledge the only One Who can really free him.

This is what gives the simultaneously tragic and scowling mask to our century. Tragic, for in seeking liberty without and against God, the world leaps into a servitude which is more formidable every day − as in ancient tragedy, man calls destiny upon himself in the very act of summoning it. He aspires to peace and wastes himself in horrible wars. Though the number of rivals diminishes, the gulf between them widens. Even if man were to succeed someday in uniting all people, it would be at the price of a terrifying destruction, compromising and extinguishing man's most authentically personal aspiration. Such a unity would always be precarious, for this aspiration, swept under but not suppressed, would manifest its explosive power some other time. Thus man (without God), far from progressing toward perfection, watches the expanding gap which separates him from himself, an internal emptiness, a metaphysical lack from which evil emerges like a diseased exhalation. The more powerful man becomes, the more this void grows to terrifying depth. Command of material energies, which should have guaranteed human freedom and inaugurated an era of happiness, has become instead a source of new anguish. The effort of peoples to free themselves from secular rulers and to forge their own destiny has led to dictatorship. Although tragic, the face of our century is also scorning. For, as a result of having opposed the source of value, man winds up denying all values. Finally he presents an image where hardly anything remains of his primitive beauty – an image turned in upon a blasphemous will. Many contemporary works of art and literature offer telling examples. Complacency in absurdity; systematic exploration of all that is least human in man; deliberate choice of sin, degradation and profanity. Let us continue; in the world of tomorrow, planned and undoubtedly possible through technical progress, many features appear as caricatures of Christian hopes. The end of all this: sadness and despair, tempered only by a lost commitment to a cause which one knows perfectly well to have no meaning.

Will this hard experience of so many failures suffice to bring man back to the path of true liberty? Instead of willing to become god without God, will he allow himself to be divinized by God become man? Will he open himself to charity? It would take a strong dose of optimism to believe that humanity is on the brink of conversion. We have not seen how far a liberty with the help of grace refuses to change the world. God has too much respect for the creature to prevent Satan's possibilities, written in our finitude and contingency, from coming to light. Certainly evil itself has a place in the order of Providence, and manifests itself only within limits established by Divine Wisdom. But we do not know what these limits are and we know that they are wide enough and leave enough play to the malevolent activities to offer a brilliant demonstration of what man becomes when he pretends to do without Being.

Perhaps humanity will continue for a long time in its sorrowful path. But the Christian believes that his work is not in vain and that his suffering has a meaning. He believes that the good will conquer and that creation will appear finally as a magnificent success. But this success is not awaited here below.

Nevertheless, even here, world history teaches that the improbable often triumphs. Life is a paradox in the sphere of physical forces; grace is another more disconcerting one for sin-laden nature. Here and there a rising force bursts up at the heart of a downward movement. Divine liberty remains intact and has not ceased bringing about surprises. Doctrines of necessity are only doctrines of despair. And what is despair except a future as rigid and determined as the past. No one who sees an Unconditional being at the source of things, a being of Unlimited power whose will cannot be deceived or enchained, has the right to say: this will not be. That which has never been seen will be seen. Dried bones may come to life. We are no longer prisoners of monotonous cycles. To believe in Divine Liberty, which is Wisdom and Love, total Liberty whose glory is to free us by giving itself gratuitously to us: this is to preserve, amid all deception, an unchangeable freshness of hope in one's soul. If so many courageous people waver, if so many others withdraw before the effort, if so many are defeated in advance by a determinism, which their very surrender renders omnipotent, it is because they do not rely on the primary Liberty which alone can free them. The greatest need of our age, so passionately in love with liberty is, perhaps, first of all to believe in liberty.

CONCLUSION

From the above, it appears that the contribution of a metaphysics of freedom lies in establishing the ground of freedom and pointing to its necessary alliance with truth and with goodness. Existentialism and phenomenology have their own contributions to make both to our understanding and to our achievement of freedom. That these contributions have not yet been fully made indicates the need to develop in the future an ever greater awareness of the concrete conditions of any realistic freedom. Though it is true that we do not have power over another's freedom, it is now seen that we have more power than formerly we either realized or used over the conditions that allow freedom to be transformed from an illusion to a reality.

Moreover, contemporary writers have made it abundantly clear that growth is a primary characteristic of freedom and that personal freedom is individually structured. Only a philosophy of the individual, of growth, and of becoming can add what is wanting to a philosophy of human nature.

Existential phenomenology is a method for knowing whatever is unique, whatever is within time and space, and whatever is organically related or complementary to metaphysics. It is concerned, not merely with methodology, but also with content because of its concern with the human in all its embodied aspects. In order for one's freedom to be realistically directed, one must appreciate the meaning not only of being in general, but of being in one's own immediate situation.

Phenomenology prides itself on being open to the findings of the sciences, especially of the biological and psychological ones. But it is not

239

enough for the philosopher to be impressed by the successes of the sciences, he must consider himself to be forced as a philosopher to rethink in the light of these achievements the future of human freedom. Has philosophy drawn sufficiently upon psychoanalytic theory, Jean Piaget's genetic program for child development or the possibility of what the evolution of mankind means and will mean for freedom? The question is now being asked whether we have fully admitted to ourselves the impact of our bodily structures and of individual environments upon our thinking? We must extend this to the question of whether we have fully realized this same impact upon our freedom?

We have seen that most contemporary scientists and philosophers tend to affirm the existence of freedom. In view of this, what is now needed is a serious in-depth study of the development of freedom. If man is an historical being, nothing about him, least of all his capacity for decision-making, can be known apart either from his cosmic, genetic, or psychological history or from a certain intelligent interpretation of the future. Projected discussions of freedom will need to take into account not merely the autonomy of human agency but man's material dependence, for adaptations in the bodily structure make for a changing inheritance of neuro-muscular patterns and affect motor behavior. The human infant's developmental series of motor patterns have evolved over immense periods of organic history; they are programmed into its body and come into action in an ordered series of developments. Perhaps upon first learning of evolutionary theory we have looked too long at the past and it is now time to consider the structured change in which we ourselves are involved.

Not only does science predict change, it makes possible an accurate study of its structure. Novelty is not intrinsically divorced from stability. In the emergence of the new there is a physiological order, and the drive to discover order is at work in the philosophical enterprise. This drive is not unrelated or in contrast to our living experience. On the contrary, it is in continuity with physiological existence where, indeed, order is not opposed to life. Nor is order imposed upon human existence in opposition to its freedom. When one experiences order in one's body, it is not surprising to find that it is connatural to our freedom, where it includes the integration of both intellect and feeling.

As feelings are or can be bridges between people, they will need to be studied more carefully as we deepen our understanding of freedom as creative responsibility and use community as the model for a mature form of freedom. Feelings have an important part to play in interpersonal and inter-group responses; they cannot be dismissed if one hopes to achieve mutual understanding. The phenomenologists have begun their study of what we need to know about human feelings if freedom is to grow. We can say that unless you feel, you will not understand; and unless you understand other men, you will not be free. There is a wisdom that the body has acquired through long ages, but which each man must consciously appropriate if he ever hopes to be spiritually free. Without this body-consciousness, there can be no realistic or adequate self-consciousness. In the past body-consciousness has been largely a pre-verbal experience, but it can now be seen that unless man becomes articulate to himself about his entire human experience, there can be no wholehearted self-acceptance.

All this indicates that any future philosophical discussion of freedom will have to include a deep reflection upon what it means to be human in an integral way. Biologists, psychologists, evolutionists, geneticists will enter into this discussion, and not without offering opposition to the existence of freedom as a possibility. Especially, however, it can be expected that their contribution will be a positive one to the identification of freedom as a more universal reality, and even to the development of higher levels of freedom.

There is no justification for thinking that the relation of man to transcendent Personal Being belongs only to abstract discussions of freedom or to so-called metaphysical analyses. The relation of man to God enters indirectly but truly into any study of the concrete conditions for freedom, for no concrete study of human emotions, decisions, and actions — such as phenomenology declares itself to be — can overlook the evidence of faltering, failing man. Paul Tillich attributes the scars and wounds of human effort to the fallen state of finite freedom that characterizes the structure of human life as such. Though philosophy does not show any inevitable connection between freedom and the fall, it has shown, as we saw, that only through the creative use of freedom can man realize his destiny to be human. While the fall of man is impossible apart from the aim of divine creation that reconciles both freedom and destiny, the reality of the fall is wholly man's doing. It would be superfluous to refer to it as a fault if man had not been free, and if there is no human essence, as some existentialists claim, the fall as an estrangement from God would be unintelligible. This estrangement took place, according to Tillich, when man separated himself from the divine ground in the very act of realizing his destiny. The effects of this estrangement, which are open to various phenomenological investigations, are rooted in the ontological disorder in which man's existence is no longer in full harmony with his essence.

It is the work of freedom to overcome the estrangement that is apparently characteristic of man and makes sense only within the framework of man's relationship to God. That from which man fell was the order of right love. The relation of man to God, and thereby to others, is the personal structure which orders the dynamic exuberance of man's creative energy, his élan vital. Without the restoration of this order of love there can be no full expression of that creativity which is both human in character and of ultimate and everlasting value.

Bibliography

BOOKS

Adler, M. J. *Freedom*: A Study of the Development of the Concept in the English and American Traditions (Albany, N.Y.: Magi Books, 1968).

Augustine, St. *Problem of Free Choice* (Westminster, Md.: Newman, 1955).

Ayers, M. R. *Refutation of Determinism:* An Essay in Philosophical Logic (New York: Barnes & Noble, 1968).

Berdyaev, Nicolas *Slavery and Freedom* (New York: Scribner, 1944).

Bergson, H. *Time and Free Will* (New York: Harper & Row, 1960).

Berofsky, B., ed. *Free Will and Determinism* (New York: Harper & Row, 1966).

Bidney, David, ed. *The Concept of Freedom in Anthropology* (The Hague: Mouton and Co., 1963).

Black, Max *Philosophy in America* (Ithaca: Cornell University Press, 1965).

Campbell, C. A. *In Defense of Free Will* (New York: Humanities Press, 1967).

Cassirer, E. *Determinism and Indeterminism in Modern Physics* (New Haven: Yale University Press, 1956).

————. *Christianity and Freedom*—A Symposium (London: Hollis and Carter, 1955).

Clark, M. T. *Augustine, Philosopher of Freedom* (New York: Desclee, 1959).

Cranston, M. *Freedom* rev. ed. (New York: Basic Books, 1968).

D'Arcy, E. *Human Acts* (Oxford: Clarendon Press, 1963).

Davis, W. H. The Freewill Question (The Hague: Nijhoff, 1971).

Delesalle, J. Liberté et Valeur (Louvain: Publications Universitaires de Louvain, 1950).

Dobzhansky, T. The Biological Basis of Human Freedom (New York: Columbia University Press, 1956).

Enterman, W. F., ed. Problem of Free Will (New York: Scribner, 1967).

Edwards, J. Freedom of the Will (New Haven: Yale University Press, 1957).

Erasmus, D. & Luther, M. Discourse on Free Will (New York: Ungar, 1961).

Farrelly, Dom M. J. Predestination, Grace and Free Will (Westminster, Md.: Newman Press, 1964).

Farrer, A. The Freedom of the Will (New York: Humanities,1958).

Festugière, A. J. Liberté et Civilisation chez les Grecs (Paris: Editions de la Revue des Jeunes, 1945).

Frank, J. Fate and Freedom (New York: Simon & Schuster, 1945).

Franklin, R. L. Free Will and Determinism: Study of Rival Conceptions of Man (New York: Humanities, 1968).

Friedrich, C. J., ed. Liberty. American Society for Political and Legal Philosophy (New York: Atherton, 1962).

Gaith, J. La Conception de la liberté chez Grégoire de Nysse (Paris: Vrin, 1953).

Gilson, E. La Liberté chez Descartes et la théologie (Paris: Alcan, 1913).

Guardini, R. Freedom, Grace and Destiny (Chicago: Regnery, 1965).

Focus on Freedom (Baltimore: Helicon, 1966).

Hampshire, S. Freedom of the Individual (New York: Harper & Row, 1965).

Hare, R. M. Freedom and Reason (New York: Oxford University Press, 1965).

Hatt, H. E. Cybernetics and the Image of Man (Nashville, Tenn.: Abingdon, 1968).

Havard, René Les Problèmes de la liberté (Paris: Desclee, 1956).

Hobbes, T. Leviathan ch. 6 & 21: Questions concerning Liberty, Necessity and Chance.

Hook, S., ed. Determinism and Freedom in the Age of Modern Science (New York: New York University Press, 1958).

Hospers, J. Human Conduct (New York: Harcourt Brace, Jovanovich 1961).

Hume, D. Treatise of Human Nature, Bk. II, Part III, ch. 1 & 2.

Inquiry concerning Human Understanding, Section VIII.

Kant, E. *Fundamental Principles of the Metaphysics of Morals*, Part III. *Critique of Pure Reason*, Second Division, Bk. II, sec. 9, III.

Kolenda, K. *The Freedom of Reason* (San Antonio, Texas: Principia Press of Trinity University, 1964).

Krause, S. J., ed. *Determinism in American Literature* (Ohio: Kent. State University Press, n.d.).

Kung, H. *Freedom Today* (New York: Sheed & Ward, 1966).

Kurtz, Paul *Decision and the Condition of Man* (New York: Dell, 1968).

Laird J. *On Human Freedom* (London: Allen and Unwin, 1947).

Lamont, C. *Freedom of Choice Affirmed* (New York: Horizon, 1967).

Lehrer, K., ed. *Freedom and Determinism* (New York: Random House, 1966).

Leibniz, G. W. *Theodicy*: "Essays on the Justice of God and the Freedom of Man in the Origin of Evil" and "Reflexions on Mr. Hobbes' Work: 'Freedom, Necessity and Chance.' " (Indianapolis: Bobbs-Merrill, 1966).

Lewis, H. D. *Freedom and History* (London: Humanities Press, 1962).

MacConaill, M. A. *Bodily Structure and the Will* (London: The Aquin Press, 1960).

MacKay, D. M. *Freedom of Action in a Mechanistic Universe* (Cambridge: Cambridge University Press, 1967).

Malinowski, B. *Freedom and Civilization* (Bloomington: Indiana University Press, 1960).

Maritain, J. *Freedom in the Modern World* (New York: Scribners, 1936).

Mauchaussat, G. *La liberté spirituelle* (Paris: Presses Universitaires de France, 1959).

McDonagh, E. *Freedom or Tolerance*: The Declaration of Vatican Council II on Religious Freedom (Albany: Magi Books, 1967).

Melden, A. I. *Free Action* (London: Humanities Press, 1961).

Melsen, A. G. van. *Physical Science and Ethics* (Pittsburgh: Duquesne University Press, 1968).

Mill, J. S. *On Liberty* and *Logic of Liberty*, Book VI, ch. II.

Monod, J. *Chance and Necessity* (New York: Knopf, 1971).

Morgenbesser, S. & Walsh, J. *Free Will* (Englewood Cliffs, N.J.: Prentice Hall, 1966).

Morris, H., ed. *Freedom and Responsibility* (Stanford University Press, 1961).

Muller, H. J. *Freedom in the Ancient World* (New York: Harper & Row, 1961).
————. *Issues of Freedom* (New York: Harper & Row, 1960).
Munn, A. M. *Free Will and Determinism* (Toronto: University of Toronto Press, 1961).
Murray, J. C., ed. *Freedom and Man* (New York: Kenedy, 1965).
Nucho, F. *Berdyaev's Philosophy: The Existential Paradox of Freedom and Necessity* (New York: Doubleday, 1966).
Ofstad, H. *Inquiry into Freedom of Decision* (London: Humanities, 1961).
Oppenheim, F. *Dimensions of Freedom* (New York: St. Martin's Press 1961).
Pears, D. F. *Freedom and the Will* (London: Macmillan, 1964).
Polanyi, M. *The Logic of Liberty* (London: Routledge & Kegan Paul Ltd., 1951).
Pontifex, M. *Freedom and Providence* (New York: Hawthorn, 1960).
Priestley, J. *Free Discussion of the Doctrines of Materialism and Philosophical Necessity* in a correspondence between Dr. Price and Dr. Priestley (New York: Kraus Reprint, 1968).
Rankin, K. W. *Choice and Chance* (London: Humanities Press, 1961).
Ricoeur, P. *Freedom and Nature: The Voluntary and the Involuntary*, tr. E. Kohak (Chicago: Northwestern University Press, 1966).
Roberts, M. *Responsibility and Practical Freedom* (Cambridge, 1965).
Rosenthal, F. *The Muslim Concept of Freedom* (Leiden: E. J. Brill, 1960).
Schopenhauer, A. *Freedom of the Will*, tr. K. Kolenda (New York: Bobbs-Merrill, 1960).
Simon, Y. *Freedom and Community*, ed. C. O'Donnell (New York: Fordham University Press, 1968).
————. *A General Theory of Authority* (Notre Dame: University Press, 1962).
————. *Freedom of Choice* (New York: Fordham University Press, 1969).
Skinner, B. F. *Beyond Freedom and Dignity* (New York: Knopf, 1971).
Spakovsky, von, A. *Freedom, Determinism, Indeterminism* (The Hague: 1963).
Spinoza. *Ethics*, Part IV, Prop. 67, Proof & App. IV & XXXIII. Part II, Prop. 48; Part I, Def. 7; Prop. 17, note; Prop. 31.
Thielicke, H. *The Freedom of the Christian Man* (New York: Harper & Row, 1963).
Thomas Aquinas. *Summa contra Gentiles*, II, ch. 64-73; 85-93.
Toulmin, S. *The Philosophy of Science* (New York: Harper & Row, 1960).

Vivian, F. *Human Freedom and Responsibility* (London: Chatto & Windus, 1964).

Ward, B. *Faith and Freedom* (New York: W. W. Norton, 1954).

ARTICLES

Al-Azm, S. "Whitehead's Notions of Order and Freedom." *Personalist*, 48 (Fall, 1967): 579-591.

Anscombe, G. E. M. "The Two Kinds of Error in Action." *Journal of Philosophy*, 60 (1963): 393-401.

Aune, B. "Abilities, Modalities, and Free Will." *Philosophy and Phenomenological Research*, 23 (1962-1963): 397-413.

Austin, J. L. "Ifs and Cans." *Philosophical Papers* (Oxford, 1961).

Ayer, A. J. "Fatalism." *The Concept of a Person* (London, 1963).

Baier, K. "Could and Would." *Analysis Supplement*, 23 (1963): 20-29.
"Action and Agent." *The Monist*, 49 (1965): 183-195.

Baillie, D. M. "Philosophers and Theologians on the Freedom of the Will." *Scottish Journal of Theology*, 4, no. 2, June, 1951.

Barth, K. "The Gift of Freedom." *The Humanity of God* (Richmond, Va.: John Knox Press, 1960).

Beardsley, E. L. "Determinism and Moral Perspectives." *Philosophy and Phenomenological Research*, 21 (1960-1961): 1-20.

Beck, L. "Agent, Actor, Spectator and Critic." *The Monist*, 49 (1965): 1-20.

Bennett, J. "The Status of Determinism." *The British Journal for Philosophy of Science*, 14 (1963-1964): 106-119.

Berlin, I. "From Hope and Fear Set Free." *Proceedings of the Aristotelian Society*, 64 (1963-1964): 1-30.

Berlinger, R. "What is Freedom?" *Philosophy Today*, 3, no. 4 (1959).

Berofsky, B. "Determinism and the Concept of a Person." *The Journal of Philosophy*, 61 (1964): 461-475.

Boring, E. G. "When is Human Behavior Pre-determined?" in D. E. Dulany (ed), *Contributions to Modern Psychology* (Oxford, 1963).

Bradley, R. D. "If's, Cans, and Determinisms." *The Australasian Journal of Philosophy*, 40 (1962): 146-158.

————. "Determinism or Indeterminism in Microphysics." *The British Journal for the Philosophy of Science*, 13 (1962-1963): 591-594.

Brandt, R. and Kim, J. "Wants as Explanations of Action." *The Journal of Philosophy*, 60 (1963): 425-435.

Bronaugh, R. "Freedom as the Absence of an Excuse." *Ethics*, 74 (1964): 161-173.

Burkle, H. R. "Schaff and Sartre on the Grounds of Individual Freedom." *International Philosophical Quarterly*, 5, no. 4 (Dec. 1965).

Campbell, C. A. "Moral Libertarianism: A Reply to Mr. Franklin." *The Philosophical Quarterly*, 12 (1962): 337-347.

Canfield, J. "Determinism, Free Will and the Ace Predicter." *Mind*, 70 (1961): 412-416.

————. "Knowing about Future Decisions." *Analysis*, 22 (1961-1962): 127-129.

————. "The Compatibility of Free Will and Determinism." *Philosophical Review*, 71 (1962): 352-368.

————. "Free Will and Determinism: Reply." *Philosophical Review*, 72 (1963): 502-504.

Cohen, M. F. "Motives, Causal Necessity and Moral Accountability." *The Australasian Journal of Philosophy*, 42 (1964): 322-334.

Dalbiez, R. "Le moment de la liberté." *Revue thomiste*, 48 (1948): 180-190.

Danto, A. C. "What We Can Do." *Journal of Philosophy*, 60 (1963): 435-445.

Daveney, T. F. "Choosing." *Mind*, 73 (1964): 515-526.

Davidson, D. "Actions, Reasons, and Causes." *The Journal of Philosophy* (1963): 685-700.

Dempf, A. "Freedom and Value." *Philosophy Today*, 3, no. 4 (1959).

De Munnynck, M. "La demonstration metaphysique du libre arbitre." *Revue neo-scolastque de Louvain*, 20,(1913): 13-38; 181-204; 279-293.

De Raeymaeker, L. "Le problème de la liberté personnelle et le principe de sa solution." *Giornale metafisique* (1949): 481-590.

De Waelhens, A. "Une philosophie de la volonté." *Revue philosophique de Louvain*, 49 (1951): 415-437.

Dilman, I. "The Freedom of Man." *Proceedings of the Aristotelian Society* London: Harrison, 1918; Johnson Reprint Corporation, 1963 (1961-1962): 39-62.

Donceel, J. F. "Determinism and Freedom in the Age of Modern Science." (ed. S. Hook). *International Philosophical Quarterly*, 1, no. 3 (Sept. 1961).

Dore, C. "On the Meaning of 'Could Have'." *Analysis*, 23 (1962-1963): 179-181.

—————. "Is Free Will Compatible with Determinism?" *The Philosophical Review*, 72 (1963): 500-501.

Edwards, R. "Agency without a Substantive Self." *The Monist* (1965): 273-289.

Evans, J. L. "Choice." *The Philosophical Quarterly* (1955): 303-315.

Ewing, A. C. "May Can-Statements be Analyzed Deterministically?" *Proceedings of the Aristotelian Society* (1963-1964): 157-176.

Forest, A. "Le réalisme de la volonté." *Revue thomiste* (1946): 457-476.

Franklin, R. L. "Dissolving the Problem of Free Will." *The Australasian Journal of Philosophy*, 39 (1961): 111-124.

Friedrich, C. J. "Responsibility." *Nomos*, 3 (New York: 1960).

Gallagher, K. T. "On Choosing to Choose." *Mind*, 73 (1964): 480-495.

Ginet, C. "Can the Will be Caused?" *The Philosophical Review* (1962): 49-55.

Gonseth, F. "Necessitarian Philosophies and Experience." *Philosophy Today*, 3, no. 3 (1959).

Gustafson, D. F. "Voluntary and Involuntary." *Philosophy and Phenomenological Research*, 24 (1963-1964): 493-501.

Hanly, C. M. T. "Phenomenology, Consciousness and Freedom." *Dialogue*, 5 (1966): 323-345.

Herztein, R. "The Phenomenology of Freedom in the German Philosophical Tradition, Kantian Origins." *Value Inquiry*, 1 (sp. 1967): 47-63.

Hoare, F. R. "Physical Determinism and Free Will." *Irish Ecclesiastical Record*, 43 (1934): 27-35.

Holmes, E. "Freedom and Growth." *Hibbert Journal*, 17 (1919): 626-641.

Huby, Pamela. "The First Discovery of the Free Will Problem." *Philosophy*, 42 (Oct. 1967): 353-362.

Jaspers, K. "Freedom and Totalitarianism." *The Future of Mankind* (Chicago: University of Chicago Press, 1961).

Kanner, L. "Causality, Determinism and Freedom of the Will." *Philosophy* (1964): 233-248.

Ladriere, J. "Déterminisme et liberté: Nouvelle position d'un ancien problème de modèle de Popper." *Revue Philosophique de Louvain,* 65 (Nov. 1967).

Lottin, J. "Le Libre Arbitre et les lois sociologiques." *Revue neo-scolastique de Louvain* (1911): 479-515.

Mailloux, N. "Psychic Determinism, Freedom and Personality Development." *Canadian Journal of Psychology,* 7 (1953): 1-11.

Marcel, G. "Truth and Freedom." *Philosophy Today,* 9, no. 4 (1965);

Margenau, H. "Quantum Mechanics, Free Will and Determinism." *Journal of Philosophy,* 64 (Nov. 9, 1967): 714-725.

Mary Aloysius, Sr. "Freedom and the I: An Existential Inquiry." *International Philosophical Quarterly,* 3, no. 4 (Dec. 1963): 571-599.

Mayo, B. A. "The Open Future." *Mind* (1962): 1-14.

McGill, V. J. "Conflicting Theories of Freedom." *Philosophy and Phenomenological Research* (1959-1960): 437-452.

Menache, T. J. "Bergson and Free Will." *The Personalist* (1939): 20-28.

Metz, J. B. "Freedom as a Threshold Problem between Philosophy and Theology." *Philosophy Today,* 10, no. 4 (1966): 264-279.

Munson, T. "Freedom: Philosophic Reflexion on Spirituality." *Philosophy Today,* 9, no. 1 (1967).

Myers, F. M. "Three Types of Freedom." *Inquiry,* 10 (Winter 1967): 337-356.

O'Connor, D. J. "Possibility and Choice." *Proceedings of the Aristotelian Society,* Supplement 34 (1960): 1-24.

Perry, D. "Prediction, Explanation and Freedom." *The Monist* (1965): 234-247.

Pitcher, G. "Hart on Action and Responsibility." *The Philosophical Review* (1960): 226-235.

————. "Necessitarianism." *The Philosophical Quarterly* (1961): 201-212.

Potter, K. H. "Freedom and Determinism from an Indian Perspective." *Philosophy East and West,* 17 (Jan. 1967): 113-124.

Rankin, M. L. "Metaphysical Freedom and the Determination of Responsibility." *Journal Value Inquiry,* 1 (Winter 1967-1968): 184-189.

Robinson, C. K. "The Polar Context of Freedom." *International Philosophical Quarterly*, 6, no. 4 (Dec. 1966).

Roxbee-Cox, J. W. "Can I Know Beforehand What I am going to Decide?" *The Philosophical Review* (1963): 88-92.

Ryan, A. "Freedom." *Philosophy* (1965): 93-112.

Schouborg, G. "Bergson's Intuitional Approach to Free Will." *Modern Schoolman*, 45 (Jan. 1968): 123-144.

Shute, C. "The Dilemma of Determinism after 75 Years." *Mind* (1961): 331-350.

Skinner, R. C. "Freedom of Choice." *Mind* (1963): 463-480.

Smart, J. J. C. "Free Will, Praise and Blame." *Mind* (1961): 291-306.

Somerville, J. "Marxist Ethics, Determinism and Freedom." *Philosophy and Phenomenological Research*, 28 (Sep. 1967): 17-25.

Strawson, P. F. "Freedom and Resentment." *Proceedings of the British Academy*, 48 (1962): 187-211.

Swiggart, P. "Doing and Deciding to Do." *Analysis*, 23 (1962-1963): 17-19.

Taylor, R. "Deliberation and Foreknowledge." *American Philosophical Quarterly*, 1 (1964): 73-80.

Thalberg, I. "Freedom of Action and Freedom of Will." *Journal of Philosophy* (1964): 405-415.

Whittier, D. "Causality and the Self." *The Monist* (1965): 230-303.

Williams, C. J. F. "Logical Indeterminacy and Free Will." *Analysis* (1960-1961): 12-13.

Index